Susie Dent is the resident word expert in Dictionary Corner on Channel 4's *Countdown* and *8 Out of 10 Cats Does Countdown*, and has been on every programme about words: *15 x 15*, *Word of Mouth*, and *More or Less*. Susie also writes regularly for the *Radio Times*, *The Week Junior* and the *i paper*, and her Word of the Day has attracted over one million followers on X (formerly Twitter).

Also by Susie Dent

INTRODUCTION

'How do you *feel*?' It's the question that punctuates our lives, the ultimate summary of every life event and situation, asked repeatedly of anyone who has been bereaved, promoted, dumped, or struck down by flu. Usually, the answer will involve varying degrees of happiness, sadness, disgust, surprise, fear, or anger – the six basic emotions that for thousands of years were thought to govern our behaviour. But if the last few years have taught us anything, it's that our emotions rarely come neatly packaged and on their own.

In the struggle to respond, it can feel like words are failing us. But take it from a lifelong dictionary obsessive, those terms are out there, we just need to track them down. And finding them can mean everything. There is in folklore a Law of Names, which states that the knowledge of a name for something or someone allows us to magically govern them. This is the Rumpelstiltskin effect, in which a mother can only rescue her child from the clutches of a malevolent imp by learning his true name.

Fairy tales as usual go straight to the heart of things: recent research has made it clear that the ability to 'name' how we feel is directly proportional to our happiness. What is at play here is our 'emotional granularity', a term coined by psychology professor Lisa Feldman Barrett whose work has shown that those who draw on a wider range of vocabulary to express their emotions are far more able to cope with them. Emodiverse people are less likely to lash out in anger (or hit the bottle in misery) and much less likely to visit the doctor. Those with a high EQ are apparently happier, healthier, and more popular than the rest of us. You are what you feel, as long as you can describe it.

This book is intended to help you find that word you need *when* you need it. I would like it to be a new kind of dictionary – a human one, that attempts to chart the stories of the emotions we know all too well, and to name those we don't. In another recent study, subjects subliminally primed on the Japanese expression *shinrin-yoku*, forest bathing, were far more likely to get up early and go for a forest walk. In the same way, knowing that there is a word for the pang of emotion that hits when you smell a familiar perfume, or hear a certain song, might help you experience it more fully (this is the **stound**, a momentary beat that can stop you in your tracks).

But what exactly is an emotion? Is it an inner sensation, or more of a social scenario? Are emotions innate, or a way of behaving that we learn as we grow up? Do we feel something and then name it, or is it the other way round? Until the nineteenth century, the word **boredom** didn't exist: so did listlessness *feel* different before then, when it was expressed as the more languishing world-weary *ennui*?

Putting a label on our emotions has never been straightforward. Even when we find a name, its meaning can shift. We may assume that we have always acted and felt as we do today, but behaviours have changed so much over time. Smiling, for instance, was once less a sign of pleasure and more the grin of fear, exhibited by primates in the face of danger. Happy smiles emerged only later, and even then were usually tight-lipped thanks to the lack of good dentistry. Similarly, while yawning today may be a sign of tiredness or boredom, a yawner amidst Shakespeare's contemporaries was more likely to be open-mouthed with astonishment. Earlier still, such noisy 'oscitation' risked opening oneself up to the devil (think of 'the yawning gates of Hell'), while French troubadours in the twelfth century would yawn vigorously to demonstrate the depths of their love. Our emotions, and our bodily responses to them, are as fluid and inconstant as we are.

The evolution of emotions can be dramatic. Four hundred years ago, a curious illness known as *mal du Suisse*, 'the Swiss illness', began to be observed amongst Swiss mercenaries who were considered the most highly prized soldiers in Europe. Their particular brand of homesickness included fevers, abdominal pain, fainting, vomiting, and even death. Military physicians attributed the singular malady to brain damage caused by the continuous clanging of cowbells since childhood. In fear of the soldiers deserting in droves, the penalty for even singing a Swiss shepherd's song was death. Jean-Jacques Rousseau later described how the mercenaries 'who sang it dissolved in tears, deserted, or were left heartbroken, so powerfully did the song arouse in them the ardent desire to see their homeland once more'. In 1688, the Swiss physician Johannes Hofer decided to rename this condition **nostalgia**. Today, this once existential malady is used to describe 1970s disco nights and album covers. Nostalgia (really) ain't what it used to be.

Across two intense years of Covid lockdowns, immersing myself in the language of feeling took me on a parallel emotional rollercoaster, spinning all the way from Italian *abbiocco* (the drowsiness you feel after a big meal) to **zwodder**, a West Country word for the laziness of a hot summer's day. Reading ancient dictionaries I have travelled from the envious staring at a companion's plate (**groaking**), through the terminology of falling in love at first sight (**limerence**), to the seven deadly sins and the reasons behind **cloud nine**. Some, like **desiderate** (to long for something now lost), have been languishing and forgotten for centuries, while others need to be borrowed from different languages – those like the evocative Japanese description of making too-frequent trips to the fridge: *kuchisabishii*, whose literal translation is 'lonely mouth'.

Words like these cry out to be shared. And, of course, these are only the merest tip of the iceberg: a truly exhaustive Emotional Dictionary would run to many volumes and feel rather exhausting to boot (an emotion I definitely don't want to inspire). Equally, I am no historian or psychologist: my passion is entirely lexical. This is not a history of emotion –

there are wonderful history books out there already.* I call this book a dictionary, but it is an entirely idiosyncratic one. I have spent decades charting language as objectively and impersonally as I can, but I wanted this book to *feel* different.

Rather than try to nail down every emotion, I have approached the language of feeling emotionally, concentrating on the words that particularly sang to me, as well as those with a surprising backstory – the intriguing (and phallic) history of **fascination**, for example, or the original colour of **jealousy**. I've written about the emotions we run from, like **churlishness** and **crapulence** (the extreme end of **hungover**), and the ones we run towards, such as **confelicity**, joy in another person's happiness, or **respair**, a recovery from despair. And there are those that we didn't know existed, but might recognize – the **well-woulder**, for example: someone who wishes another success, as long as it's not more success than them, or **resistentialism**, the feeling that inanimate objects can sometimes have it in for us.

As for the names of those six basic emotions, while their meanings may have shifted, they still do their job. But, as the narrator of Jeffrey Eugenides' novel *Middlesex* points out, they are never going to be enough. 'I'd like to have at my disposal complicated hybrid emotions, Germanic train-car constructions like, say, "the happiness that attends disaster". Or: "the disappointment of sleeping with one's fantasy." I'd like to show how "intimations of mortality brought on by aging family members" connects with "the hatred of mirrors that begins in middle age" … I've never had the right words to describe my life, and now that I've entered my story, I need them more than ever.'

An Emotional Dictionary can help with some of these. There's **gruglede**, for example, Norwegian's answer to a mixture of happiness and dread, while the disappointment of sleeping with one's fantasy is surely embraced in **anticipointment**.

---

* Thomas Dixon's fascinating *Weeping Britannia* in particular.

That intimation of mortality might find echoes in the German *Torschlusspanik* ('gate-shut-panic'), which expresses the middle-aged feeling that life is passing you by. **Idiorepulsive**, meanwhile, describes the shock of catching your own reflection in the mirror.

This book will also name the urge to shout 'bollocks!' when you've stubbed your toe, and the joy of sunshine on your back; the blues that descend on a Sunday evening, along with the ecstasy of looking up at a canopy of trees. It offers light and dark, and the many tones between. For while it is undeniable that my much-loved library of dictionaries leans towards sadness – it seems as if there are more than fifty shades of grey – I believe strongly that it's never too late to change. A lexicon of lost positives is waiting, like Superman in the ice, to be brought back to life. Take words such as 'gormless', 'feckless', and 'disgruntled': they are the dark offspring of terms that once described hopeful and happy states of mind. You might be **gruntled** or **gormful**, or full of **ruth** and **feck**. Over time, such happinesses were abandoned in favour of their antitheses, but if psychologists are right, giving them new life now may allow us to experience them once more. As the story of Rumpelstiltskin shows, the power of a true name can break an evil spell. We just need to choose our words better. If ever there was a time to release the magic of **respair**, it is surely now.

Susie Dent
Oxford, July 2022

abbiocco [Italian: ab-biok-ko]: the drowsiness you feel after a large meal.

The long, delicious lunch is over and the lively conversation slows to a gentle, lazy pace. You're full and happy and entirely comfortable. So comfortable, in fact, that your eyelids are beginning to droop. This is *abbiocco*, an Italian word that is defined variously as 'post-prandial lethargy', a 'general afternoon drowsiness', or, as *far venire l'abbiocco*, 'to make someone sleepy'. The most common usage is for what we might today call a 'food coma'. The term is an etymological relation of another Italian word, *chioccia*, used of a 'broody hen' that sits snugly upon her nest. However you use it, *abbiocco* is all about the lolling head of a human as they try in vain to resist the seductive pull of sleep.

abdabs: the horrors.

'Abdabs' usually come in the screaming variety. First recorded as 'habdabs' in the anxious 1940s, the word articulates a state of extreme agitation or horror. Its origins may lie in its sound, which is suggestive of the spluttering, wobbly speech of someone caught up in an acute abdabs attack.

For a time, in the 1960s, the expression 'don't come the old abdabs with me' was a warning against trying to pull the wool over someone's eyes. While that sense faded from view, the descriptive power of 'abdabs' to articulate utter disgust and impending doom remains undiminished, rivalled only by a similar phrase from the 1920s: **heebie-jeebies**.

abhorrence: loathing and revulsion.

From its first entrance into English in the early fifteenth century, 'abhor' has been freighted with repugnance. Its root lies in the body's physical reaction to something frightening or repulsive: in Latin, *horrere* meant to 'bristle' or 'shudder' to the extent that the hairs on your body stood on end, a process technically known as 'horripilation' or 'piloerection'. Put another way, all such 'horrid', 'horrible', and 'abhorrent' emotions will give you 'goosebumps': a none-too-pleasant nod to the pimply skin of a plucked goose.

acatalepsy: the impossibility of comprehending the universe.

'It's big, space, isn't it?' The physicist Brian Cox regularly points out that we still don't know what 96 per cent of the universe is made of. We talk airily about 'dark matter' but, as with the Dark Ages, 'dark' here is simply adjectival shorthand for 'shrouded in obscurity' and hence 'we haven't a clue'. Most of us these days would accept that humans still have an enormous amount to learn. The earliest people to grasp this were the ancient Sceptics, who argued that unknowability was a characteristic of all things. Human knowledge, they believed, can never amount to certainty, only to probability. The fact that nearly all of the writings of the Sceptics no longer exist feels entirely fitting.

From Greek, 'acatalepsy' is made up of *a*, 'without', and *katalēpsis*, the 'ability to grasp fundamental concepts about life'. In reality, life offers both acatalepsy and katalepsis. Perhaps, in the end, it was Socrates who got it right when he said, 'The only true wisdom is in knowing you know nothing.'

accismus: the impulse to refuse something you really want.

The last chocolate éclair, a single ticket to the gig of your favourite band, the only seat left at a football match: have you ever declined something out of courtesy when you really, really wanted it? This is known as 'accismus', defined in the *Oxford English Dictionary* as 'the pretended refusal of something one keenly desires'. First recorded in the sixteenth century, it stems from the Greek *akkismos*, meaning 'shyness' or 'prudery'.

Accismus was for centuries a social convention, where restraint was a virtue and modesty everything. Jane Austen's novels are full of female accismus – a feigned or restrained coyness that society expected. The nineteenth-century German writer Jean Paul Friedrich Richter, whose work both venerated and patronised women, decided that a woman 'requires no figure of eloquence – herself excepted – so often as that of *accismus*'. Many of us still practise accismus in polite company, even if the stakes are no longer quite as high as an offer of marriage.

acedia [uh-seed-yuh]: apathy of body and spirit.

Most of us would put our hand up to at least a couple of the seven deadly sins. There were even more to begin with, for their story originates in 'the eight evil thoughts', written down by a fourth-century monk named Evagrius Ponticus as a warning to other monks of distractions that could lead to the death of the soul. The eight in question were gluttony, lust, avarice, anger, sloth, sadness, vainglory, and pride.

In the sixth century, Pope Gregory I – later St Gregory the Great – removed sloth, added envy, and gave pride an over-arching role as the ruler of the seven remaining sins. But their journey was still not over, for they were revisited by the thirteenth-century theologian Thomas Aquinas, who rejected sadness and determinedly brought back sloth. The latter was not quite the same as the general apathy and laziness we think of today; rather it was a far more spiritual affliction, and it also went by the name of 'acedia'. For Evagrius Ponticus, acedia was 'the most troublesome' of all, and 'the last of the sins to conquer'.

'Acedia' is founded upon the Greek *a*, 'without', and *kēdos*, 'care, concern'. More than physical laziness, it encompassed a dangerous dejection of spirits or spiritual malaise that could lead to both inaction and frustration; some even personified it as an actual demon.

For the Benedictines, the rule was that any monk displaying the outward signs of acedia should 'be reproved a first and a second time. If he does not amend, he must be subjected to the punishment of the rule so that the others may have fear.' The attempt to achieve such 'amendment' was at times intense. Peter Damiani, a Benedictine monk in the eleventh century, recorded that St Rodulphus could overcome the temptation of acedia only by 'tying ropes to the ceiling of his cell, putting his arms through, and singing the psalms'.

'Acedia' has motivated drama and literature for centuries. The critic Walter Benjamin saw it as the decisive factor in *Hamlet*, and the catalyst for the prince's downfall. The writer Aldous Huxley considered it a disease of the modern age, while more recently the spectacular downfall of a few business giants has also been ascribed to acedia and the indecision it induces.

addiction: a physical or mental dependence upon something.

At the heart of 'addiction' is the Latin *dicere*, to 'say', which has bequeathed us many words in English, including the unlikely couple 'dictator' and 'dictionary'. In the Roman Republic, 'addiction' implied devotion, a giving-over to a higher power. An 'addict' was someone assigned by decree to another, just as a debtor or gambler might become a slave to their creditors. It was this notion of the relinquishment of control that underlies the sense of 'addiction' today, be it to a noxious, potentially fatal, substance or to a TV show. Carl Jung saw every form of addiction as toxic, 'no matter whether the narcotic be alcohol, morphine, or idealism'. Or, indeed, *EastEnders*.

adorable: inspiring affection and delight.

Who really wants to be labelled 'adorable'? While clearly fine for puppies and kittens, it is a far less attractive adjective for anyone who wants to be taken seriously. But it wasn't always that way – not least because it begins, of course, with 'adore', a word that combines the two strands of love and prayer. Its roots are the Latin *adorare*, to 'worship' (from *ad*, 'to', and *orare*, to 'speak' or 'pray'). When 'adorable' first came into use in the early seventeenth century, it too carried the weighty meaning of 'worthy of divine worship'. The idea of 'lovability' and inspiring great affection emerged soon after, with a good dollop of 'cuteness' thrown in. *See also* **gigil**.

aduantas [Irish: ah–dwon–tez]: a feeling of unease at being in new surroundings.

At some point most have us have felt the discombobulation of encountering somewhere for the first time and feeling completely out of place. The Irish *aduantas*, rooted in *aduaine*, 'unfamiliarity', encompasses the mixture of feelings you might experience when you find yourself in strange surroundings and out of your comfort zone. Perhaps this accounts for the lookalike Irish pubs in most corners of the globe, providing a much-needed familiarity for travellers far from home. *See also* **dépaysement**.

adulation: excessive admiration or flattery.

First recorded in English in the fifteenth century, 'adulation' came to us from the Latin *adulari*, to 'fawn on', and was used specifically of affectionate dogs. As the canine associations receded, so human flattery took over. Adulation may be a form of worship and devotion, but it has blind subservience built in.

affection: endearment and warm-heartedness.

Today's 'affection' is a gentle affair: a general fondness or liking for someone or something that began with the Latin *affectus*, a 'mood' or 'state of mind'. In medieval theology and the philosophy of the Enlightenment, intense 'passions' and 'lusts' were unfavourably contrasted with milder and generally more virtuous 'affections'. By the thirteenth century, 'affection' had settled happily on caring, tenderness, and goodwill. C. S. Lewis firmly believed that 'affection is responsible for nine-tenths of whatever solid and durable happiness there is in our natural lives.'

affronted: offended.

The verb 'affront' was borrowed from the Anglo-French *afrunter*, which in general terms meant to 'defy', but which also had the very specific sense of slapping someone across the face. All becomes clear when you know the word's Latin origins, a combination of *ad*, 'to' or 'towards', and *frons*, 'forehead'. For some reason, English declined to adopt the literal sense, although the earliest uses of 'affront' did involve insulting someone *to* their face, a sense that survives today when we are 'affronted' by someone's rudeness (so much so, to continue a theme, that it brings to mind the German *Backpfeifengesicht*, a 'face deserving of a slap').

afterclap: a nasty and unexpected surprise.

An 'afterclap' is something unpleasant that arrives after you thought a situation or matter was settled: a late invoice, say, or a damning letter from your ex months after your relationship ended. Perhaps Samuel Johnson defined it best, in *A Dictionary of the English Language* from 1755: 'Unexpected events happening after an affair is supposed to be at an end'. No matter how you interpret it, no one wants an afterclap.

after-wit: a realization that comes too late.

'After-wit' is the opposite of the 'fore-wit' that gives us foresight and prudence. It is essentially the realization of a truth that comes after an event and is therefore too late to influence anything. The companion emotion to *l'esprit d'escalier*, it offers at best a lesson for learning, and at worst a self-administered kick in the teeth.

agelast [ad-ji-last]: a person who never laughs.

If laughter keeps you young, you might consider the seventeenth-century 'agelast' a bit of an oxymoron, for it describes someone who has no sense of humour at all. All of which might suggest a slightly crabby and petulant face marked with frown lines, rather than one that stays forever youthful, but in fact the word has no relation to the English 'age' and 'last'. It is based on the Greek *a*, 'without' or 'not', and *gelastos*, 'laughing'. If you are 'agelastic', you are a definite party-pooper. The moral of the story is to always exercise your 'gelastics' (laughter muscles).

age-otori [Japanese: aah-gey-oh-toh-ree]: looking worse after a haircut.

Hairdressers famously put you on the back foot with their 'Who cut your hair last?' But if today's trips to the salon feel perilous, they are as nothing compared to visits of the past. Barbers in particular required nerves of steel, for they were cutters of far more than hair. Up until the eighteenth century, alongside routine surgery and dentistry, the barber also offered blood-letting, a supposed cure-all for balancing the fluids of the body. Indeed, blood was so central to the barber's profession that he would place bowls of the red stuff from his clients in his shop window as a reminder to others that their own bloody appointment was due. Outside the premises would stand the now-famous barber's pole: striped in red (for blood) and white (for the bandages applied afterwards). The brass ball at its tip symbolized the basin used to collect the blood.

While any tribulations today pale in comparison with visits to those demon barbers, immortalized in the nineteenth-century figure of Sweeney Todd, we surely need a word for the nodding approval we automatically give our own hairdressers once their work is done, even while we are dying a little inside. English sadly provides none, but we can at least take some masochistic pleasure in the Japanese *age-otori*, which goes some way towards expressing the misery of leaving the hairdressers looking far worse than when you went in.

agony: excruciating pain.

In earliest English, 'agony' referred specifically to the anguish of Christ in the Garden of Gethsemane, and to a mental rather than physical struggle. As the word developed, it took on bodily pain, including the 'mortal agony' that describes the throes of death. Its beginnings lie in the Greek *agōn*, a 'public gathering'. The Greeks attached enormous prestige to sports and athletic competition, and competitive events were traditional at gatherings on festival days. The intense struggle for victory in such contests came to be called *agōnia*, as did the pain that went with it – be it physical or mental. For those of us who are not at our best at parties, the idea that public gatherings are literally agony might resonate.

alert: watchful; vigilant.

The roots of 'alert' lie in the Italian military command *all'erta*, 'to the watchtower!', an order therefore to 'be on the lookout!' It is thus very similar to 'alarm', from the Italian *all'arme!*, 'to arms!', a warning of imminent attack, or, alternatively, the insistent buzzing on your bedside table.

allergic: relating to an allergy; feeling a strong dislike for something.

Today we can declare ourselves to be allergic to almost anything we don't fancy – Brussels sprouts perhaps, or getting up before midday. For those with medical allergies, the new laxity of the word might be pretty irksome, although it might brighten their day to find out that 'allergy' and 'orgy' are close linguistic relatives. Both look back to the Greek for 'energy' or 'work'. The *all-* of 'allergy' means 'differently', because an allergy involves an abnormal reaction that 'works against' a foreign antigen, whilst an 'orgy' (originally a secret rite held in honour of Bacchus, the god of wine) requires an altogether different kind of energy. Today, 'allergic' is also used metaphorically to indicate a strong antipathy towards something – including work (of the non-orgiastic variety).

all-overish: generally ill-at-ease and unhappy.

An issue of the *Tickler Magazine* from 1820 carries a tale by Henry Lee about a pastor who seeks to educate a shepherd boy on the morals of the Bible. After listening to the story of Cain and Abel, in which Cain murders his younger brother and is exiled, the boy exclaims:

> 'Excuse me, zir, but when this tale I hear,
> I somehow feel all-overish and queer!'

This is our earliest record of an expression that is as relatable as it is transparent. If you are feeling 'all-overish', you are overwhelmed by an unease that extends to the entire body. Later on, it was interpreted more broadly, to mean generally ill-disposed and off-colour in a vague, undefinable way. *See also* **frobly-mobly**.

aloof: cool and distant.

Seven hundred years ago, a 'luff' was an implement used to alter the course of a ship, while to 'wend the luff' was to change course ('wend' being a synonym at that point for 'go', still preserved in our past tense of 'go', 'went'). In the late seventeenth century, the cry of 'a luff!' was an order by a ship's captain to keep the bow close to the wind in order to keep it clear of the shore. It's from here that we inherited the modern sense of the word, one of keeping at a safe emotional or physical distance, or of keeping our cards close – if not to the prevailing wind, then to our chest.

altruism: disinterested or selfless concern for others.

There is 'egotism', behaviour intended to satisfy ourselves, and there is 'altruism', designed to help somebody else. Both came to us via French but are rooted in the Latin *ego*, 'I', and *alter*, 'other'. In its earliest days, 'altruism' was used in reference to the work of the philosopher of science Auguste Comte, who founded the doctrine of positivism. Like 'philanthropy', 'altruism' has retained all its goodness, with none of the edge that occasionally accompanies 'charity'. 'Every man must decide whether he will walk in the light of creative altruism,' wrote Martin Luther King Jr, 'or in the darkness of destructive selfishness.'

alysm: the boredom that comes from being unwell.

When you're on your way back to health, a lazy day under the covers with your favourite box set can seem almost idyllic. Rewind to when you were really unwell, however, and you might have found yourself unable to relax at all. For those days there is 'alysm': rooted in a Greek word for 'anxious' and describing a feeling of frustrated disquiet when confined to bed.

ambition: the determination to succeed.

'Ambition' comes with a dark side. While trying to get on in life is a largely positive attribute, if you call someone 'ambitious' you bring a whole load of preconceptions into the mix, especially the desire to succeed at the expense of other people.

It has always been this way. 'Ambition' began with the Latin adjective *ambitiosus*, 'eager for public office or favour; ingratiating', which itself came from *ambire*, to 'walk around'. Both terms referred to political hopefuls who would swish about Rome in their pristine white togas, pressing as many hands as possible in order to secure the votes they needed.

amok: out of control.

In the course of his voyage around the world, Captain James Cook witnessed a terrifying phenomenon amongst the Malay people that was known as 'amock'. To 'run amock', he later wrote in his journal, 'is to get drunk with opium and then sally forth from the house [and] kill the person or persons supposed to have injured the amock . . . in a frenzied attack.' Such attacks typically took place in crowded areas, making them even more murderous, and ended when the assailant was captured or took their own life.

The impulse for such frenzy is as debated now as it was at the time. The Malay people put it down to an evil spirit known as *hantu belia*, said to enter the body of the afflicted and inspire an indiscriminate rampage. To outsiders, 'amok' remained an anthropological and culture-bound curiosity until it was later classified as a psychiatric condition. In mainstream English, the word has become so diluted that anyone running amok these days tends to be more disruptive than murderous, and it is applied most often to groups of animals or children who play havoc.

amour propre [French: a-moor-prop-ruh]: self-esteem or vanity.

The French have long had the linguistic edge when it comes to love. And not just love for other people – their language also serves us well when we need to express the love we hold for ourselves. *Amour de soi*, according to the philosopher Jean-Jacques Rousseau, is a self-esteem that protects our individual well-being but that is neither selfish nor competitive. It is not contingent upon the judgement of others, and, for Rousseau, is crucial for survival. Self-esteem that is reliant upon outside approval, on the other hand, is known as *amour propre*. For those hunting down likes and shares on social media, it is this, a self-respect that is nonetheless conditioned by the (literal) views of other people, that perhaps belongs most powerfully to our times.

angry: annoyed; displeased; hostile.

'There are three words ending in -*gry*. Two of them are "hungry" and "angry". What is the third word in the English language?' So runs a question that has been bending minds for decades. There is in fact no third word ending with -*gry* – other than a handful of highly obscure terms that were never really on the table. The puzzle was described by US linguist Richard Lederer as 'one of the most outrageous and time-wasting hoaxes in our nation's history', and it requires only a literal reading of the question 'what is the third word in "the English language"' to reveal the answer: 'language'.

Thankfully there is no such mystery about the emotion 'anger', nor the word itself. Its beginnings belong to the Vikings, for whom *angra* was to 'vex'. For them the feeling was one of annoyance rather than rage, and when 'anger' slipped into English in the thirteenth century it likewise meant to 'irritate', like an angry rash or swelling. Not until a few centuries later did the word escalate to its current meaning of 'wrath'.

'Anger' was a favourite word of Shakespeare's, for whom it was 'like a full hot horse' (*Henry VIII*). Overpowering rage features prominently in his works, particularly one that back-fires: 'Heat not a furnace for your foe so hot/That it do singe yourself.' Such fiery images descend straight from the Bible, where anger is pithily described as 'hot displeasure'.

angst: a feeling of dread or unease.

Whenever we encounter the German borrowing 'angst', chances are it will be prefaced with 'teen', for it has come to be seen as an unavoidable rite of passage for the adolescent years. But this has also meant a level of dismissiveness that neither the word nor teenagers deserve. For true Angst, to give it its Germanic capital letter, is a serious thing indeed.

The concept of Angst was central to the work of the existential philosopher Søren Kierkegaard. He argued that an individual only becomes truly aware of their potential through the experience of Angst, because 'Whoever has learned to be anxious in the right way has learned the ultimate.'

If you stand and look over a cliff's edge, you fear falling but also recognize the opportunity to jump. Kierkegaard believed we experience the same dual response when confronting every significant choice, describing it as 'the dizziness of freedom'. Angst, he believed, needs to be embraced, because restricting ourselves to the safe and the ordinary means living a lie. Arguably this was something that Kierkegaard pursued in his own life, when, at great personal cost, he deliberately decided not to marry his childhood sweetheart, Regine Olsen, and to dedicate his life instead to philosophy.

Angst slowly percolated into English, where it was first recorded in a description in the *Boston Medical & Surgical Journal* from 1872, regarding a patient who 'was accustomed to a sort of panic (angst), coming over him suddenly'. At this time the term was used to describe an existential anxiety and morbid fear about the human condition. A few decades on, its meaning had broadened to encompass a range of psychological stresses, or even, as one literary work put it, 'remorse about the past, guilt about the present, anxiety about the future'. In other words, pretty much any worry at all.

By the 1970s, the word was sufficiently well known to be chosen as the name of a music genre, 'angst rock', whose lyrics focus on frustration and despair. Given its long and earnest history, it is perhaps best reserved for days of extreme unease – as the actor Jim Broadbent put it, 'You can't be angsty all day, or else it becomes a sort of pale angst.'

anhedonia: the inability to feel pleasure.

From the Greek for 'without pleasure', 'anhedonia' is a characteristic of psychological disorders such as depression. *Hedonia* is also at the root of the more familiar 'hedonism', which sits at the opposite extreme and means the pursuit of pleasure at the expense of everything else. *See also* **nikhedonia**.

animated: full of movement and activity.

In one of the most popular stories from Greek myth, the chief deity Zeus gives the task of creating man and the animals to the Titan Prometheus (whose name means 'forethought') and his brother Epimetheus (whose name means 'afterthought'). Prometheus shapes man out of mud, while Epimetheus gives all the animals special gifts for protection, such as shells for turtles and claws for bears. But the cupboard is bare when it comes to living man, until Athena, the goddess of wisdom, breathes into Prometheus's figure of clay and humanity is born. When we talk about 'breathing' life into something we are echoing the literal meaning of 'animate', which descends from the Latin *animare* – for the Romans, the *anima* was 'air', 'breath', and 'soul'. Consequently, to be 'animated' is to be full of vigour, just like the characters in a cartoon that are given life by the animator's touch.

annoy: to vex or irritate.

Something 'annoying' is still a long way off being 'hateful'. Its cause might be any old disturbance (or what English dialect might call a **joblijock**), but in most cases the effect will be temporary, and at worst simply irritating. That is not, however, how it all began. The Latin phrase *mihi in odio est* was the Romans' way of expressing extreme distaste – it meant 'it is hateful to me'. In other words, 'annoyance' was at the odious (from *odium*, 'hatred') end of the spectrum. *In odio* eventually moved into Old French in the mangled form of *anoier*, which is how English ended up with 'annoy'. In a parallel move, it also travelled to both languages in another guise: **ennui**.

antagonistic: hostile or argumentative.

The Greek struggle or contest known as an *agōn*, the root of **agony**, also gave us the 'antagonist', one who openly contends against another. The original reference was to opposition in battle or sport, but in the seventeenth century it was extended to any human conflict. The leading person in such a contest, or in a dramatic story, was the 'protagonist', from the Greek *prōtos*, 'first'.

anticipointment: disappointment in something eagerly anticipated.

A large percentage of new words today are a mash-up of one or more elements of an existing word with one or more of another. These are otherwise known as 'portmanteaus', a term coined by Lewis Carroll that rests on the metaphor of a folding suitcase that brings two compartments into one. He himself created many, including 'chortle', a joyful confection of 'chuckle' and 'snort'. Modern English is full of them, and they have proved particularly useful in conveying emotions. One such is 'anticipointment'.

'Anticipointment' is used in two ways. Firstly, it can summon the almost-inevitable sense of disappointment that comes from looking forward to something so much that you find yourself whipped up into unrealistic expectations. Alternatively, 'anticipointment' is the disappointment you already know will descend even before the event. Either way, the word is a pithy descriptor of longing for something to turn out as good as your dreams, only to find that it falls decidedly short of the mark.

antipelargy: the love between a child and its parents.

'Antipelargy' is an odd-looking word on the face of it, particularly for something as positive as the reciprocal love between parent and child. Things become even more curious when a bird comes into the mix, namely the *pelargos*, Greek for 'stork'. This doesn't, as you might expect, refer to the superstition that babies are carried to us from the skies by a stork. Rather it looks back to the bird's reputation in antiquity as one of the most affectionate and fiercely loyal of all creatures. Classical legends tell of young storks bearing in flight the weight of their parents as they reach old age; indeed, a law of ancient Greece known as the Pelargonia dictated that children must always care for their elderly parents. Perhaps we need a simpler word for one of the most instinctive and spontaneous of all loves – although it is nice to know that one exists.

antsy: agitated.

In the 1930s, to be restlessly impatient, especially in a lustful sense, was to have 'ants in your pants' – a reference to the extreme energy and activity of the industrious insect. It soon shifted to encompass any form of fidgety eagerness, as in James Brown's 'I Got Ants in My Pants (and I Want to Dance)'. 'Antsy' emerged a couple of decades later as part of teenage slang, with the same idea of restless impatience and just a hint of irritation.

anxiety: fear or nervousness about what might happen.

A pandemic, climate peril, war in Europe, widespread food poverty – over 20 per cent of adults today rank their daily anxiety as 'high', with a third of us likely to experience an anxiety disorder during our lifetime. The Age of Anxiety is surely now, even though that term has preoccupied lexicographers for decades, not least thanks to W. H. Auden's 1947 poem of the same name, set during the Second World War.

But what exactly is 'anxiety'? The anatomists of feelings at the Centre for the History of Emotions, which studies modern emotions through the lens of the past, believe that even in the notoriously complicated world of emotions, anxiety is especially problematic. Its causes may be tangible or totally indefinable. It is an emotion predicated on what *might* happen, yet historians in particular know how things *did* pan out in the past, adding a perspective that many of us who feel a slave to anxiety can only long for. Even so, the things that caused such stress in the past may seem alien to us now. Fifteenth-century society was eager to identify those thought particularly prone to anxiety, such as witches, or women with a wandering uterus (*see* **hysteria**). The fear of being buried alive, meanwhile, was acute in the late nineteenth century, at a time when both undertakers and doctors rushed to verify a death.

While the term 'anxiety' itself is recorded from the fifteenth century, the emotion's formal beginnings are generally considered to date from the 1860s, when the American neurologist George Beard explored 'neurasthenia', a condition caused by an excess of nervous energy. Before then, patients with anxiety clearly existed, but were diagnosed with other labels, such as 'melancholia', 'mania', and 'the vapours'. Soldiers in the American Civil War were thought to suffer from 'irritable heart syndrome' – what would now be diagnosed as post-traumatic stress.

Today, the diagnoses of anxiety disorders are constantly revised, and interventions such as cognitive behavioural therapy have thankfully replaced the electro-shock therapies and lobotomies of the past (although one cure for the wandering uterus syndrome survives in the modern vibrator).

The roots of the word 'anxiety' are not quite as complex. They lie in the Latin verb *angere*, to 'constrict', as well as the related adjective *angustus*, meaning 'narrow'. All of these words derive from an Indo-European root that also produced *Angst* in modern German and related words in Dutch and Scandinavian languages. Rippling through each is the sense of a chokehold of dread; not for nothing is the heart condition 'angina' a close relative.

apanthropy: an aversion to others and love of solitude.

Between loneliness and aloneness lies an ocean of difference, and each has its own, very distinct thesaurus. 'Apanthropy' belongs firmly in the latter camp – it is voluntary solitude, born of a desire not just to be by oneself, but to be free from the intrusion of other people. It is made up of the Greek *apo*, 'away from', and *anthrōpos*, 'man'. In a medical glossary of 1839, 'apanthropy' is neatly defined as 'a species of melancholy characterised by a dislike to society'. It is, in other words, the state of being 'peopled out'. Any modern 'humgruffin' or misanthrope will relate to that.

apathy: indifference and lethargy.

It is often said that the opposite of love is not hate but apathy. Derived from the Greek *apathēs*, 'without feeling', 'apathy' is used to describe an emotionless insensibility to anything at all. Combine that with an indolence of mind and a sluggishness that is hard to shake off, and you have what the newspaper editor Horace Greeley described as 'a sort of living oblivion'.

For the ancient Stoics, however, apathy was a positive ideal of passionlessness. A Stoic sage had such control of their mind that they were never perturbed or deranged by human feelings of fear, hate, or anger. Instead, they could enjoy the perfect peace of mind and detachment of *apatheia* – aware of their passions but never slaves to them. Perhaps today we're just not approaching it right.

apophenia: the tendency to perceive meaningful connections between random things.

'Apophenia' is often linked to gambling, where a random outcome can appear to be dictated by preceding events. If, for example, three coin-tosses reveal three successive 'tails', it can seem more likely to the gambler that the next coin-toss will reveal itself to be 'heads', despite bearing an unchanging 50 per cent statistical likelihood. In other words, apophenia is a reflection of the human need to find connections, even in entirely unrelated information.

l'appel du vide [French: la'pell du veed]: the call of the void.

The French have an affinity with the abyss and its hypnotic effects. They have, for example, a term for the reproduction of an object within an object, often in endless reflections that recede into infinity. This is *mise en abîme*, meaning 'placed into the abyss' – you will find it on the cover for Pink Floyd's album *Ummagumma*, which utilizes the infinity effect through a large mirror.

An even more evocative term is *l'appel du vide*, 'the call of the void', which describes the impulse to jump off a cliff as you stare down from its summit, or to drive into the path of oncoming traffic. It can be as strong as it is irrational, and thankfully few of us give in to it. But the mind is seduced by the abyss as if by some strange compulsion, perhaps as a reverse affirmation of the desire to live. We consider doing something life-destroying precisely in order to dismiss it and appreciate life more fully.

appetite: an instinctive desire or craving to eat.

Appetite is different from hunger: as the writer Rabelais put it, 'Appetite *comes* with eating ... but the thirst goes away with drinking.' The relationship between appetites, passions, and emotions has been fluid over the centuries. For Thomas

Aquinas, passions and affections were different parts of the soul, where one represents physical appetite and the other the intellectual kind; both represent a search or desire for more. Indeed, 'seeking' and 'desire' come together in the very word 'appetite', which derives from the Latin *appetitus*, 'desire for', itself from *appetere*, to 'seek after'. Yet for all that we seek to desire, our cravings must always be kept in check: in Shakespeare's *Troilus and Cressida*, the appetite is given life as the 'universal wolf' that 'last eat up himself'.

apricity: the warmth of the sun on a winter's day.

The physiological effects of sunshine are well proven. We are sadder when deprived of it, and swimming with serotonin when basking in it. That basking, centuries ago, was known as 'apricating', and it is a word with a beautiful relative. There is just a single record of 'apricity' in the *Oxford English Dictionary*, from 1623, where it is presented simply as 'the warmeness of the Sunne in Winter'. The sound of 'apricity' is almost as exquisite as the feeling it describes.

Arcadian: idyllically innocent, simple, and untroubled.

It was the Roman poet Virgil who described a particular mountainous, landlocked region of Greece so remote and untouched that it provided the ideal backdrop to pastoral poetry. The region was known as Arcadia, and over the centuries many writers found themselves equally inspired. The poems of Arcadia speak of an unruffled, idealized existence, far removed from the turbulent passions of the outside world. Here, sighs of pleasure emanate from pan-pipers as they play to coquettish nymphs, while shepherds and goatherds sing harmonies to their animals.

An Arcadian existence is therefore one of peaceful pleasure, characterized by a total harmony with nature. Above all, it is a life of utter tranquillity. When Marie Antoinette started keeping her own flock of very clean cows at Trianon, a picturesque French farm free of dirt, disease, or poverty, she was trying perhaps to cling on to an Arcadian fantasy of a simpler life and to ignore the warning signs of impending revolution. Unfortunately, the rich queen pretending to be a milkmaid proved the final straw for an angry and starving populace. Even Arcadia has its price.

aroused: excited; stimulated.

The word 'rouse' is a borrowing from the Normans, for whom it was a hunting and hawking term. When a hawk 'roused' it shook its feathers, whilst gamekeepers 'rousing' birds would be 'putting them up', or chasing them from cover. From here came the general sense of stirring oneself into action, or of becoming active (voluntarily or otherwise) after a period of rest. 'Arouse' came about as an extension of 'rouse' on the pattern of 'arise', but when, in the sixteenth century, 'rousing' veered closer to a state of excitement or heightened emotion, 'arouse' happily took over the sexual side of things.

arsle: to go backwards.

For those days when you seem to be achieving the very opposite of progress, and to be going instead in entirely the wrong direction, there is always the verb 'arsle', which means simply to go backwards on a task, or 'arsewards'.

aspectabund: wearing your emotions plainly.

In his history of the theatre, published in 1708, John Downes declares of one actor, 'On the Stage, he's very Aspectabund, wearing a Farce in his Face.' The 'farce' in question was copious face paint, based on another meaning of the word, 'forcemeat' or 'stuffing', since the comedic farces were 'stuffed' into interludes during more serious dramatic performances. As for 'aspectabund', its definition is simple: 'expressive of face'. The word is made up of 'aspect', meaning 'look', and the deliberately ornate '-bundus', modelled on such Latinate words as 'moribund': 'in terminal decline'. When you are 'aspectabund', your expressions betray your current mood as clearly as if they were actors on a stage.

astonish: to astound.

In its early days, 'astonish' was a boomingly effective word. It originated with the Romans and the Latin *ex*, 'out', and *tonare*, to 'thunder', as though astonishment came directly from Jupiter, god of the sky and storms. Amongst its offspring is the shorter form 'stun', which neatly describes the effects of 'astonishment' in the sixteenth century, when it meant to 'deprive a person of every sensation' to the extent that they were stupefied or paralysed. As the word progressed, so its meaning began to shift and soften, moving from thunderous stupefaction to setting someone's teeth on edge, and on to shock or wonder.

ataraxy: calmness untroubled by mental distress.

Recent years of despondency and fear have pushed 'serenity' to the very corners of our dictionary. But you don't have to be a yogic master to achieve nirvana. Central to several ancient Greek philosophies is the concept of *ataraxei*, generally translated as 'imperturbability', 'equanimity', or 'tranquillity'. For the Epicureans, who were famously focused on pleasure, this lucid state of freedom from distress and worry was the key to achieving perfect happiness. In non-philosophical usage, the term could describe the ideal mental state for soldiers entering battle. It is founded upon the Greek *a*, 'not', and *tarassein*, to 'disturb'. In other words, an 'ataraxic' state is one of absolute calm, when emotions are as unruffled and peaceful as the halcyon days of the past.

aware: having knowledge or perception.

To be *ware*, in Old English, was to be 'informed and conscious'. It stems from an ancient root meaning to 'take care' (a little like **gorm**). To 'be well ware' meant to 'take note'; when the 'well' dropped out, we were left with 'beware'. As for 'ware' itself, it took on two further forms in the words 'wary' and 'aware' – both descriptive of someone alert and on their guard. Such attention to the moment is a key tenet of mindfulness, where we are taught to 'observe what is', as the actor Bruce Lee once remarked, 'with undivided awareness'.

awkward: uneasy; tricky; embarrassed.

Throughout history, left-handers have been given a particularly bad rap. The word 'sinister' came to us directly from the Latin for 'left', while 'dextrous' comes from *dexter*, meaning 'right'. Depending on where you are in Britain, you can be 'kay-pawed', 'cack-handed', and 'caggy-handed', as well as a 'cuddy-wifter' or 'pally-duker'. The word 'awkward' is another in this mould. It comes from the Vikings' *awk*, 'the wrong way round' – another disparaging nod to those seen to be on the wrong side of everything. 'Awks', the modern contracted version, has become shorthand for any difficult and embarrassing situation.

awumbuk [Baining: a-WOOM-book]: emptiness and lethargy after loved ones depart.

One of the most complex human emotions is surely empty-nest syndrome, when a formerly busy, buzzing house is suddenly devoid of the children whose activity once filled it. Then there is the more fleeting emptiness when much-loved visitors leave and silence descends. Such emotions of loss, for the Baining people from the mountains of Papua New Guinea, are captured in the word *awumbuk*: a form of emotional hangover after company has been withdrawn.

The Baining believe that departing visitors, in an effort to travel lightly, shed their heaviness as they leave, which then lingers in their wake and creates melancholy and apathy among those left behind. As an antidote, a coconut shell of water is left overnight in the house of the hosts, which is believed to absorb the charged air. The next morning, the occupants ceremonially empty the water into the forests, purging sadness and allowing for the resumption of normal life.

backendish: wet, windy, and appropriate for the end of the year.

In its literal sense, 'backendish' describes weather that is simply 'blah': damp and dreich, and full of grey. This description from Yorkshire dialect can also be neatly transferred to the general feeling of **frobly-mobliness** that can set in during the slow, dark days of winter.

backfriend: a secret enemy.

In *A Dictionary of the English Language* from 1755, Samuel Johnson defines a 'backfriend' as 'a friend backwards; that is an enemy in secret'. The predecessor to today's 'frenemy', the backfriend represents the ultimate in betrayal (a word that itself began with the Latin *trahere*, 'to hand over'). As Anonymous once noted: 'The saddest thing about betrayal is that it never comes from your enemies.'

badkruka [Swedish: bad-kroo-kah]: a cowardly bather.

If you live in fear of the **curglaff** – Old Scots for the almighty shock of cold water hitting you – then you may well also be a *badkruka*. This Swedish word is made up of *bada*, meaning 'bathe', and *kruka*, literally a 'pot' or 'jug', and itself a slang term for a coward. A *badkruka* is therefore someone who gingerly lowers themselves into water to make the curglaff as bearable as possible.

bamboozled: deceived; hoodwinked.

'Bamboozle' arrived out of nowhere in the early 1700s, appearing in an article in the *Tatler* magazine by the author Jonathan Swift, in which he decried 'the continual Corruption of our English tongue'. On the list of words Swift held up for criticism, alongside 'bamboozle', were 'banter', 'sham', 'mob', 'bubble', and 'bully' – all considered by Swift to be fancy concoctions dictated by fashion rather than sense.

Where do the origins of 'bamboozle' lie? Several theories have been put forward, including the Scots 'bumbaze', which has a similar meaning, while others look to beginnings among the Roma community. Last of the contenders is a very old French word, *embabouiner*, meaning to 'make a baboon of'. No solid evidence for a connection with any of these has been discovered, but it's hard to resist the idea that bamboozling someone is, metaphorically speaking, making a monkey out of them.

bào fù xìng áo yè [Chinese: pao fu hsing ao yeh]: staying awake as revenge.

When we feel an inability to control the world around us, we tend to turn to things closer to home. We might choose, for example, to stay up far too late as a way of regaining an ounce of the freedom we feel has been denied to us during the day. The Chinese have an expression for exactly this. *Bào fù xìng áo yè* translates as 'suffering through the night vengefully' – in other words, this is revenge bedtime procrastination.

Barbados, been to: intoxicated.

This curious phrase has echoes of a Victorian euphemism for going to the toilet: 'visiting the Spice Islands'. But although the Spice Islands might be a detour on the way back from Barbados, the expression belongs in *The Drinker's Dictionary*, published in an edition of the *Pennsylvania Gazette* from 1737, a paper owned by a rising young publisher called Benjamin Franklin. Franklin prefaced the list of 228 terms picked up from taverns across the country with a statement that there is 'Nothing more like a fool than a drunken man'.

   The Drinker's Dictionary is as curious as it is comprehensive. Under 'J', for example, you will find 'Jolly', 'Jagg'd', 'Jambled', 'Going to Jerusalem', 'Jocular', 'Been to Jericho', and 'Juicy'. A victim of strong liquor might also be 'Piss'd in the Brook' or have even 'Been too Free with Sir Richard'. As for Barbados, its celebrated export of rum frequently appeared on the editorial pages of the *Gazette*, so it is little surprise, perhaps, that its name became equated with the causes of **crapulence**.

basorexia: a sudden appetite to kiss someone.

The Greek suffix *-orexia* denotes a hunger or appetite and is typically used in medicine: to suffer from 'anorexia' is to be without (the Greek *an*) appetite, while 'orthorexia' describes an extreme desire to eat healthy or 'straight' (*orthos*) food. Occasionally the appetite encompasses other impulses, such as 'basorexia': the overwhelming desire to kiss someone.

befuddled: confused; perplexed; tipsy.

The *Oxford English Dictionary* makes no bones about the state of being 'befuddled', which it defines as 'to be made stupid by tippling'. The word is an extension of a sixteenth-century verb, to 'fuddle', meaning to 'have a drinking bout; to tipple or booze'. It was used particularly in the expression 'to fuddle it', meaning, essentially, to go out on the lash, while a pub was popularly known as the 'fuddle shop'. Over time 'befuddled' has been used more and more to describe a confusion that may not always come from a bottle.

benighted: feeling heavy sorrow or disappointment.

'Benightment' is all about the descent of darkness, be it physical, intellectual, or moral. John Milton offers a suitably ominous description in *Comus*:

> He that hides a darke soule, and foule thoughts
> Benighted walks under the mid-day Sun.

For the rest of us, dark souls or no, to be 'benighted' is to be plunged into a darkness obscuring all hope. Happily, however, the historical dictionary offers some respite close by with 'bedawned', to 'be refreshed by dawn', and 'beday', to 'let in daylight'.

beochaoineadh [Irish: bay-oh-keen-you]: a lament for the living lost.

For the Romans, a *lamentum* was a 'weeping' or 'wailing', which became a set kind of mourning in the form of a lament for the dead. The Irish *beochaoineadh* is a different kind of mourning, even if the emotions it describes are just as strong. It is, essentially, a eulogy for the living – for someone who, although not dead, has gone away and is keenly missed.

berserk: wild, frenzied, and out of control.

Going 'berserk' is today more of an action than an emotion, but for the Vikings it was a matter of both. Norse literature tells of groups of warriors who fought with wild and uncontrolled ferocity, and who entered combat in a manic frenzy known as a *berserkr* rage. *Berserkr* itself translates as 'bear-coat', and alludes to the bearskins worn by the warriors in battle that were believed to convey superhuman strength. Consequently known as 'berserkers', these fearsome enemies were said to become so intoxicated by battle lust that they would dig their teeth into inanimate objects, attack boulders and trees, and even kill each other while waiting for the formal fight to begin. One of the twelfth-century chessmen found on the Isle of Lewis in the Scottish Hebrides depicts a warrior biting down hard on his shield. In the thirteenth-century *Volsung Saga*, a legendary saga written in Old Norse, it is said of the berserkers that they 'went without armour, were as mad as dogs and wolves, they bit their shields, were as strong as bears or oxen, they killed everybody, and neither fire nor iron bit them; this is called going berserk'.

betwattled: confused.

There are few better articulations of feeling addled, bewildered, and generally befuddled than 'betwattled', an inexplicably rare word from seventeenth-century English dialect. It is tempting to link its etymology to feeling like a bit of a twat, but it seems instead to rest on 'twattle', meaning both to 'gossip' (or 'tittle-tattle') and to 'stand idly about'. The latter sense of disengagement filtered through into what could be one of the most useful adjectives of our time.

betweenity: a state of in-betweenness or indecisiveness.

'It is really provoking', snarled a critic in the *Quarterly Review* in 1824, 'to find [Miss Mary Russell Mitford using] such low and provincial corruptions of language as "Betweenity".' The offending word in question had but a moment in the spotlight before vanishing fairly conclusively. Which is a pity, because it neatly conveys a sense of being neither one thing nor another – either as a permanent characteristic or a temporary phase of transition. 'Betweenity' thus suits both the banal and the important, whether it's an indecisiveness over what to choose from a menu, or the act of treading water while waiting for something significant to drop.

betwittered: overcome with pleasing excitement.

Before social media, 'twitter' was all about the birds. Like the word 'jargon', which began with the Norman French *jargoun*, meaning the indecipherable chattering of birds, 'twitter' denoted a light, tremulous but persistent chirruping. In human terms, such a sound might translate into a state of nervous excitement or agitation. To be 'in a twitter' was therefore to be all 'aflutter'.

Little surprise, therefore, that 'betwittered', in Yorkshire dialect, took on similar notes of excitement and nervousness. In Joseph Wright's *English Dialect Dictionary*, published between 1898 and 1905, it is defined as 'excited, frightened, or overcome with pleasing excitement'. That's quite a range of potential emotions, which some might say matches the modern-day 'beTwitterment' very well.

bewildered: lost and confused.

The origin of 'bewilder' is hiding in plain sight. At its heart are the words 'wild' and 'wilderness'. The latter, from the Old English *wilddeornes*, originally referred to uncultivated land occupied by undomesticated animals (*deor* here, the ancestor of 'deer', originally meant any animal). To 'wilder' was to lead someone astray or into 'the wild'. Someone 'bewildered' therefore, metaphorically at least, is thoroughly lost in the wilderness.

black dog: melancholy and depression.

Winston Churchill famously referred to his bouts of low spirits as his 'black dog'. His encounters with melancholy would often last several months, during which he functioned only with extreme difficulty. In a letter to his wife Clementine in 1911, upon learning that a friend's wife had been treated for depression by a German doctor, he wrote, 'I think this man might be useful to me – if my black dog returns. He seems quite away from me now – it is such a relief. All the colours come back into the picture.'

'Black dog' has been a synonym for depression for hundreds of years, but the belief in spectral canine tormentors dates back further still. Roman poetry describes the dark dogs of misery, while the animal has at various times been regarded as a gatekeeper to the realm of death and as one of the manifestations of the Devil.

Having 'the black dog on one's shoulder' was experienced by many before Churchill, including the lexicographer Samuel Johnson, who plaintively wrote of this unwelcome visitor, 'When I rise my breakfast is solitary, the black dog waits to share it, from breakfast to dinner he continues barking.'

blahs, the: despondency and low spirits.

Some things give you **all the feels**, while others bring on a case of 'the blahs'. This nattily descriptive term from US English emerged in the 1960s to mean low spirits and a generally depressed state of mind.

bliss: joy in the highest degree.

'Bliss' has become a real multi-tasker for most of us. We experience it in everything from eating a slice of cheesecake to dropping into a holiday hot tub. You might consider this a distance away from the original, heavenly, kind of bliss, but in fact such ordinary pleasures, for all their joy, are in keeping with the first meaning of the word, which focused very much on earthly delights including a 'lightness of countenance' and a 'smile'.

The roots of 'bliss' are the ancient Indo-European *blithiz*, meaning 'gentle' and 'kind', which also gave us 'blithe'. Thanks to its closeness in appearance to 'bless', it later became tightly bound to spiritual joy, and notably the joy of heaven. Today, it has come back around to secular felicity, and in our hyperbolic age can describe anything from the feel of fresh sheets to a true state of elation.

blues, the: melancholy and despondency.

There is an unexpected demonic influence behind a number of English words and expressions. When our grandparents exclaimed 'What the Dickens!' they were referring not to the great nineteenth-century novelist, but to the Devil himself – named indirectly for fear that use of his true name would summon him. The 'blue devils' were similarly feared, popularly conceived as harmful demons that induced despondency as well as hallucinations in an alcoholic. The 'blue devils' was eventually shortened to the 'blues', an evocative term for depression and low spirits.

The association of the blues with music is deep-rooted in African-American history. Plantation workers, toiling for long hours in the sun, often sang in a form of long, musical moan that was known as a 'shout' or 'holler'. Labourers on prison chain gangs and railroads continued this practice long after the end of slavery. Like spirituals, they conveyed stories of sorrow and struggle.

Such were the foundations for the Blues, a title that was harnessed suddenly and sensationally in the 1910s when it became a hit trend on the music scene. Built on those old folk songs, these Blues felt nonetheless new and different. Two of the primary figures responsible for popularizing them were William Christopher 'W. C.' Handy and Gertrude 'Ma' Rainey – the former's 'Memphis Blues' lit up what was already becoming a national craze, with all memory of the 'blue devils' long forgotten.

But why were those devils blue in the first place? The link between the colour and melancholy emerged in the fifteenth century, and may be connected to the use of 'blue' to describe skin that had a leaden colour as the result of disease or exposure to the cold. Blue, as the *New English Dictionary* of 1885 notes, was also 'the distinctive colour for the dress of servants, tradesmen, etc., also of paupers, charity-school boys, almsmen, and in Scotland of the king's almoners or licensed beggars'. The colour was equally chosen for the uniform worn by prostitutes sent to prison, which might in turn have informed the idea of a 'blue joke'. In fact, the list of undesirables that were described as 'blue' was vast, from plagues and pestilence to poverty. Little surprise, then, that the demons besetting alcoholics were similarly conceived.

bluthered: having a face swollen by weeping.

To 'bluther', according to the *Dictionaries of the Scots Language*, is to 'soil or disfigure the face with tears, blood, etc.' – in other words, a 'bluthered' face is one messed up by something wet, particularly as the result of heavy weeping. In its uses it is not unlike 'blubber', an unsympathetic description of crying that dates back to the sixteenth century. In the 1550s, the future Archbishop of Canterbury Matthew Parker stated in a sermon that to weep for the dead was to deny the resurrection, declaring it 'womanish', 'childish', and 'beastly' to 'use any howling or blubbering' for the deceased, 'in the manner of the heathen'. As for 'bluther', the *Dictionaries* offer another useful definition: 'to make a noise with the mouth in taking in liquid' – that is to give out a highly annoying slurp.

blutterbunged: confounded.

There is astonishment, and there is open-mouthed amazement – a state once described in some parts of northern England as being 'gloppened'. For the articulation of being overwhelmed, whether by shock, disgust, or happiness, 'blutterbunged' is the word you need. Originating in Lincolnshire, it describes a state of being utterly overtaken by surprise.

boffola: a hearty, unrestrained laugh.

A 'boffola', as you might expect, is a little 'boff'. The latter emerged in the USA in the 1940s as a word for a joke or punchline (also known as a 'boffo') that elicits uproarious laughter, the kind you can't contain. A 'boffola' can equally mean the unchecked laughter that a deeply funny joke provokes.

The suffix '-ola' has proved highly useful since its beginnings in 'pianola'. Although it was used in the latter to mean 'little', as with 'boffola', the suffix came to be a versatile intensifier too, producing slang's 'schnozzola' (the nose), 'cashola' (money), and the 'noisola', a jukebox.

boredom: tedium; ennui.

'Boredom' didn't exist until the nineteenth century – at least not as we know it today. The word is first recorded in 1853, when Charles Dickens employed it in *Bleak House* as a 'chronic malady'. The noun 'bore' had been around for almost a century by then, and was used slightly differently from today. To be 'in a bore' was to suffer a bout of ennui. The latter, typified by world-weariness and lassitude, was seen as an exclusively 'French' malady at the time, while 'boredom' was to become its less sophisticated English cousin.

Whereas ennui suggests a languishing and listlessness – even a sense of futility – boredom can be a passing moment, spurring us on to look for distraction or fulfilment. Boredom is also usually outside ourselves, rather than the result of a moral or physical deficiency. By contrast, the antidotes for ennui, insisted upon by Victorians alarmed at the decadence and aestheticism of the end of the nineteenth century, were moral earnestness and a strong work ethic. The cure for boredom was far less certain, as Lord Byron must have lamented when he wrote in *Don Juan*:

> Society is now one polish'd horde,
> Formed of two mighty tribes, the *Bores* and *Bored*.

boreout: chronic boredom.

Most of us are familiar with 'burnout', the result of a work/life imbalance and excessively long hours, but 'boreout' may be less familiar – at least in name. This recent coinage describes the effects either of an insufficient workload or an overwhelmingly repetitive one. In 2020, an employee at a luxury perfume-maker won substantial damages from his employers for subjecting him to the boreout of having so little to do that it gravely affected his mental health.

brabbag [Manx: bravvag]: the pleasure in warming oneself by the fire.

Where English dialect has 'cloffin', Manx has *brabbag*. Both describe the simple and instinctive pleasure of an open fire.

With 'brabbag', the delight seems to be in specifically warming the back of one's legs in front of it.

braggadocio [brag-uh-doh-chi-oh]: a blustering boaster.

Take a fairly ordinary English word, add a dash of Italian, and you end up with something exotic. So it is with 'braggadocio', which was formed in the sixteenth century by combining the English 'brag' with a twist on the Italian *-occio* for extra pizzazz. A 'braggadocio' is an empty, idle boaster, a swaggerer. If ever a word strutted its stuff just like the person it describes, this is it.

breedbate: someone looking for an argument.

'Bate' is a fifteenth-century word for strife or discord. It comes either from a shortening of 'debate', or from the Old French *batre*, meaning to exchange physical blows or verbal fisticuffs. If you 'breed bate', you are looking for a fight, which makes a 'breedbate' the last person you want around if you're after a quiet life. Breedbates are also the reason why the mute button exists on social media.

bugbear: a cause of excessive fear or irritation.

The first 'bugbears' were recorded in the middle of the sixteenth century. They appear in a spine-tingling description of a range of terrors from a play of that period: *Hob Goblin, Rawhead, & bloudibone, the ouglie hagges Bugbeares, & helhoundes* . . .

A 'bugbear', then, was no trivial thing. Rather, it was conceived as an imaginary evil creature said to devour children who misbehaved. The 'bug' is a variation of 'bogy', while the 'bear' added to the spectre of ferocity. From here, 'bugbear' became a source of fear or dread.

Today's examples, often involving linguistic pedantries, are more pet hates than terrorizing beasts – a 'bête noire', if you like, which once carried the same potency, coming from the French for 'black beast'.

bully: one who seeks to intimidate someone vulnerable.

There are no upsides to bullying, no hint of anything good about an intimidation and aggression that can ruin lives. And yet 'bully' was once a term of real affection, having started out as the Dutch *boel*, 'lover'. The word was even used as an unofficial title in personal names, such as Shakespeare's Bully Bottom in *A Midsummer Night's Dream*. Later it was frequently used as an affectionate moniker between male friends – an admiring description of a 'fine fellow' or 'gallant'. This byword for 'mate' or 'brother' continued in English dialect right up until the nineteenth century, but in mainstream English the rot had already set in. A 'bully' was not just a gallant, but a blustering, swaggering one – a 'bravo', 'hector', or 'swashbuckler' of the kind we still loathe today.

bumfuzzled: confused or bewildered.

The state of utter bewilderment has attracted many synonyms over the centuries. Amongst the most expressive is 'bumfuzzled', first recorded in an Indiana gazette from 1878 in reference to one unfortunate J. M. Golden (Honorable), described as 'the worst bumfuzzled man in ten states'. The adjective is likely to be a take on **bamboozled**, only with less of the trickery and more of the confusion.

Bunbury: an excuse or alibi.

'Excuses are like assholes, Taylor: everybody's got one' – the conclusion of Sgt O'Neill in Oliver Stone's *Platoon*. If you're the sort of person who frequently feels the need to escape an obligation, 'Bunbury' may be the word for you. Oscar Wilde famously came up with it as the name for an imaginary person in *The Importance of Being Earnest*: 'I have invented an invaluable permanent invalid called Bunbury, in order that I may be able to go down into the country whenever I choose,' explains Algernon in Wilde's play, before making 'Bunbury' a particularly useful verb, too: 'I have Bunburyed all over Shropshire on two separate occasions.' Such allusions may now be lost to most of us, but the very sound of 'Bunbury' makes it too good to resist whenever we might need a spurious alibi.

burnout: a state of emotional and physical exhaustion.

'If you subtract your ability to work, who are you? Is there a self left to excavate?' asks Anne Helen Petersen in *Can't Even: How Millennials Became the Burnout Generation*. There she explores the condition of being so exhausted from overwork that it destroys us as effectively as a fire guts a building, leaving behind nothing more than a shell. The effect of burnout, Petersen writes, is 'more than just addiction to work. It's an alienation from the self, and from desire.'

busy: occupied; having a great deal to do.

For all that it defines our modern lives, no one knows precisely where 'busy' comes from. Its story began with the Old English adjective *bisig*, which in its earliest use could also mean 'careful', 'eager', and 'anxious'. There is a sense here of intensity, an element of which can be found in other languages – the German *bisen*, for example, once meant to 'run around wildly or bolt'. All may come from an ancient root meaning to 'tremble' or 'shock', and there is still a panicked edge to much of our busy-ness these days. (If, on the other hand, you are busy doing nothing, see **quiddling**.)

buzzed: tipsy; overstimulated.

'Buzz' has proved a useful set of letters. For Shakespeare's contemporaries, it was a common exclamation of impatience or contempt, expecially when someone was spinning a yarn – the Jacobean equivalent of 'pish!' or 'fie!' In the eighteenth century, to 'buzz' was to finish the very last drop in a bottle, while if you were 'buzzed' a hundred years later, you had probably fallen victim to a pickpocket. Today, being 'buzzed' can either mean feeling high from drugs or alcohol, or simply to be buzzing with excitement. In these senses, the reference is to the busy 'bombilating' or humming of a highly social insect. Anyone who is a 'buzzkill', on the other hand, dampens all enthusiasm and enjoyment and is a total killjoy.

cacafuego: a braggart or swaggering boaster.

In 1578, Sir Francis Drake, at the helm of the *Golden Hind*, passed through the Strait of Magellan and sailed into the Pacific Ocean below the radar of the Spanish authorities. *El Draque*, as he was known to them, was able to secretly garner information as to the whereabouts of a 120-ton Spanish galleon called *Nuestra Señora de la Concepción* (Our Lady of the (Immaculate) Conception). The ship, which Drake knew to be laden with silver and jewels, was nicknamed the *Cacafuego*, 'fire-shitter' or 'spitfire', thanks to its considerable arsenal. In the event, when Drake caught up with his target and opened fire, such was the crew's surprise that he encountered little resistance, and the *Cacafuego* became one of his most famous conquests. It took six days to unload the galleon's treasure. This triumphant escapade ensured that 'cacafuego' slipped into English to describe any braggart whose bluster and bravado ultimately amount to nothing, just like the eponymous ship.

cacoethes [ka-ko-ee-theez]: the irresistible desire to do something unwise.

Few words beginning with 'cac' or 'kak' in English promise anything positive, for *kakos*, their root, is Greek for 'bad'. A 'cacophony' is a discordant din, while a 'kakistocracy' is a government run by the worst of citizens. 'Cacoethes' is no exception. Borrowed directly from the Greek *kakoēthes*, 'an ill habit or itch', the term perfectly describes the compulsion to behave in a way you know will ultimately do you no good whatsoever. You might have a 'cacoethes' for smoking, for example, or for making a knee-jerk response to a situation when taking a breath would have been far more sensible.

If 'cacoethes' is just a little too hard to pronounce, English has come up with an easier term for doing something you already know is a mistake: **pregret**.

callomania: an excessive regard for beauty.

The opposite of the Greek *kakos* is *kalos*, meaning 'good' or 'beautiful'. We may not know it, but 'callomania' is everywhere. It is defined in medical dictionaries in two ways: as either an attraction to someone purely on account of their beauty, or as a delusional belief in one's own attractiveness. The term is typically used within medicine for a manifestation of psychosis, but in its undiagnosed form it is surely one of the foundations of social media, where we are rendered instantly beautiful by filters and momentarily deluded into thinking we actually look like that.

calophantic: pretending to be better than you actually are.

A useful adjunct to the callomaniac is the 'calophantic': a word from Tudor times for someone who makes a fine show of excellence but goes no further. In other words, they like to flaunt their own superiority despite all evidence to the contrary.

candour: openness and honesty.

'Candour' comes from the Latin *candor*, 'brilliance', and *candidus*, a perfect, shining white. In grimier Roman times, this colour was both precious and infinitely harder to maintain, adding to its cachet. The heavy woollen togas that ordinary citizens wore once they reached adulthood were generally cream; those running for political office, on the other hand, wore a special and dazzlingly white *toga candida*. Such a pure white was achieved by a bleaching process involving sulphur, while those keen to improvise might rub chalk on their togas. From *candidus* we have derived both 'candidate' and 'candid', for those political hopefuls wishing to appear honest and true – whiter than white. For 'candour', it was a small step from shining whiteness to a figurative sense of complete integrity and openness. 'All faults may be forgiven of him who has perfect candour,' wrote the poet and essayist Walt Whitman.

cantankerous: ill-natured and quarrelsome.

'Cantankerous' has triumphed in the vocabulary of peevish contrariness for over 300 years. Too grumpy to be confined to dictionaries, it seems to be the much-improved result of a Middle English word, *conteck*, meaning 'quarrelling' or 'strife', changing its form later under the influence of such words as 'rancorous' and 'cankerous'. Another theory has it as a blend of the Anglo-Irish *cant* ('auction') and 'rancorous' (that must have been a *very* bad-tempered auction).

Whatever its origin, 'cantankerous' is pleasingly pithy. In Oliver Goldsmith's eighteenth-century comedy *She Stoops to Conquer*, one character is summarily dimissed with 'Ecod! I know every inch about her; and there's not a more bitter cantankerous toad in all Christendom.'

capricious: unpredictable.

It's a strange linguistic journey that takes in both a whim and a hedgehog, but 'capricious' does just that. It came to us from the Italian *capriccio*, made up of *capo* 'head', and *riccio* 'hedgehog'. A 'hedgehog-head' is one whose hair stands on end, just like the prickly creature's spines. In human terms, this is usually the result of being horrified or alarmed, and *capriccio* described a state of 'shuddering', later picked up in the musical lexicon to mean 'lively' and 'free in form'. In its English incarnation, 'caprice' came to mean any sudden and dramatic change. A 'capricious' person is therefore a whimsical one, inclined to dart from one idea or action to another, much like the word itself.

care: attention; consideration; anxiety.

'Don't care was made to care,' goes the old nursery rhyme, a cautionary tale for grumpy children tired of being told what to do by adults. 'Care' is a confusingly flexible word; its many faces occupy a range of emotions encompassing both happiness and grief. We are 'careful', 'careless', and 'carefree'; we 'take care', are 'full of care', 'couldn't care less', and occasionally 'couldn't care a fig'.

They each began with the Old English *carian*, which is related both to the Old High German *chara*, to 'grieve' or 'lament', and to the Viking word *kor*, meaning 'sickbed'. The earliest emotional states that 'care' described were thus to do with sadness and ailing. To be 'in care', in the eleventh century, was to be in a state of unease, whilst 'clothing of care' was a synonym for mourning dress. You could equally be 'care-pined', 'care-worn', 'care-wrinkled', and 'care-crazed'. It followed, then, that 'careless' initially meant 'free of anxiety and apprehension'; like 'gormless', however, the word grew to mean 'heedless' and 'negligent', whilst 'carefree' took on the insouciant, untroubled side of things.

carnaptious: bad-tempered and argumentative.

Little needs to be said about 'carnaptious' other than that it is made up of the intensifying prefix *car-* and a version of *knap*, to 'bite' or 'snap'. Any 'carnaptious' person will neither need nor want further explanation.

catastrophize: to imagine the worst possible conclusion from an event or circumstance.

'What is the most likely outcome?' Ask this question of a catastrophizer, and there is only ever one answer: that outcome will be the absolute worst. Catastrophizing involves a cognitive distortion that exaggerates the bad and underplays the good in any situation. In other words, this is a thinking error, and an extremely seductive one at that.

When English speakers first borrowed the Greek word *katastrophē*, from *katastrephein*, 'to overturn', in the 1500s, they used it for the conclusion of a dramatic work, in particular that of a tragedy. In time, the meaning of 'catastrophe' broadened to describe any ending that was at best unhappy or at worst totally ruinous. Our tendency for linguistic inflation ensured that it was the latter definition that took hold, so that by the mid 1700s the word was harnessed exclusively for any devastating event such as a war or earthquake. But the tide has begun to turn back again, and 'catastrophe' is today frequently applied to things that are only mildly unpleasant, from an embarrassing date to a burnt omelette. As a verb, 'catastrophize' manages to combine the calamitous consequences of the original meaning of 'catastrophe' and the overegging inherent in its current, diluted sense. Whichever end of the scale it sits on, however, the expectation of the very worst is at the core of much of our modern anxiety.

catchfart: a servant; one who follows the political wind.

We have all encountered a 'catchfart' or two – the obsequious individual who sucks up to anyone they consider important. This pungent term, which dates back to the seventeenth century, began as a mocking nickname for a foot-servant, specifically one who followed their master or mistress so closely that they were in the firing line for a lot more than they bargained for.

cautious: prudent and heedful.

The word 'caution' was originally, in the thirteenth century, all about security and guarantees, specifically for the carrying-out of a pledge or promised engagement. By Shakespeare's time it had become a notion of warning and an admonition to take heed – a sense it carries to this day. After a warning comes care and wariness, which is where 'cautious' comes in – displaying a prudence in regard to danger.

There are plenty of expressive synonyms for 'cautious' available in the historical thesaurus, from 'averty' in the fourteenth century and 'hooly' in the fifteenth, to the still current 'chary', 'gingerish', and 'pussy-footed'.

cavoli riscaldati [Italian: ka-vo-li ris-kal-da-ti]: the pointless attempt to revive a romance.

The temptation to return to a former love affair, and the blind confidence that all the problems that once defined it will have completely disappeared, is known in Italian as *cavoli riscaldati* – literally 'reheated cabbage'. In other words, the promise of something delicious turns out to be entirely misplaced.

charitable: generous, tolerant, or lenient.

> Though I speak with the tongues of men and of angels, and have not charity, I am become as sounding brass, or a tinkling cymbal. And though I have the gift of prophecy, and understand all mysteries, and all knowledge; and though I have all faith, so that I could remove mountains, and have not charity, I am nothing.

Wedding guests have long pondered the rolling cadences of St Paul's Epistle to the Corinthians, famously also read by Prime Minister Tony Blair at the funeral of Princess Diana. Why is charity so all-important, and what might matrimony have to do with it? The answer is that 'charity' really began not at home, but in church, and with *caritas*, the Latin for 'dearness' and 'love'. In its earliest senses, in the twelfth century, it meant specifically Christian love and the support of fellow people.

The act of giving has been around since the beginning of time. The ancient Hebrews self-imposed a tax designed to help the poorest, while the word 'philanthropy' originated in Greece, where it meant 'a love of mankind'. In 1180 CE, Maimonides wrote the *Mishneh Torah* and, within it, the 'Eight Levels of Tzedakah' (the Hebrew word for 'charity'), in which the ultimate goal is Level One, whereby a charitable donor gives someone in need the wherewithal to support themselves. By the 1600s, charitable giving was beginning to be formalized, and the focus moved from feudal lord and dependant to a new social order, and from religious institutions to the state.

With such profound changes to social structures, the meaning of 'charity' was on the move, embracing not just theological support but also the secular virtues of altruism and humanitarianism. The seventeenth-century writer John Bunyan, author of the Christian allegory *The Pilgrim's Progress*, lived at a time that straddled the two. His writings mark the shift from the state to the individual: 'You have not lived today,' he wrote, 'until you have done something for someone who can never repay you.'

charmed: unusually lucky or happy.

Some people lead a charmed life, as though protected by a magic force. That magic is of course central to the idea of a 'charm', which began with the Latin *carmen*, a 'song' or 'incantation'. By the seventeenth century, the word encompassed any quality or attribute that exerts a fascinating influence – a meaning crafted in the full knowledge that **fascination** was once also all about supernatural powers (and penises).

cheer: optimism and confidence.

'Cheer' is a fundamentally happy word, variously attached to celebrations and friendship, support from the sporting sidelines, and lifting the spirits of someone who's sad. Yet its past wasn't all about joy and comfort. Its story began with the Greek *kara* and the Latin *cara*, both meaning 'head' or 'face'. It travelled into French as *cheir* and from there into English as 'cheer', where it described someone's facial expression, interpreted as a reflection of their inner feelings. Most of the earlier references linger on the sad side – in a fifteenth-century reworking of the story of King Arthur, Sir Lancelot departs with a 'heavy cheer'. Others in the same period are recorded as having a 'sad and sori' cheer, or even a 'waylinge and lamentable' one.

It wasn't until another couple of centuries had passed that 'cheer' began to be applied to anything that gladdened the heart. To 'cheer someone on' was to shout words of encouragement; to 'give three cheers', as early as the nineteenth century, was to celebrate a triumph or achievement. To utter 'cheers' to someone as a thank you or sign-off was simply to wish them 'good cheer' upon parting.

'Cheer' remained a term for the face and the mood it expressed well into the nineteenth century, when 'what cheer?' was a common greeting that meant 'how are you?' or, more literally, 'what's your mood?' It was this that was eventually worn down to 'wotcher', a salutation that belongs so memorably to the 1900s that it's hard to believe its story began thousands of years ago.

cherish: to hold dear.

'Cherish' is a kissing cousin of 'caress' and 'charity' – all from an ancient root meaning to 'love' or 'desire'. 'Cherish' came to English from the Old French *chierir*, from *chier*, 'dear' (*cher* and *chère* in modern French), and ultimately from the Latin *carus*, meaning 'dear' and 'beloved'.

cherubimical: happy-drunk.

If we had to choose what type of drunk we would want to be, many of us would opt for the 'cherubimical' kind. One of the many expressions in the eighteenth-century *Drinker's Dictionary*, it describes the drinker who becomes so happy and affection-ate that they go around hugging everyone. *See* **been to Barbados**.

cheugy [chew-gee]: demonstrating the need to try too hard.

'Cheugy' is said to have been the confection of a US high school student, who was searching for a new adjective to describe something off-trend and uncool, as seen in those who feel compelled to try too hard. Those who are 'cheugy' are consequently 'cheugs': behind the times or offputtingly conventional. To quote the *New York Times*, if you have a 'Keep Calm and Carry On' poster in your bedroom, call your friend a 'bestie', or announce the end of the week as *Fri-yay*, then you are probably a 'cheug'.

Like other insults of its kind, such as 'chav', 'cheugy' has become politicized, the subject of debate as to whether it is classist or misogynistic. Others see it as part of the ongoing 'war' between Gen-Z and millennials. Either way, 'cheugy' perhaps comes closest to another damning adjective of the 2020s: 'basic'.

chipper: cheerful and lively.

There is something undeniably reassuring about 'chipper'. It is the perky relation of 'kipper' from northern English dialect, used to mean 'nimble', 'lively', and 'in good spirits'. By the early 1800s, to be 'as chipper as a bird' was to be chirrupingly carefree and full of life.

chivalrous: courteous and gallant.

'Courtesy' is a word that wears its heart on its sleeve. It was essentially the code of etiquette demanded in royal company – if you were 'courteous', then your manners were fit for 'court' (at which you might 'curtsey', itself a simple variation on 'courtesy'). 'Chivalry' was also expected, a term that is etymologically a little more adventurous. In its earliest guise, the Old French *chevalerie*, lies the key to its inspiration – a *cheval* or horse, used by mounted men-at-arms and knights in battle. The meaning of 'chivalry' and 'chivalrous' extended to embrace bravery or prowess in war and, from there, knightly skill and manners. Historically, at least, the age of chivalry is indeed long dead.

choleric: bad-tempered and fiery.

For more than two millennia, medicine was founded upon the perceived influences of the four bodily humours. These were fluids organized around the four qualities of cold, hot, moist, and dry, which were believed to govern the physical health of all living beings.

The fluids in question were blood, phlegm, choler (yellow bile), and melancholy (black bile). Each needed to be kept in strict balance to avoid excessive emotion. A preponderance of blood, for example, was thought to lead to an overly sunny and optimistic disposition — hence 'sanguine', from the Latin *sanguineus*, 'bloody'. And an excess of yellow bile would make one nauseated ('bilious') or 'choleric'.

'Choler' was absorbed into English in the fourteenth century via the Anglo-Norman *colere*, but was ultimately from the Latin *cholera* (later a disease thought to cause large secretions of bile). A predominance of choler, believed to be hot and dry in nature, was said to cause irritability or irascibility of temper. To call someone 'choleric' today is to imply that they are hot-tempered and fiery, as well as red-faced through anger — the medieval predecessor, perhaps, of today's puce put-down 'gammon'.

chop-logical: disputatious and argumentative.

We have all encountered those who love nothing more than an argument for argument's sake (*see* **breedbate**). In the sixteenth century, a particularly specious discussion was known as a 'chop-logic', because the participants chopped subjects into tiny detail and, to borrow a different metaphor, were forever splitting hairs. The adjective 'chop-logical' soon developed to describe someone who kicks off a debate without any real skin in the game, and merely for the sake of bandying words back and forth.

churlish: mean-spirited; surly.

Churlishness tends to involve a sullen begrudgement or rude resentment. Its history, however, is about much more than mulish unhappiness.

In Saxon days, a *ceorl* was a peasant as opposed to a man of noble rank. As a label, it was fairly neutral: a statement of fact rather than anything inherently classist. Like most descriptions of its kind, however, it acquired insulting overtones over time. Just as the original 'villain' was simply a servant attached to a 'villa', so the 'churl', regarded as the lowest of the low, became associated with all manner of negative qualities, from uncouthness to outright dishonesty.

To be 'churlish', then, in Chaucer's day, was to be both brutish and surly. By the sixteenth century it had extended its meanings to embrace stinginess and ungraciousness too. Today, if you are feeling 'churlish', you are mean-spirited and generally **ill-willy**. The only trace of its prejudiced past is a hovering sense of 'beneath you' about it all.

circumbendibus: a pointless, circular exercise or debate.

A 'circumbendibus' is not, as you might think, an articulated bus built like an accordion that curves effortlessly around corners. It does, however, involve roundabouts, albeit of the verbal kind. Rather like a circumlocution, in which someone goes round and round the same point, a 'circumbendibus' is a seventeenth-century term for an entirely circular argument that never gets to the point, and whose emotional impact is to induce acute frustration in its audience.

clamihewit: a misfortune or disappointment.

The very sound of 'clamihewit', also spelt 'clamyhooit' and 'clamyhuic', shouts commotion and unhappiness. It appears in the *Scottish National Dictionary* where it is usefully described as 'an accident or disappointment to anyone'.

clevers, fit of the: a sudden rush of activity.

The French know it as a *charrette*, while in the seventeenth century it was also called a 'fire-flaught'. But by far the clearest articulation of a sudden flurry of energy, required when you realize the clock is ticking down, is a 'fit of the clevers', which comes to us from nineteenth-century Scotland and which is surely due a revival.

clinomania: the overwhelming desire to lie down.

Dictionaries tell the stories of hundreds of 'manias', a word that began with the Greek *mainesthai*, to 'be mad'. Among the most relatable is surely 'clinomania', a term hitherto restricted to medical textbooks, where it is defined as the irresistible desire to lie down. It is closely linked to anxiety disorders and depression, so is not always to be taken lightly. Nonetheless, its application to daily life is slowly nudging the term into the mainstream, where it sits alongside 'dysania': the intense longing to stay in bed.

cloud nine, on: blissfully happy.

'Cloud nine gets all the publicity, but cloud eight is actually cheaper, less crowded, and has a better view.' Wise words from the comedian George Carlin – in fact, wiser than he perhaps knew, for some of the earliest iterations of 'cloud nine' involved both 'cloud eight' and, especially, 'cloud seven'.

But why a numbered cloud in the first place? One theory involves a meteorological guide published in 1896 called the *International Cloud Atlas*. The guide classified ten basic types of cloud, with the lofty fluffy cumulonimbus coming in at number nine. Whether or not that holds water, the expression 'on cloud nine' was popularized by a 1950s US radio show in which a character called Johnny Dollar, a fictional insurance investigator, was continually coming unstuck through various misadventures. Every time he was knocked unconscious, Johnny was taken to 'cloud nine', where he recovered.

Nine, then, seems to be an arbitrary choice – as George Carlin mooted, we might have been just as delirious on cloud eight. Or, as it happens, in **seventh heaven**.

coddiwomple: to travel purposefully without a clear destination.

Dip into the lexicon of pootling and you'll never simply 'potter' again. Centuries of frittering away time have produced 'moodling', 'picking a salad', and 'thrumming caps', as well as 'piddling', 'puddling', and 'pingling'. What you won't find yet is the word 'coddiwompling': a much more recent invention whose sound surely makes it worthy of mention. 'Coddiwompling', to give it its popular definition, is to 'travel in a purposeful manner towards a destination as yet unknown'. It is, in other words, all about the journey, which makes it a cousin of such words as 'roaming' and 'roving', or the Irish *seachrán*, to 'wander' or 'stray'. Whilst all of these suggest something aimless and dawdling, however, 'coddiwompling' has far more determination. You may not know where you're going, but wherever it is, you'll get there.

cold feet: a loss of nerves or confidence.

The first record of 'cold feet' in our modern, idiomatic sense is from 1896. Of course, there were plenty of references to physically cold feet for centuries before, including many an advertisement for curing them. Its new use, however, quickly became popular as a metaphor for losing one's nerves, particularly during the First World War, whose mental and physical horrors included trench foot as a result of long immersion in freezing mud. Little wonder, then, that 'getting cold feet' operated on more than one level.

There is another theory, however, which connects the phrase to the gambling table. Players whose luck was waning were said to leave the table with the excuse of having cold feet.

Whatever its history, there is a lot of truth in the adage that it is better to have a cool head and a warm heart than a hot head and cold feet.

collywobbles: queasiness or intense anxiety.

The glorious-sounding 'collywobbles' is a fanciful concoction of 'colic' and 'wobbles'. Originally, in the nineteenth century, it referred to a terrible upheaval of the intestines – or, as people once evocatively put it, a 'grumbling of the groozlins'. As the word's physical associations began to fade, so mental disturbances took over, and an attack of the collywobbles today usually involves a state of high anxiety, albeit expressed with a smile.

comedy: entertainment designed to make an audience laugh.

'Life is a tragedy when seen in close-up, but a comedy in long shot': Charlie Chaplin saw that comedy and tragedy have always been two sides of the same coin. For the ancient Greeks, they were two of the three fundamental genres of drama, offered alongside the satyr plays that combined elements of both and that were sandwiched between parts of a tragedy to make fun of the plight of the drama's main characters (all the while dressed as satyrs, half-human and half-goat figures who sported giant phalluses for light relief).

Like the satyr plays, comedy was also designed to lampoon, only the focus here tended to be on public and political figures of the day, who would be mercilessly criticized under the disguise of buffoonery. Comedy's function was to be corrective, and to hold a mirror up to society and its many foibles. For Aristotle, tragedy imitated those who are better than average, while comedy imitated those who are worse, meaning that part of the surprise and pleasure of comedy is the feeling of superiority it induces in its audience.

By the Middle Ages, 'comedy' was shifting from satirical plays with a happy ending to performances whose main focus was on provoking laughter, even while the use of the term by such writers as Dante and Shakespeare retained the core idea of triumph over adversity. The buffoonery of those ancient comedies was preserved in the sixteenth-century *commedia dell'arte*, comic Italian plays in which masked actors portrayed stock characters such as Arlecchino and Pulcinella, the predecessors of Harlequin and Punch who were later to reappear in England's Punch and Judy puppet shows. They in turn looked ahead to the slapstick comedy of pantomime actors and clowns who entertained the masses in the nineteenth century.

Modern comedy, be it stand-up, surreal, romantic, burlesque, or situation, still holds true to a function of the kind that tickled the crowds in ancient Greece: it provides what the Russian critic Mikhail Bakhtin described as 'an officially sanctioned holiday' from the rules of normal life. These ideas of release and abandon are echoed in the term's etymology, the Greek *kōmos*, 'revel', and *aoidos*, 'singer', thanks to the revels associated with the ancient dramatic festivals held in honour of the god Dionysus. Shared laughter and merry-making can be as cathartic as the tears shed over tragedy. Humans, after all, are the only animals that both laugh and weep.

compassion: sympathetic concern for the sufferings of others.

As emotions go, passion and compassion feel wildly different, yet both derive from the same Latin root, *pati*, to 'suffer'. 'Compassion' is built upon *compati*, to 'suffer alongside'.

In ancient Greek philosophy, motivations based on 'pathos' ('feeling; passion') were frequently mistrusted, and reason was generally considered to be the proper guide to conduct. The figure of Justice is often depicted as blindfolded, because she is without passion and prejudice.

In Roman society, compassion was particularly viewed as a vice when expressed as 'pity' rather than 'mercy'. In other words, showing empathy to someone deserving was considered virtuous, whereas directing it to someone unworthy was immoral and weak. Perhaps in partial reaction to this, universal and unjudgemental compassion is central to many religions. The teachings of Christianity, Judaism, and Islam all stress the compassionate nature of God. The famous parable of the Good Samaritan describes a Samaritan traveller who 'was moved with compassion' at the sight of a man who was beaten. Today, compassion is still seen as the cornerstone of collective morality.

Even such an apparently worthy emotion has had its critics. The Greek philosopher Plato, who pictured the human emotions as a chariot propelled by the often conflicting demands of horses and driver, believed compassion to be potentially destructive, while Immanuel Kant viewed its inherent soft-heartedness as weak and misguided. The latest continuation of the spectrum is 'compassion fatigue': a burnout born from witnessing too much suffering and the compulsion to empathize, or – true to the emotion's etymology – 'suffer alongside' its victims.

confelicity: pleasure in another's happiness.

Most of us have heard of **_Schadenfreude_**, the one-word German articulation of the pleasure we take in someone else's pain. Few, however, know of a word for its far nicer flip side: finding joy in another person's happiness. Gratifyingly, one does exist, and its failure to catch on is as surprising as it is regrettable. You may find 'confelicity' in watching children opening their Christmas stockings, or in their nervous smiles during their first nativity.

The word is made up of the Latin *con*, 'with', and 'felicity' – based on the French (and ultimately Latin) for 'happiness'.

content: pleased; satisfied.

Are you content with the contents of your life? Despite their vastly different meanings, these two uses of 'content', pronounced with different stresses, share the same roots. Both grew from the Latin *continere*, to 'contain'. The connection with the 'contents' of a suitcase is a direct extension of the Latin, while being 'content' draws on the idea of being 'filled up' with satisfaction.

contumacious: reproachful, insolent; full of resentment.

For all its pretty sounds, the Latin *contumelia* has never been a happy word. Meaning 'abuse', 'insolence', or 'reproach', it has given us a raft of terms for contempt. The rare verb to 'contumely', in the fifteenth century, was to feel such reproach towards someone that you longed to humiliate them, while to be 'contumacious' was to be positively spiteful. The word 'contumax', meanwhile – surely a perfect name for the haughtiest of gladiators – meant 'insolent', 'obstinate', and 'utterly contemptuous of the law'.

cordial: from the heart.

A textbook from 1751 entitled *The Art of Distillation* lists some of the most effective tonics for the heart. They include 'Dr Burges' plague water' and the 'palsy water' of Dr Mathias. 'Godfrey's Cordial', meanwhile, originally prepared by Thomas Godfrey of Hunsdon in Hertfordshire in the early eighteenth century, was a tincture of opium with sassafras and treacle. It was to become hugely popular: the *Oxford Dictionary of National*

Biography notes that 'its sweetness and agreeable flavour, added to its ability to knock out the senses of the most fractious patient, made it a boon for distraught mothers and lazy nurses.'

Most cordials were a lot simpler. Lavender water was an antidote to 'falling sickness', what we would today call epilepsy. 'Surfeit water', consisting of poppies, raisins, and spices steeped and distilled in alcohol, was recommended as a hangover cure, while 'hysterical water' addressed women's complaints, and Mr Cornwell's Oriental Vegetable Cordial claimed to be 'especially efficacious against excruciating pains in the bowels'.

What has all of this to do with feelings? The answer is the seat of emotions, for 'cordial' is from the Latin *cordialis*, 'belonging to the heart'. Cordials such as those readily imbibed in the eighteenth century were viewed above all as tonics for the heart, which in turn would stimulate or comfort the entire body. Someone who is feeling 'cordial', meanwhile, will act sincerely, 'from the heart'.

coup de foudre [French: coo-duh-foo-druh]: falling in love at first sight.

In 2014, Google Translate assessed that we are far more likely to go to French than any other language for the articulation of love. French is not just a Romance language, one of a family derived from the language of the Romans, it is also, it seems, *the* language of romance and of sexual sauciness. 'Pardon my French' has become a standard apology for less-than-respectable language, while French knickers, kisses, and letters still hold erotic sway in the dictionary. And so it seems entirely fitting that the articulation of the thunderous moment in which we fall in love should belong to it too. The literal meaning of *coup de foudre* is 'stroke of lightning', an appropriate metaphor for the breathtaking and blindsiding awareness of love at first sight.

crambo–clink: poor-quality conversation.

For the Romans, any news described as *crambe repetita* was simply 'repeated cabbage' – second-hand, regurgitated, and distasteful (*see cavoli riscaldati*). Centuries later, the term found its way into English as 'crambo', a forfeit game in which one set of players has to guess a word agreed upon by the other set, after being told what word it rhymes with. The pastime, pronounced by Ben Jonson to be one of those 'Devil's games', nudged 'crambo' into English as a byword for useless or irritating repetition. Scots took it a step further, creating 'crambo-clink' to mean either doggerel or tedious conversation (the kind that might make you resort to **nod-craftiness**).

cranky: bad-tempered and irritable.

For the Anglo-Saxons, a *crancstæf* was a weaver's implement, the predecessor of the mechanical crank. 'Crank' is a relative of *crincan*, to 'bend', and the primary sense of the word is of 'something bent together'. The individual who is a 'crank' is fraudulent and therefore 'not straight', while to be 'cranky' was to be 'eccentric', and later, thanks to US English, 'bad-tempered' or 'bent out of shape' (the related German *krank* is still used of someone who is ill and out of sorts).

crapulent: hungover.

If ever a word had a dual personality it would be 'crapulental'. Half 'crap', and half 'monumental', it doesn't quite seem to know what it wants. Knock off the suffix, however, and you are left with 'crapulent', which leaves you in no doubt that this is nothing other than bad. The seventeenth-century adjective is defined in the *Oxford English Dictionary* as 'suffering from excess drinking, eating, etc.' (presumably the 'etc.' can cover a multitude of similar sins). 'Crapulence' is, in other words, a mighty hangover, a legacy of what one medicinal manual from 1694 described as the result of 'a drunken Debauch'.

The *OED* provides one possible further use of 'crapulent', which describes the debauchery itself rather than its after effects. Defined as 'given to gross intemperance', it offers just one terse record, from 1888: 'The crapulent monks'.

craven: contemptibly lacking in courage.

'Craven' is a distant relative of 'crepitation', meaning a 'crackling, bursting, or rattling sound' (or, bizarrely, the explosive ejection of fluid from the abdomen of a bombardier beetle). To 'crepitate' was also to 'break wind', which you might imagine to be the nervous reaction of a coward to any challenge. The more likely link between a craven person and crepitation, however, is the idea of bursting – in the case of a coward, being utterly defeated, with all strength evacuated.

crazy: mad; angry; foolish; infatuated.

Writing 'Crazy', the song that Patsy Kline was to make world-famous, Willie Nelson felt on the brink of physical and mental collapse. He was juggling three jobs to support his wife and three children, and success had never felt further away. Desperately writing songs on his long night commutes to play at clubs, and rueing his situation compared with those of his contemporaries, he recalls in his autobiography asking himself whether he was 'crazy' to continue hanging on for his big break. Such was the inspiration for his song.

Across the centuries the meaning of 'crazy' has veered between total insanity and mild foolishness. First recorded in the sixteenth century, when it meant 'cracked' or 'flawed', its root is the verb 'craze', meaning to 'break in pieces' or 'shatter' – a sense retained in our modern 'crazy paving'. A crazy person, therefore, has had their sanity shattered. Whether this is manifested by excitement, wild behaviour, infatuation, or stupidity is as fluid now as it was 400 years ago.

crestfallen: sad and dejected.

'O how meager and leane hee lookt, so creast falne, that his combe hung downe to his bill': such was the writer John Lyly's sixteenth-century description of a bird with a drooping 'crest' – the tuft of feathers on its head. The image behind the sorry adjective 'crestfallen' is just the same: of someone so dejected, abashed, and cast down that they resemble a defeated fighting cock. The ancient antithesis, 'crest-risen', meaning 'proud' or 'lusty', never quite caught on. Today, the crestfallen droop may be as much spiritual as physical, but the pervasive sense of dejection is very much the same.

cringy: worthy of disgust or embarrassment.

'Cringy' is surely the universal teenage adjective of choice to describe parents. Fittingly, perhaps, the word is a relative of 'cranky': both carry the idea of being bent out of shape – in the case of 'cringe', by bending one's head or body in fear or apprehension. To 'cringe', of course, is also to feel an inward shiver of utter embarrassment: the body's instinctive response to anything or anyone deemed 'cringy' – or, more modern still, **cheugy**.

crocodile tears: fake or insincere sorrow.

We have been crying 'crocodile tears' since the sixteenth century. The odd expression stems from an ancient belief that crocodiles regularly weep in order to lure prey, which is then promptly devoured, again with a show of tears. In *The Travels of John Mandeville*, the most widely circulated piece of travel writing in medieval Europe, a knight from St Albans sets off on a journey to the Holy Land and on to Asia and Africa. Of an encounter with crocodiles, the narrator notes, 'These serpents slay men, and then eat them weeping.'

But can a crocodile really weep? The experts say yes: they have tear glands like most other animals. And zoologists have recorded alligators, close relatives of crocodiles, shedding tears while they're eating. Crucially, though, rather than being an emotional response, the weeping seems to happen as a result of ingesting food: the animals huff and hiss as they blow out air, and their tear glands may empty at the same time. In other words, crocodile and alligator tears are unrelated to inner feelings. In human terms, 'crocodile tears' are perceived to be ones not of sorrow but of deceit – they too, albeit for different reasons, are entirely false.

croochie-proochles [kroo-chi-proo-chuls]: an uncomfortable feeling of restlessness.

'Croochie-proochles' is an unmistakably Scots expression for the 'discomfort from sitting in a cramped position', as well as general 'restlessness and fidgetiness'. Thought to be an altered version of 'crooky prickles', it's surely one for the Zoom generation and those of us who tried to set up a makeshift home office under the stairs. And if it all becomes too much, you might borrow another Scottish term, 'crinkie-winkie', which handily is 'a poor excuse for not achieving anything at all'.

crotchety: irritable and peevish.

As with 'cranky', the image behind being 'crotchety' is of something bent out of shape – in this case the shape of a hook. The musical note 'crotchet' acquired its name because of its 'hooked' shape, while the weaving of 'crochet', another relative, involves using a hooked needle.

crumpsy: cranky and irritable.

'Crumpsy' is a Cheshire synonym for 'grumpy'. The *English Dialect Dictionary* records one correspondent who states that 'fratchetty and crumpsy' is said of a 'tiresome, cross, child'. Now consigned to the margins, 'crumpsy' can still offer a pithy description of being irritable, creased, and probably in desperate need of coffee.

crush: a crowd of people pressed closely together; an intense feeling of love.

It's a strange journey that takes us from a violent compression to a romantic infatuation, but 'crush' has moved quite neatly from destruction to love in the course of its six centuries. The link, of course, is passion, and an emotional intensity that has informed 'crush' from the start. Its roots are just as fervent: the Old French *cruissir*, to 'gnash one's teeth'.

cupboard love: insincere affection to gain an advantage.

'A cupboard love is seldom true,' ran an eighteenth-century adage. 'Cupboard love' is the insincere kind, used to describe the false profession of love for the sake of gain. A cupboard lover is the opposite of the nineteenth-century 'bread and cheese friend', who will stick with you through feast and famine. The *Merriam-Webster Dictionary* offers a vivid description of exactly what the self-interest behind cupboard love might entail, from an eighteenth-century court record, *The Proceedings at the New Bayley*:

> Now, there is a Kind of Love in the Old Stile, termed Cupboard Love; and it often happens, that what People judge to be an Intrigue with a young Woman, turns out, on a nearer View, to be only an Intrigue with a Leg of Mutton and Turnips.

curglaff: the shock of cold water.

Scots has a knack of filling gaps in English that you either never quite knew existed, or that would otherwise take an entire sentence to describe. Take 'dreich', for example – the one-word evocation of a day that is miserable and wet. The bibulous amongst us might also be fond of the word 'bonailie' – a drink taken just before parting from friends. A 'bumfle', meanwhile, is an unsightly bulge in your clothing (perhaps best concealed by a 'cover-slut' – seventeenth-century speak for something worn over the top of a garment that is no longer presentable).

And so it is with 'curglaff', which neatly expresses the shock of cold water as you plunge into it – be it a pool, a sea or lake, or even the shower. It is made up of the prefix 'cur-', often applied when something or someone goes awry (think **curmudgeonly**), and 'glaff', a sudden blast of cold.

curious: eager to know or learn.

'Curiosity' was once all about care. Its source is the Latin *curiosus*, 'careful', which ultimately stems from *cura*, 'care' (indeed it was 'care' that originally 'killed the cat', rather than 'curiosity'). Simple enough, yet 'curious' has had a variety of meanings over the centuries, including 'skilfully made', 'accurate or precise', and 'having an exquisite taste' – all bearing the idea of close attention to detail. Today, 'curious' lives a double life, describing both inquisitiveness and something strange or unusual. This last meaning emerged in the eighteenth century, when 'curious' became a euphemistic term among booksellers for a work that was erotic or pornographic. As for 'curiouser and curiouser', this has never quite lost its moorings from Alice and her adventures in Wonderland, who 'was so much surprised, that for the moment she quite forgot how to speak good English'.

curmudgeonly: bad-tempered and mean-spirited.

In his 1755 *Dictionary of the English Language*, Samuel Johnson described a 'curmudgeon' as 'an avaricious churlish fellow; a miser; a niggard'. The word's etymology, he maintained, was a mangling of the French *cœur méchant*, or 'evil heart'. As origins go, it is fairly ingenious, but there is no evidence whatsoever to back it up.

If not from an evil heart, where did 'curmudgeon' originate? The answer, sadly, is unknown, and a host of early spellings – 'curmudgin', 'cormogeon', and even 'cormullion' – make the trail even trickier. It may be a nod to the Scots 'curmurring', a low growling sound, such as you might pick up from a cantankerous curmudgeon.

cursed: expressing annoyance or irritation; subject to a curse.

From the evil eye to menstruation, the mark of Cain to the Hope Diamond, curses have been invoked and feared for as long as humans have pondered the supernatural world. The belief in vengeful spirits and malevolent gods has inspired spells and maledictions for millennia. Curses were found carved upon the tombs of the pharaohs (Tutankhamun's Tomb was believed to be afflicted by 'The Mummy's Curse', said to unleash fire, floods, and even deaths amongst those excavating it), whilst at the Roman baths at Bath, 130 ancient 'curse tablets', or *defixiones*, have been unearthed, upon which are inscribed messages wishing for the death and destruction of an enemy. *Defixio* is from *defiger*, to 'fasten', because it was believed that, through a curse, evil would bind itself to the enemy. Those enemies were most commonly thieves, whose booty ranged from tools to bathing tunics. One tablet, inscribed by a citizen called Docimedis whose gloves had been stolen, requests that the gods ensure not just the return of the items but also the loss of the perpetrator's mind and eyes. Other curses are even more heartfelt: 'May he who carried off Vilbia from me become liquid as the water. May she who so obscenely devoured her become dumb ... and have all intestines eaten away.'

It is little surprise, then, to find that the word 'curse' has been present in English for over a thousand years. Where it came from is, fittingly perhaps, a mystery. It is first recorded in religious terms in the Charter of Leofric, an eleventh-century Earl of Mercia and husband of Lady Godiva. At this time 'curse' embraced variously the vengeance of a deity, excommunication by the Church, and the uttering of a profane oath. All of which might suggest a link between 'curse' and 'cross', but no connection has yet been found.

Whatever the real backstory, curses have been cast in thousands of different forms and contexts ever since. As for the adjective 'cursed', its meanings occupy two extremes – of irritation on the one hand ('those cursed phone updates'), and the feeling of being blasted by malevolence on the other.

curt: rudely brief.

'In more temperate climes, hair is curt,' wrote Sir Thomas Herbert in his 1665 account of his travels in Africa and Asia. Rather than describing temperamental locks, however, his description reflects the original meaning of 'curt', namely 'short' or 'shortened'. The word is from the French *court*, with the same meaning, which in turn comes from the Latin *curtus*, 'cut short, abridged' – or, 'curtailed'. Today's use of 'curt' takes the idea of terseness and ups the ante with a healthy dose of brusque bad manners.

cwtch [Welsh: rhymes with 'butch']: more than a hug.

It is regularly named as Wales's best-loved word, has been used in wedding vows and football commentaries, and is emblazoned across mugs and T-shirts that tell you that 'Everyone can hug; only the Welsh can cwtch.' *Cwtch* has no literal English translation, and its origins are in fact French, where *coucher* means to 'hide' or 'snuggle' (a relative of 'couch'). While its primary meaning in modern Welsh is a 'hug' or 'embrace', it is also much more than that. The word doubles up to mean a 'cubbyhole' or 'cupboard': a small space in which to store things safely. Blend the cosy space and an embrace and you get a better idea of its range: a *cwtch* involves the wrapping of arms around someone to make them feel safe and cherished.

daffle: to act inanely.

In Yorkshire dialect, 'daffling' involves both silly behaviour and futzing about. A possible twist on 'daft', 'daffle' is also used for elderly people considered superannuated – otherwise known as the 'dafflers'.

daft: silly; foolish.

'Daft' is one of those English words that has performed several somersaults in the course of its long history. In its earliest days, around the eleventh century, it meant simply 'meek' and 'humble' – akin to 'nice' and 'silly', which meant largely the same thing. Its first change began some 300 years later, when an inoffensively 'daft' individual was assumed to be lacking in intelligence. Nor did the downward trajectory stop there: 'daft' went on to encompass someone whose perceived stupidity was born of an unsound mind. Yet some of the word's earlier innocence was to slowly creep back in, beginning in the sixteenth century when 'daftness' also embraced a carefree sense of merriment and mirth – a 'giddiness' that could pass uncensored. The 'daft days' were ones of gaiety enjoyed at Christmastime. Today's often-affectionate uses – 'don't be daft!' – retain that sense of unabashed silliness, with a fair bit of affection thrown in.

dardledumdue: a daydreamer.

'Dardledumdue' is a beautiful old East Anglian word that conjures up an image of a happy country-dweller, straw drooping from their lips and a donkey's battered straw hat keeping off the bees, ambling along some country lane singing a tuneless 'dumdeedumdee'. They are, as they might put it in Afrikaans, in a 'dwaal' – a dreamy, dazed, and thoroughly absent-minded state.

daring: bold; having the courage to do something.

'Who dares wins,' exhorts the motto of the SAS. 'Those who dare to fail miserably can achieve greatly,' said John F. Kennedy, echoing words of his predecessor Theodore Roosevelt. In ancient times, the Roman Stoic philosopher Seneca declared, 'It is not because things are difficult that we do not dare; it is because we do not dare that they are difficult.'

Today, 'daring' wears its history more lightly, found in the dares swapped by children at school, in the *Eagle* comic's Dan Dare, or in such terms as 'daredevil' – once someone who was recklessly daring but now an affectionate moniker for anyone who pushes the boundaries.

The roots of 'daring' are as deep as they come, however, for the word is related to forms with similar meanings in Greek and in Sanskrit, the ancient language of India, which all descend from a root meaning 'bold'. From the start, daringness has involved having the courage to risk danger in order to succeed.

'Dare's' swashbuckling sibling is 'derring-do', a coupling

that grew out of a series of misunderstandings and misprints beginning with Chaucer. Romantic writers enthusiastically adopted 'derring-do' as a synonym for what a sixteenth-century glossary called 'manhood and chevalrie', as well as 'desperate courage'.

decent: respectable or moral; of an acceptable standard.

'Decency', thundered the dramatist George Bernard Shaw, 'is Indecency's conspiracy of silence.' It is an unfortunate reflection on human behaviour that the word 'indecent' is used far more frequently than its better half. In its earliest incarnation, 'decent' simply described what was fitting or appropriate to circumstances – the Latin *decentia* meant just that: 'being suitable or becoming'. Over time it became shorthand for moral integrity, good taste, and proper (if slightly dull) behaviour. 'Are you decent?' even became a theatrical euphemism for 'are you wearing any clothes?', shouted before barging into backstage dressing rooms. And so 'decent' came to mean 'good', or at least 'good enough'. Unusually, however, this is a word that is getting stronger as it ages: 'that's a decent wine' is today often high praise indeed.

dejected: dispirited or depressed.

The Latin *jacere*, to 'throw', and its successor in French, *jeter*, have produced a useful English brood. They include 'abject': 'thrown away'; 'eject': 'throw out'; 'ejaculate': 'spurt forth'; 'project': 'throw forth'; and 'subject': 'throw under'. To be 'dejected', then, is to be 'thrown down', as though our feelings of melancholy cast us to the very ground.

delirious: in an acutely disturbed state of mind; wildly happy or ecstatic.

The now obsolete English verb 'delire' was surely too useful to throw away. It meant to 'go astray', either morally, or by going off-topic in a conversation. At its heart is the Latin *lira*, a 'ridge or furrow produced by ploughing'. Add on a *de* and you introduce the idea of deviating *from* those furrows. In other words, to 'delire' is to leave the conventional track and become a little erratic. It is this drifting that gave the spin-off 'delirium', the sense of 'madness' or 'disorder', either as a permanent condition or one induced by a drug or disease. Those who are 'deliriously happy', meanwhile, are emotionally off-kilter by being in a state of wild excitement or enthusiasm.

demoralized: having lost confidence or hope.

You'd think that abandoning your morals might be fun once in a while, but being 'demoralized' has always been a serious business. Its beginnings coincided with the French Revolution, where *démoraliser* expressed a corruption of prevailing morals as well as an undermining of morale. The US dictionary-maker Noah Webster translated it into English, having become thoroughly disillusioned with revolutionary practices and all too aware of the dangers of political reform, even while he supported its aims. 'The nation is now so totally demoralized by the current philosophy of the age,' he wrote in his pamphlet *The Revolution in France*. Much later, when asked how many words he had personally contributed to the English language, he responded, 'Only one. To wit, "demoralize".'

demure: reserved and modest.

It is always women who are 'demure', never men. A byword for being shy, reserved, or modest, in appearance as well as nature, it is based upon the Latin *maturus* and the French *mûr*, meaning 'ripe' or 'mature' – the implication being that 'demureness' is largely acquired as women age.

denial: the refusal to acknowledge an unpalatable truth or emotion.

'Denial' is for many of us our first line of defence. We ignore the reality of a situation in order to protect ourselves and avoid emotional overload. The phrase 'in denial' is often a value judgement made by others, directed at an individual who fails to recognize the consequences of their own behaviour. These uses of 'denial' in emotional contexts are entirely in keeping with the word's etymology – the Latin *denegare*, from *de-*, one sense of which is 'formally', and *negare*, to 'say no'. While much of our denial may be unconscious rather than 'formally' acknowledged, we could agree with the conclusion of Tyrion Lannister in *Game of Thrones* that 'Most men would rather deny a hard truth than face it.'

dépaysement [French: day-pays-mon]: a feeling of not belonging; disorientation.

A traveller often seeks out the new and the strange as a means of broadening their horizons. But with the new can also come a feeling of disquiet – a sense of being out of one's comfort zone. *Dépaysement* literally means 'decountrification', a state of physical removal from one's country, and the intense and unsettling feelings that change provokes. The emotion is not entirely negative, however, for it can equally involve the desire to escape to somewhere completely fresh and new, as a means of waking ourselves up (*see* **aduantas**).

depression: despondency and a profound dejection of spirits.

'Hello, darkness, my old friend, I've come to talk with you again' – the introductory lines to Paul Simon's 'The Sound of Silence' might offer a helpful contribution to the definition of 'depression', a condition whose emotional darkness can be as familiar as it is unwelcome.

The name for this mental condition, one characterized by feelings of intense despondency and hopelessness, is founded upon the Latin *deprimere*, to 'press down' – a potent expression of the crushing effects that depression can bring. The word appeared in this sense in the mid sixteenth century, and the condition was formally diagnosed within psychiatry in the early twentieth century, but the state it describes has existed for millennia, recorded by the ancient Greeks, Romans, Chinese, Babylonians, and Egyptians.

For each of these cultures, depression was seen largely as a result of demonic possession, requiring treatment by priests rather than physicians. Remedies ranged from gymnastics and donkey's milk to starvation and beatings. Not everyone saw depression as the result of evil: the Greek physician Hippocrates diagnosed 'melancholia', as it was known, as the result of an imbalance of bodily humours. Nonetheless, belief in supernatural influence continued to percolate through the Middle Ages and on to the Renaissance, torturously manifested in the burning of witches and the locking-up of those considered mentally aberrant.

By 1621, when Robert Burton published his *Anatomy of Melancholy*, a more formalized search was under way for the natural causes of depression. Burton was ahead of his time in recognizing the benefits of exercise, travel, and a good diet (although bloodletting was also high on his list).

It was the German psychiatrist Emil Kraepelin who in 1911 formally recognized 'manic depression', known today as 'bi-polar disorder'. For Sigmund Freud, general depression was the result of loss and the anger it inspires. More recent diagnoses involve a complex combination of causes, both biological and psychological, but there is still much to be learned.

In language, while 'that's depressing' has become an under-whelming throwaway for anything disheartening, 'depression' itself has lost little of its power, nor its demons.

derisive: ridiculing.

Imagine an evil laugh and you are halfway towards the root of 'derisive', which is based on the Latin *de*, meaning 'down', and *ridere*, to 'laugh'. To 'deride' someone is therefore to laugh at them in contempt or mockery.

desiderate: to yearn for something now lost.

At the heart of 'desiderate' is the Latin *sidus*, 'constellation', suggesting a sense of gazing at the stars in longing and hope. Indeed, celestial bodies were once taken so seriously that their influence was believed to bring not just love, but also 'disaster', a word that is built upon the Greek and Latin *aster*, 'star', for disastrous events were believed to result from their unfortunate alignment at certain times. In modern terms, 'desiderate' allows us to articulate a longing for something we regret ever having let go. *See* **desire.**

desire: to want, covet, or crave.

We have been 'desiring' since the thirteenth century. The word's applications are many and its gamut runs from intense longing to hoping and on to appetite: a refugee desires safety, a lover craves their heart's desire, a host desires a guest's attend-ance, and a child desires sweets.

'Desire's' roots are the Latin *desiderare*, to 'long for' or 'miss', which makes it a relative of **desiderate**. It too is usually understood to have celestial roots thanks to the connection with *sidus*, 'constellation'. This links both words with the ancient world's augurs and *auspices*, who foretold the future through omens – including those believed to be narrated by the stars.

There is, however, another theory that accounts for 'desire', involving an older use of *sider* for a 'target' or 'goal' – in which case, to 'desire' would be to focus on a goal but end up missing it. Most of us would surely prefer the more romantic interpretation of wishing upon the stars.

despair: the complete loss of hope.

In an illustration accompanying a treatise on 'The use of passions' from 1649, Reason is seated as a crowned woman upon a chariot, the angel of Divine Grace blessing her from above. Sorrow, Feare, Hatred, Desire, Love, and Choller are all figures in chains, writhing just feet away from the unfettered smiles of Joy and Hope. But it is the figure of Despaire that really catches the eye – his head thrown back while his hands pull hard upon a rope he has tied around his neck.

Within Christian teachings, despair was cast as a deadly sin, one of the most unforgivable manifestations of **acedia** or **sloth**. Despair was also the one sin that could not be forgiven, for it was seen to directly contradict the will of God and his promise of redemption. One of despair's frequent outcomes, as so chillingly depicted in that seventeenth-century engraving, was suicide, another mortal sin in Catholic theology, whose Church dictated that the goods and land belonging to suicides should be confiscated and made as anonymous as the victims themselves, buried in unmarked graves. In John Bunyan's allegory *The Pilgrim's Progress*, the characters of Christian and Hopeful are thrown into a dungeon in Doubting Castle by Giant Despair, where they are starved and beaten. They are locked in as much by their own doubts as by their physical fortress, until they discover they have had the key all along, one known as 'Promise'.

Fundamentally, 'despair' means a total loss of existential hope, a sense enshrined in its earliest form – the Latin *desperatio*, 'a falling away of hope'. The emotion has continued to preoccupy writers for centuries. The poet Emily Dickinson distinguished despair from fear through the metaphor of a shipwreck, expressing the difference as the one 'between the instant of a Wreck, and when the Wreck has been'. In other words, despair is what is left behind.

despondent: losing heart; dejected.

The Slough of Despond has always run deep. Clearly the Slough here is not a reference to the town, despite the poet John Betjeman despising it so much that he called for bombs to fall on it. Rather this Slough is a fictional, deep bog in John Bunyan's *The Pilgrim's Progress*, where Christian sinks under the weight of his sins (and which may have been inspired by Squitch Fen, a wet and marshy area near Bunyan's cottage in Bedfordshire which he had to cross on his way to church).

If a 'slough' is a place or state into which a person sinks, 'despond' and 'despondency' are the emotions that might swamp you when you get there. Both come from the Latin *despondere*, to 'lose heart', in which *spondere* meant to 'promise' – the loss is therefore of confidence and hope.

dès vu [French: day-voo]: the knowledge that something will become a memory.

Memories. Often we can feel one in the making, as though we can already look back on it from the future. This is the basis of the concept of *dès vu*, recently coined by John Koenig in his *Dictionary of Obscure Sorrows* as a step on from *déjà vu*. The translation of the French phrase is simply 'as soon as seen'.

devil-may-care: cheerfully reckless.

The Devil occupies many pages in the dictionary, and few of them offer a smile. Those dining with him are well advised to bring along their own long spoon; put a foot wrong and we may have him to pay, while if we speak of him we dare him to appear. 'Devil-may-care' is an exception to the rule, an expression that emerged in the late eighteenth century for a spirit of reckless abandon or cheerful bravado, ready to take on anything in its path.

devoted: loving; loyal.

To 'vote', in the sixteenth century, was to 'make a wish' – its ancestor is the Latin *votum*, a 'promise' or 'vow'. From these beginnings came not just the word 'vote' itself, but also 'devout': 'promised to a religion', and 'devote': to 'formally dedicate or consecrate'. Of course, wishes can be bad as well as good, and so devotion could also involve an allegiance to evil. The second and third meanings of 'devote' in Samuel Johnson's *Dictionary of the English Language* (1755) are 'to addict, to give up to ill' and 'to curse, to execrate; to doom to destruction'. While its religious applications continue strongly, 'devoted' has also acquired a distinctly secular sense of passionate allegiance to a person or activity, whatever they may be. When *Grease*'s Sandy sings to Danny that she is 'hopelessly devoted to you', no one could ever doubt her commitment.

disappointment: sadness arising from the non-fulfilment of hopes.

Politics is full of disappointment. Sometimes quite literally, for had our governments been around in the fifteenth century, their 'disappointment' would involve a physical removal from office – an 'unappointing' of their official role in which they were also formally disrobed or 'divested' of power (by literally having their official 'vests' removed). Only later did 'disappointing' take on a more generalized sense of thwarted actions and frustrated intentions, by which someone is unseated in an emotional rather than a bodily sense.

discombobulation: the state of being unsettled; unnerved.

'Discombobulate' regularly tops the polls of Britons' favourite words. Its bouncy sound allows us to express a degree of confusion that disconcerts but does not topple us. Emerging from US slang in the 1830s as a fanciful alteration of 'discompose' or 'discomfort', 'discombobulate' was one of several playful inventions of the time. Others include 'absquatulate': to 'leave somewhere in a hurry', **dumfungled**: 'utterly used up', and 'hornswoggle': to 'bamboozle'.

It is natural to wonder whether we could, in the past, also be 'combobulated'. Sadly, the dictionary doesn't yet offer that possibility, but Mitchell airport in Milwaukee has masterfully introduced a 'Recombobulation Area', in which passengers exiting the security checks can take a moment to gather both their belongings and their thoughts before moving on.

disdain: the feeling that something, or someone, is unworthy of our consideration.

To 'deign' to do something is tantamount to saying you consider it to be 'infra dig' (literally, 'beneath your dignity'), and indeed the word is a close relative of 'dignity' itself. 'Disdain' comes from the same family, with its sense of considering someone unworthy of respect. Despite strong competition in the historical thesaurus of scorn, including 'despication', 'unworthhead', and the rather wonderful 'byscorn', 'disdain' remains the popular choice for describing aversion accompanied by a generous dash of contempt.

disgraced: fallen from favour or honour; discredited.

'Life with disgrace is dreadful,' wrote Horatio Nelson. The many words in English that have, over the course of their lifetime, lost their original bite and intensity – words like 'awesome' or 'horrible', for example – are said by linguists to have been 'semantically bleached'. 'Disgraced' is not amongst them. To be disgraced today is to fall as spectacularly and profoundly from favour as anyone in the sixteenth century, when the word first emerged. Its story began with the Italian *disgraziare*, from *dis-*, here denoting a reversal, and *grazia*, 'grace'. It is consequently used to describe any situation in which someone loses their rank, prestige, or authority, the predecessor perhaps to today's 'cancelled'.

disinterested: not influenced by considerations of personal advantage; uninvolved.

Some couples are more prone to fight than others, and so it is in language. The argument over the 'incorrect' use of 'disinterested' to mean 'uninterested' has been raging for centuries. The unexpected truth is that the version most considered wrong today was in fact its earliest meaning in the sixteenth century – to be 'disinterested' was to be 'without interest or concern'. It took just a few decades for a second meaning to emerge, that of being 'impartial' or 'unbiased'. But if language teaches us anything, it is that it is as much dictated by fashion as our clothes, and we may soon be right back where we started.

dismayed: concerned; distressed.

Can you be 'mayed' as well as 'dismayed'? The answer is yes. 'May' as a verb joins the long list of English 'lost positives', for in Old English it meant to 'be able to do or be'. Take that away and the result is a faintness of heart from the knowledge that you are simply unable to cope.

distress: extreme anxiety, sorrow, or pain.

If you are 'stressed', you are strung out. If you are 'distressed', you are entirely pulled apart. Both metaphors stay faithful to the etymology of the 'stress' family, which begins with the Latin *distringere*, to 'hinder', 'stretch', or 'draw asunder'.

disturbance: an agitation in body or spirit.

'Disturbances' are all about 'trouble', and both words come from the same family, which also counts 'perturb' and 'turbulent' among its members. 'Disturbed' involves the Latin combination of *dis-*, 'utterly', and *turbare*, 'to throw into disorder'. In its earliest uses, in the thirteenth century, to 'disturb' someone was to send them into a state of extreme physical agitation. The extended sense of destroying their mental equilibrium followed soon after.

dolce far niente [Italian: dol-cheh far-ni-en-teh]: the pleasure of doing nothing.

Idleness has always had a mixed reception. For some, it signifies shirking and a disregard for duty. For others, it is a necessary antidote to the stresses and scurrying of daily life. Etymology prefers the former, for 'idle' is rooted in the Germanic *eitel*, meaning 'bare', 'worthless', or 'empty': in other words, idleness is devoid of any value or significance.

The lexicon of laziness is equally judgemental. There is 'lubberly', defined in the *Oxford English Dictionary* as 'coarse of figure and dull of intellect; loutish, lazy, and stupid'. And there are 'lusky', 'sweatless', 'slovening', 'shammocking', and 'pigritious' (the prerequisite to the ultimate in laziness: 'pigritude'). Dialect brings up a convincing rear, designating anyone indulging in 'slounging' (Scots and northern English for hanging about in a 'lazy, slouching manner') a 'slugabed' or 'morning-killer'.

Yet what is life without laziness? English seems to have few answers, even if it does do 'snuggling' rather well. But the Italians, as always, know better. For them, *dolce far niente* is the exquisite and necessary pleasure of doing absolutely nothing. It is idleness that is sweet, earned, and – above all – unjudged.

doldrums: a state of depression or downheartedness.

There is something stagnant about the 'doldrums', and their sense of motionlessness inspired the name of the equatorial region of the Atlantic known for its unpredictable winds and sudden calms. For sailors, being becalmed in the doldrums meant an indefinite period of dull and useless inactivity. Which is where 'the doldrums' tends to send you, into a state of despondency which linguistically began with *dold*, a sixteenth-century variant of 'dull' meaning 'stupid' or 'inert, as through age or cold'.

doolally: stir-crazy.

At the height of Crown rule in India, the British army established a military base at a sanatorium in Deolali, north-east of Bombay, which also doubled as a transit camp where soldiers would await their travel home. As boats left only between November and March, many waited for months under the scorching Indian sun or the deluges of the monsoon season. The ensuing boredom and restlessness made some soldiers become what was described as 'doolally tap': 'doolally' being the serviceman's pronunciation of Deolali, and *tap* being an Urdu word for 'malarial fever'. In other words, this was 'camp fever'. The *tap* was soon dropped, and 'doolally' moved with ease from military slang into the mainstream.

doubt: uncertainty or lack of conviction.

Doubt is not quite the everyday emotion we might take it for. When ancient philosophers introduced a new way of interpreting the world, one that extended beyond the traditional beliefs in deities and divine control, their doubt represented danger. When Socrates challenged the status quo more systematically, his stance was taken for 'impiety', a charge for which he was indicted and executed (by his own hand, for he was condemned to consume a deadly potion of hemlock).

Conflicts over the positions of faith and doubt, often perceived as binary, have informed human actions and beliefs since ancient times. Several key figures in Christianity experienced doubts about God and his promises, including Jesus himself. Doubt does not, however, necessarily equate to a lack of belief. Ambiguity is at the heart of the emotion, for it carries the dual possibilities of a healthy scrutiny and a lack of trust. 'Dual' is fitting here, for 'doubt' itself is a sibling of the Latin *duo*, 'two'. A doubtful person is in two minds, caught between one position and another and thus questioning both. Doubt can push for answers rather than take them away. Bertrand Russell put it a little more bluntly: 'The fundamental cause of the trouble is that in the modern world the stupid are cocksure while the intelligent are full of doubt.'

For some of us, the most perplexing thing about 'doubt' is its silent 'b', inserted into the French-English *doute* by Renaissance scholars who wanted to show off the word's classical origins – the Latin *dubitare*.

dowfart [Scots: dow-fuht]: lacking in spirit or courage.

The definition of the Scots 'dowfart', or 'duffart', is as satisfying as it is condemnatory: 'so much under depression of spirits as to be in a state bordering on that of an idiot'.

dread: to fear greatly or regard with awe.

'I've developed a new philosophy ... I only dread one day at a time,' decides Charlie Brown in Charles Schulz's *Peanuts* comic strip. In Old English he would have 'adreaded' rather than simply 'dreaded', for this Germanic word lost its *a-* in the Middle Ages. Its meaning, however, has remained steady, and to 'dread' something is to regard it with fear and anticipated loathing. To be 'dreadful', originally, was to be 'full of dread', before shifting to mean 'inspiring dread' in the fourteenth century. Among Rastafarians, 'dread' is reverence or awe of the Lord, as well as a deeply felt sense of alienation from society. Their favoured hairstyle of 'dreadlocks' carries a distinctly spiritual significance, a symbol for some of the same peaceful nonconformity.

dreamy: given to living in one's head.

Dreaminess may allow a temporary escape from reality, but it isn't usually equated with unalloyed delight. That, however, was how it seems to have begun, for the very first meaning of 'dream' was 'joy'. *Mann-dream*, for the Anglo-Saxons, was 'human joy', the kind rooted in the present and sourced from other people. A *wyn-dream*, on the other hand, was the height of happiness, for **wynn** itself meant 'joy' or 'pleasure'. As its journey continued, 'dream' embraced the sound of music, as well as frenzy or delirium. It is not entirely clear whether this 'dream' is the same as those we experience in our sleep, but there is a very real possibility that the meaning of the word shifted from actual joy and happiness into the illusory, story-like kind we create in our minds.

dudgeon: a feeling of offence or deep resentment.

'If your great umbrage would care to meet my high dudgeon at twelve paces, I would be happy to entertain you at dawn': words attributed to the hero turned traitor of the American Revolutionary War, Benedict Arnold. Both 'umbrage' and 'high dudgeon' have fared rather better than the memory of Arnold himself.

English has many fossil words – those that survive only in fixed expressions. Take the 'wend' in 'wend one's way', the 'spick' in 'spick and span', or the 'bated' of 'bated breath'. 'Dudgeon' is another, appearing almost exclusively in modern English in the form 'high dudgeon': a state of profound resentment or sullen anger.

The origin of 'dudgeon' is unknown. Its use in a different sense, as wood employed in the making of knife handles, has no apparent connection, for all its potential as a tool of malice. Some look to the Welsh *dygen*, also a word of resentment, but the route is unclear. For now, we can only preserve the fossil as a useful if mysterious artefact.

duende [Spanish: dwen-deh]: the power to attract through magnetism and charm.

In Spanish, Portuguese, and Filipino folklore, a *duende* is a goblin or ghost. It is thought to be an offshoot of the phrase *duen de casa*, 'owner of a house', evoking a local demon or household spirit. It was the belief in supernatural powers that endured, and *duende* has come to signify the highest inspiration, particularly in creative endeavours, where the spirit of *duende* operates like a muse. The emotion is particularly bound up in flamenco music, and the ability of a dancer to hypnotize their audience.

Spanish poet Federico García Lorca called *duende* 'a power and not a behaviour . . . a struggle and not a concept', believing that Goethe had hit on the perfect definition of it as 'a mysterious force that everyone feels, and no philosopher has explained'. For Lorca, it was as dangerous as it was inspiring, a possession that brings irrationality and the prospect of death along with creativity, and that is abundantly present in dance, music, and the bullfight.

English has borrowed 'duende' wholesale in an attempt to express the dark allure of Spanish art and, by extension, any unspoken but compelling charm or magical attraction.

dumbfounded: greatly astonished or amazed.

'Dumbfounded' is an early portmanteau or 'blend': a mash-up that combines the type of shock that renders you dumb with the gobsmacking sense of 'confounded'. The word emerged in the mid seventeenth century and has scarcely looked back since.

dumfungled: utterly exhausted.

A playful invention from 1830s America, 'dumfungled' perfectly describes a feeling of being entirely spent, used up, and probably spat out. *See also* **forswunk**.

dumps, down in the: depressed or unhappy.

In the Dutch of the Middle Ages, *domp* described a 'haze' or 'mist'. To be 'down in the dumps', therefore, was to be 'entirely lost in a fog' or 'confused'. Given that a dump is usually especially uninviting, the expression gained the extra dimension of a depression of spirits.

dust-sceawung [Old English: doost-shay-ah-wung]: a recognition of the transience of things.

Dust-sceawung is an Anglo-Saxon treasure that deserves another outing. The evocative term, a Germanic borrowing that literally means 'dust-viewing', involves a reflection on the transience of life, as through the contemplation of scattered remains – the distillation of all that has been lost.

eager: full of enthusiasm.

Vinegar and eagerness make an odd coupling, but both words are built upon the French *aigre*, meaning 'keen' or 'sharp'. *Vinaigre* is French for 'sharp wine', while *aigre* passed into English as 'eager', full of keen desire or appetite.

ebullient: cheerful and full of energy.

'Let this bottle remayne one hour in hot ebullient water,' advised *the boock of physicke* in the sixteenth century, giving us a clue that 'ebullience' is all about bubbles, whether describing a fizzing personality, a freshly poured glass of champagne, or seething water. Its root is the Latin *bullire*, to 'boil'. Each carries the idea of intense motion and unstoppable energy.

ecstasy: overwhelming happiness or excitement.

Today's throwaway 'I'm ecstatic' – whether over winning a holiday or getting the right exam result – has little of the force of the original. At its heart is the Greek *ekstasis*, which meant 'standing outside yourself'. Anyone experiencing this feeling was transported elsewhere, or was, in modern idiom, 'beside themselves'. The earliest uses of 'ecstasy' in English, in the fourteenth century, described a similar state of frenzy or distraction borne out of fear, passion, or other strong emotion. It referred particularly to a religious frenzy, and was adopted by mystical writers as the name for a state of rapture in which the body was immobilized, while the soul contemplated the divine.

Today, it is the rapture that survives, as well as highs that are artificially induced. The illegal drug Ecstasy was first mentioned in 1985 in the *Los Angeles Times*: 'You'll be hearing and reading more about yet another new drug . . . Humanistic psychologists who advocate it believe it a powerful therapeutic tool, bringing about peacefulness and an ability to trust. On the street, its name is "ecstasy" or "Adam".'

edgy: tense and irritable.

What has nervous irritation to do with edges? Probably the sense of sharp corners, for 'edginess' is all about a cutting intensity and sense of peril. In the nineteenth century, however, 'edgy' also had a more literal sense, as of a painting in which the outlines were considered too hard: an issue of *Blackwood's Edinburgh Magazine* from 1825 wrote of 'two Holbeins: flat, shadowless, edgy compositions'. The emotional sense of being testy or irritable emerged soon after. By the 1970s, 'edgy' had acquired another meaning when 'edge' was preceded by 'cutting' and became a synonym for 'avant-garde'.

Eeyorish: pessimistic and gloomy.

'It's all for naught,' says Eeyore, the permanently disconsolate but lovable donkey in A. A. Milne's *Winnie-the-Pooh*. 'The sky has finally fallen. Always knew it would.' For all his determined gloominess, Eeyore is still cherished in English as a nickname for someone whose glass will forever be half empty.

effervescent: bubbly or fizzy.

Like 'ebullience', 'effervescence' is all about bubbling, whether it's a sparkling drink or a personality that 'spills over'. It too began with Latin, this time the verb *effervescere*, to 'boil up'.

egg of Columbus: a brilliant idea that seems easy after the fact.

'The egg of Columbus' is a thing of joy that brings together the discoverer of the Americas with what Britons once liked to call a 'cacklefart'. The expression derives from an apparently apocryphal story from the sixteenth century, in which Christopher Columbus, having been told that his success could have been achieved by any number of people, devises a challenge to prove his superiority. He invites his gainsayers to take an egg and make it stand on its tip. After many botched attempts, they give up, only to see Columbus tap the egg on the table in order to give it a flat bottom – and voilà, the egg stands up. It is from this supposed incident that the metaphor of the 'egg of Columbus' moved into English, to mean something that is easy when you know how.

Eilkrankheit [German: isle-krunk-hite]: the anxiety induced by always rushing around.

We live according to the rules of time. When T. S. Eliot spoke of measuring out his life with coffee spoons, he may not have anticipated school runs, Zoom calls, and dental appointments that have us measuring our own lives with anxious glances at our watch or phone in an effort to keep to time.

It may seem ironic that it is the Germans who have come up with a word for the acute stress of rushing about, given that their national stereotype is built upon punctuality and efficiency. But *Eilkrankheit* – literally 'hurry sickness' – gives us a pithy description for something we all experience: an overwhelming and persistent sense of urgency that jangles the nerves and denies us the opportunity to breathe.

élan vital [French: ell-on vee-tahl]: the life force.

The *élan vital* is every person's animating force – the impetus of all our actions and intuitions, and vital to growth, change, and success. Coined by the French philosopher Henri Bergson in his 1907 book *Creative Evolution*, the concept became so popular in the early twentieth century that the French army incorporated the doctrine of *élan vital* into its thinking during the lead-up to the First World War, when it was believed that the spirit of individual soldiers was far more important for victory than weapons. The Ukrainian resilience during Russia's invasion inspired the same conviction that there exists in some a vital impulse that separates heroes from the rest of us.

The concept of *élan vital* wasn't met with universal warmth. The biologist Julian Huxley drily remarked that Bergson's *élan vital* is no better an explanation of life than the operation of a railway engine is explained by its '*élan locomotif*'. For most of us, however, the notion that evolution is creative, and precisely *not* mechanical, is surely as reassuring as it is mysterious.

elation: intense happiness and exhilaration.

You might think that, in language as in life, 'elation', 'inflation', and 'deflation' are very much part of the same picture. When we are 'elated' our spirits are lifted high: we are exalted or 'inflated' as a hot-air balloon, one that, at some point, will inevitably 'deflate'. But while 'inflate' and 'deflate' both involve the Latin *flare*, to 'blow' (the source of 'flatulence', too), 'elated' relies upon *elatus*, the past participle of a very different-looking Latin verb, *efferre*, meaning to 'raise up' or 'hold aloft'.

elozable: seducible; amenable to flattery.

It may be rare, but this adjective from the eighteenth century describes a state of mind that most of us have experienced when seduction overcomes sense. If you are 'elozable', you will allow yourself to be sweet-talked into doing something you normally wouldn't – or shouldn't. In other words, you are won over by **swasivious** compliments and all-round cajolery.

elumbated: weak at the knees (or elsewhere).

'Elumbated' is sparsely defined in the *Oxford English Dictionary*, as 'weakened in the loins', thereby inviting various applications. You could be 'elumbated' at the very sight of something that inspires your lust, or too infirm and weak to do anything about it. Either way, it is not a feeling to be desired.

Elysium: a state of ideal happiness.

For the Greeks, *Ēlysion* was the home of the blessed after death, the final resting place of those who had lived with integrity and purity, or who had died as heroes and were conveyed by the gods to the ends of the earth. The name of this paradise moved into Latin as 'Elysium', a name that by Shakespeare's time had come to mean a place or state of perfect happiness. The myth inspired the name of the great boulevard of Paris, the Champs-Élysées, or 'Elysian fields'. *See also* **Arcadian**.

embarrassed: perplexed or humiliated.

'Do you know that feeling: you're not completely embarrassed yet, but you glimpse tomorrow's embarrassment?' Tom Cruise as Jerry Maguire neatly articulates the keen sense felt by many of us that we may be exposed at any moment.

But red cheeks aside, embarrassment was once more physical than emotional. Although the word came into English from French, it seems to have been based on the Portuguese *baraço*, 'harness'. The first English sense was of an impediment or physical obstacle that pulled a person or object back. It was this notion of an encumbrance that led to the use of 'embarrassed' to mean 'in difficulties', particularly when one was financially 'strapped' (a word that draws on the same metaphor). By the eighteenth century, to be 'embarrassed' was to be 'awkward' and 'self-conscious', while today we have taken it further still. Through all of these, however, runs a sense of wearing a metaphorical halter or 'noose'.

emoji: a pictogram of an emotion.

In 2015, Oxford Dictionaries challenged the limits of lexicography by choosing an emoji as their Word of the Year. 'Face with Tears of Joy' 😂 had spiked dramatically on their frequency and usage graphs. The response to their choice was inevitably heated – 'an emoji is not a word!' lamented many, decrying the perceived surrender by the most authoritative of dictionary-makers to the pressures of fashion. Others reasoned that pictographs such as these, including ancient hieroglyphs, have been used to communicate since the beginning of civilization. Furthermore, emojis transcend language barriers and provide nuances that traditional language can't always convey, offering visual thumbnails that are playful, immediate, and pithy. Oxford's own editors judged emojis to be perfect for 'a digital world that is visually driven, emotionally expressive, and obsessively immediate'.

It is not just lexicographers who have entered the fray. Detailed research by scientists has linked emojis with 'emotional granularity' – an individual's capacity to precisely identify their feelings. Those with high emotional granularity, according to the findings, use a larger array of emojis, which in turn leads to a richer and healthier interaction with others. Other studies show national characteristics in emoji use, albeit ones that support existing stereotypes – the French are apparently extremely fond of the heart emoji, while Americans opt for guns and pizzas.

Love them or loathe them, emojis – from the Japanese *e*, 'picture', and *moji*, 'character' – are also one of the fastest-growing forms of language. Such is our dependence on emotional shorthand and visual soundbites that their future – at least in the short term – seems secure. Not that words have been dispensed with altogether: in some cases written descriptions of an emoji have crossed into digital slang; when 🍆 became a euphemism for 'penis' and was hurriedly removed from Instagram searches, the actual word 'aubergine' was substituted instead. Similarly the ¯_(ツ)_/¯ emoji, depicting a lopsided face with arms outstretched and palms upturned, has become known as a 'shruggie' or 'smugshrug'.

emotion: a state of feeling.

For centuries, feelings were categorized into various groups, including 'affections', 'sentiments', 'sensibilities', 'passions', and 'appetites'. It wasn't until the eighteenth and nineteenth centuries that 'emotion' became an umbrella term for all such mental feelings. Before then, the word had far more physical meanings of disturbance and agitation, particularly political and civil unrest, external to ourselves. This agitation or uprising was subsequently extended to the impulses of the body and mind that provoked such agitation, and eventually to any strong mental or physical feeling of our internal lives. Both the physical and mental are catered for by the word's roots: the Old French *esmouvoir*, to 'rouse' or 'excite', and the Latin *emovere*, to 'displace'.

One of the first users of 'emotion' in English in the early decades of the seventeenth century was John Florio, poet, lexicographer, and translator of the Renaissance philosopher Michel de Montaigne's celebrated essays. Florio felt the need to apologize to his readers for the use of various 'uncouth termes' in his English version, among them the word 'emotion'. It's not clear what the objection might have been – perhaps it was the unspecificity of the word, for he was not using it in its modern, psychological sense. Such ambivalence was to linger for over two centuries: the Scottish philosopher Thomas Brown, who did much to advance the academic study of emotional states, told his students, 'The exact meaning of the term . . . is difficult to state in any form of words.'

In the eighteenth century, the Romantic poets had enough of a grasp of the word 'emotion' to embrace it as the superior of reason, a reaction to the Enlightenment ideas of the time. Above all they cultivated passion, as well as the reverence of nature, individualism, and a sense of mysticism; William Wordsworth defined good poetry as 'the spontaneous overflow of powerful feelings'.

Today, there is much debate as to whether emotions are instinctive at all, or rather 'constructed' according to our need to label and define them. It follows, therefore, that there are as many emotions as we wish to identify. When we call a person 'emotional', on the other hand, we forget all complexity and imply simply that they are irrational and rather sentimental. 'Emotional baggage', similarly, is almost always best left with the porter.

emotional intelligence: the capacity to perceive, manage, and regulate emotions.

The ability to recognize when to be silent, and the instincts that allow us to understand the needs of others as well as manage our own feelings – such are the traits of an emotionally intelligent individual. The concept was introduced by the science journalist Daniel Goleman in his book *Emotional Intelligence*, where he identifies five key elements: self-awareness, self-regulation, motivation, empathy, and social skills. All contribute to what has become known as our 'EQ', 'emotional quotient', said to operate in tandem with our IQ. While the latter helps us succeed in the world, our EQ gives us the tools to navigate it.

empathy: the ability to share and understand the feelings of others.

In 1928, the novelist Rebecca West used the relatively new term 'empathy' to describe her feelings of soaring alongside a bird as it arched through the skies. Had she looked in the dictionary for the definition of the term, she would have found agreement, for in this period it meant the power to mentally identify with an object of contemplation, in order to better appreciate it. Which means that those living in the opening decades of the twentieth century could happily 'empathize' with a painting or a rousing view.

'Empathy' was intended as a translation of the German *Einfühlung*, 'in-feeling', borrowing from the same stable as 'pathos': 'feeling', 'apathy': 'without feeling', and 'pathetic': originally 'affecting the emotions'. 'Empathy' seemed to best capture the individual projection of one's own feelings onto something else. Were you to empathize with a mountainous panorama, for example, you might experience the heady exhilaration of looking down on the world from above; stare at a rippleless lake, meanwhile, and you might feel its icy waters close around you.

From there it was only a comparatively short step to the object of contemplation being a human being, so that the 'in-feeling' was a way of identifiying another person's emotions and participating in them. After the Second World War, the term became the popular choice for expressing unity and commonality rather than difference. The idea was of an emotional identification, and we use 'empathy' today in that same broad sense.

The term remains, however, highly flexible, and 'empathetic' is often used in the way that 'sympathetic' once was, to mean simply 'nice and considerate'. There is nonetheless a clear distinction between the two. While 'empathy' implies the ability to get inside someone's head and see their point of view, 'sympathy' (from the Greek *sym*, 'together') is more detached – a desire to be alongside someone in their suffering whilst acknowledging a separation from it. The writer Rebecca O'Donnell put it in more relatable terms: 'Empathy is walking a mile in someone else's moccasins. Sympathy is being sorry their feet hurt.'

empleomania: the compulsive desire for public office.

We have become all too familiar in recent years with individuals who have a manic desire to hold – and hold *on to* – power, no matter what the cost. There is some consolation to be had in discovering that there is a word for it. 'Empleomania' is the excessive thirst for power. It couples 'mania' with the Spanish *empleo*, 'employment' – though clearly this mania reflects much more than the desire to be at work. Described by one commentator in the nineteenth century as the 'dry rot of Spain', and by another as 'the evil which has sapped the vigour of so many nations', 'empleomania' is clearly a word for our own times.

enchanted: charmed.

We may associate sirens with the intrusive wailing of emergency vehicles, but their noise was once both magical and dangerous. The original Sirens were beautiful bird-women, whose singing lured unwary sailors to their death upon the rocks. Their 'siren song' was both irresistibly alluring and perilous, and its victims were thus 'enchanted', a term whose original meaning was 'spellbound by song'. The word is a borrowing from the Latin *incantare*, to 'sing'.

engouement [French: on-goo-mon]: an irrational fondness.

It would seem a big leap from something stuck in your throat to an irrational fondness for something or someone. But that is exactly how the French describe an infatuation that goes against your better judgement. *Engouement* is literally 'an obstruction of the throat'. Be it cheesecake for breakfast or the boyfriend you know is going to treat you badly, the term nicely describes something you know is ultimately unwise, but that you go ahead and indulge in anyway.

ennui: restless boredom.

A fluttering fan; the back of a hand pressed feebly against the forehead; a gentle swoon of the back: such are the images that tend to accompany the word 'ennui'. It is an emotion that goes deeper than 'boredom' but stings less than 'annoyance', and that conveys a mental weariness or lack of interest in one's present surroundings.

'Ennui' came into its own at the height of eighteenth-century Romanticism in Europe, when it represented a fashionable, world-weary variety of boredom. Jaded by the unrealized promises of the French Revolution, the prevailing attitude was one of lethargic, passionless disappointment. Many artists and poets demonstrated how they suffered from it; as with 'melancholy', the experience of ennui became a form of posturing, a mark of spiritual sensitivity to which the uncreative and bourgeois were immune.

There seems to be no English equivalent for 'ennui', and so we retain both the French word and pronunciation. But the French themselves have had mixed feelings towards the emotion over the centuries. Camus, Sartre, and Proust all found inspiration in the listlessness of spare hours. The poet Gérard de Nerval banished it by taking a lobster for walks in Paris's Palais Royal, and he may not have been the only one to benefit from the stroll, for Charles Darwin pointed out that many animals (particularly dogs and monkeys) can feel ennui, along with wonder, curiosity, and other 'intellectual emotions'.

Etymologically, 'ennui' shares the same ancestor as 'annoy', namely the Latin *in odio*, 'in hatred'. Perhaps the smothering weariness of 'ennui' was best summed up by Oscar Wilde in *The Picture of Dorian Gray*, when Dorian declares, 'I am tired of myself tonight. I should like to be somebody else.'

enthralled: captivated and fascinated.

When we are in someone's 'thrall', we are wholly within their power. The word comes from the Old English *thrǣl*, 'slave', brought to us as a legacy of the Vikings. To be 'enthralled', therefore, is to be 'enslaved' or 'captivated'.

enthusiastic: highly interested and motivated.

'Enthusiasm' was originally a scary thing to behold. At its heart is the Greek *theos*, 'god', and *enthousiazein* meant to 'be possessed by a god' and at the mercy of their malevolent power. When 'enthusiasm' entered English in the seventeenth century, its meaning was still far from favourable. It was seen as one of the hallmarks of religious mania, characterized at its most extreme by speaking in tongues or by 'ventriloquism' (from the Latin *venter*, 'stomach', and *loqui*, to 'speak', applied to those believed to harbour an evil spirit deep within them).

When written with a capital letter, 'Enthusiast' was a formal term in the sixteenth century for a fanatic who claimed to receive divine communications through prayer – a feature, in Britain, of Nonconformist religious sects including Quakers and Methodists. William Hogarth produced an engraving, never published, called *Enthusiasm Delineated*, a satire on Methodist preaching. A reworking of it by Isaac Mills for a 1795 collection of Hogarth's works depicts a scene in a Methodist chapel in which a weeping and ecstatic congregation, gathered before a baying preacher who holds puppets aloft, passionately kiss their religious icons as a dog howls and a fainting woman is brought round with smelling salts. At the edge of the picture a barometer publicly measures the religious enthusiasm of the congregation.

Those are quite some beginnings for a word that today is entirely positive, with a broadly secular meaning of inspiration and interest, all fanaticism and 'stomach-speaking' long forgotten.

eristic: argumentative; inclined to specious reasoning.

'Eristic' is a word many of us could do with on social media, where people love to hold forth on subjects they know little about, brooking no counter-argument. But for all its usefulness, this term from the seventeenth century has remained largely in the shadows of the dictionary. It is the product of the Greek *eristikos*, 'fond of wrangling', and can describe both an argument that sounds convincing but is logically invalid, as well as the person delivering it – one who loves nothing more than an argument for argument's sake and who causes a fair bit of strife in the process. *See also* **breedbate**.

l'esprit d'escalier [French: les-pre-des-kalya]: hind-speech; the knowledge of what you should have said.

Denis Diderot, the French philosopher and chronicler, would never forget a dinner party held by Jacques Necker, finance minister for Louis XVI and a highly influential political actor at the time of revolution. In the course of the meal, a damning philosophical remark comparing individuals who are 'ordinary' with those who are 'genius' left Diderot both disconcerted and speechless. Necker's guest only managed to recover himself – and the snappy comeback he might have made – at the bottom of the stairs. As Diderot put it in his account of the incident, *'L'homme sensible, comme moi, tout entier à ce qu'on lui objecte, perd la tête et ne se retrouve qu'au bas de l'escalier.'* ('The sensitive man, like me, overwhelmed by what was said against him, loses his head and doesn't find it again until he reaches the bottom of the stairs.') It was thanks to Diderot that we have the expression *l'esprit d'escalier*, 'wit of the staircase', which was subsequently echoed in other languages such as German and Yiddish, which offer *Treppenwitz* and *trepverter* respectively. Each describes the perfect retort that occurs to you only as you exit, and is therefore too late to be of any use at all.

eucatastrophe: a happy resolution.

J. R. R. Tolkien may be best known as the author of *The Hobbit* and *The Lord of the Rings*, but he was also Professor of Anglo-Saxon at Oxford University and a highly accomplished etymologist. '[My] real taste for fairy-stories', he once explained, 'was wakened by philology on the threshold of manhood, and quickened to full life by war.' Tolkien's harrowing experiences in the First World War (he lost two of his closest friends in the Battle of the Somme) pushed him to create his alternative world of Middle-earth. Recognizing the pressing need to find a happy ending even in the midst of darkness, he coined a word for one: 'eucatastrophe', the antithesis of a catastrophe, and an unexpectedly happy conclusion. By adding the Greek prefix *eu-*, meaning 'good' (there in 'euphemism' too), he turned a catastrophe on its head. A 'eucatastrophe,' he went on to explain in a letter, is 'the sudden happy turn in a story which pierces you with a joy that brings tears.'

euphoria: a feeling of well-being or elation.

The ancient Greek adjective *euphoros*, the root of 'euphoria', was as much about the body as the mind. It could be used of anything healthy or of good bearing – from a graceful dancer to a majestic oak.

When 'euphoria' entered English in the seventeenth century, its usage was relatively contained within the study of medicine as a specialized term relating to a patient's ability to recover. One lexicon of the late nineteenth century describes it as 'a word used to express well-being, or the perfect ease and comfort of healthy persons, especially when the sensation occurs in a sick person'. It was witnessed both in the moments before death and after the delivery of psychoactive drugs.

By the 1920s, 'euphoria' had crossed over into mainstream language as a synonym for 'pep' and 'vitality'. As the decades continued, its power increased further, eventually landing on today's articulation of a feeling of intense and extreme happiness, whether naturally or artificially induced. But it is a happiness that usually proves temporary: one of 'euphoria's' most-cited companions in linguistic databases is the word 'moment'. Still, if that's all we have, most of us would take it.

evil: profound wickedness and immorality.

Nothing can touch evil. In Old English, and indeed almost all other early Germanic languages, this word is the most comprehensive adjectival expression of disapproval, dislike, and disparagement that you will find. From the tenth century onwards, it has denoted the height of moral depravity and wickedness. With the exception of the headlines of excitable tabloid journalists, 'evil' has not lost an iota of its bite since, reserved in theology for the work of Satan or Shaytan, and in secular contexts for the extreme depravity of certain individuals or regimes ('Hell is empty,/And all the devils are here,' wrote Shakespeare).

The concept of evil, of course, is ancient, illustrated in the many expressions involving its influence. Every culture has a term for the 'evil eye', for example, believed to hold the power to inflict material harm (*see* **fascination**). The first 'necessary evil', recorded in 1547, was a woman, while scrofula, a chronic constitutional disease affecting lymphatic glands, went by the name of the 'King's Evil', as it was thought to be reversible only by the powers of the King or Queen.

In film, literature, and art, the concept continues to preoccupy us, and the struggle between the forces of good and evil is relentlessly played out. Evil is the Dark Side of *Star Wars*; it lies beyond the frontier in American Westerns, and is embodied in every 007 and Disney villain from Goldfinger to Blofeld, Cruella to Jafar.

The root of all evil, money aside, is an ancient word meaning 'up' or 'over' – suggesting an overstepping of every boundary that is reasonable, moral, and proper.

exasperated: intensely frustrated and irritated.

The Latin *asper* meant 'rough'. It sits at the beginning of 'asperity', used for the roughness of a surface or the harshness of a bad temper. Its role in 'exasperate' is more hidden, but here too it is the antithesis of smooth. If a plant is 'exasperate', it is roughened with irregular prickles, and human 'exasperation' conveys a similar idea of bumpiness or frayed edges, ones that cause nothing but irritation and frustration.

excited: very enthusiastic and eager.

Excitement involves a fair bit of motion as well as emotion, whether it's jumping up and down or shivering with anticipation. The roots of 'excite' are equally mobile – both the Old French *esciter* and the Latin *excitare* meant to 'rouse', 'set in motion', or 'instigate'. Excitement is thus the 'calling up' of feelings. Originally these feelings would have been more than a little intense, but the energy of 'excited' has gradually been sapped to the point where it needs the addition of 'uber' or 'super' to achieve extra punch. Luckily, there are all kinds of other synonyms to galvanize your vocabulary, including 'spark-plugged', 'gunpowdered', 'uproused', and the thoroughly energetic 'whomped'.

excruciating: intensely painful.

When we describe a stubbed toe or toothache as being 'excruciating', we are a long way from the pain of crucifixion, but at the crux of 'excruciate' is a cross. In fact the Latin *crux* meant just that, and the first to be 'excruciated' were those who were tormented on the cross. The punishment inherent in the word continued well into the seventeenth century, when to 'excruciate' was to torture someone on the rack. Little wonder that the word continues to signify extreme pain and torment.

exhausted: extremely tired and out of energy.

To be 'exhausted' is to be so out of puff that you feel like an empty vessel, which is exactly how the word started. The Latin *exhaurire* meant to 'draw' or 'drain out' – to use up reserves completely. In today's inflated world, 'exhausted' barely cuts it, but there is conversely an inexhaustible supply of synonyms to choose from. Why be exhausted or 'knackered' when you can be 'depooperit', 'ramfeezled', or utterly **dumfungled**?

exhilarated: intensely happy or excited.

To be cheerful in ancient Rome was to be *hilaris*; by extension, the earliest meaning of 'exhilarate' was to 'make cheerful' or 'gladden'. In a rare move for English, which usually sees a word reducing in intensity, 'exhilarate' has upped its own ante, so that today's exhilaration is far more about elation than simple good cheer. Which is altogether 'hilarious' – a word from the very same stable.

facetious: flippant, or inappropriately humorous.

The Romans loved a *facetia*: a 'jest' or 'witty remark'. When 'facetious' entered English in the sixteenth century, it was equally positive, used especially of manners that were considered polished, elegant, and highly agreeable. 'I have a letter in my hand', wrote one of the earliest settlers in New England, 'from the learned and pious and facetious Mr Charles Morton of Charles-Town.'

Before long, the idea of pleasantry shifted to encompass the modern meanings of 'facetiousness' – jokiness or flippancy, particularly when more seriousness is required. 'The proper name *Peter*,' we read in a glossary of dialect from the early twentieth century, 'is so universally used by children and facetious adults as a name for the penis that it never quite loses this significance.'

fair: just and appropriate; attractive.

We might make a 'fair' decision, have 'fair' hair, and do a 'fair bit of' sleeping after a night out. All of these senses of the word 'fair' are, surprisingly, related. Its story begins in Old English in the sense 'pleasing, attractive', as well as 'proper'. In these early days its main purpose was as the opposite of 'foul', a duality that persists in 'fair play' and 'foul play', both of which first appeared in the late sixteenth century.

What does being proper or pleasing have to do with fair hair? It seems blondes still have all the fun, a trope of movies from *Gentlemen Prefer Blondes* to *Clueless* which play on three stereotypes: the blonde bombshell, the ice-cold blonde, and the dumb blonde. Each of them rests, to varying degrees of misogyny and playfulness, upon that earliest meaning of 'attractive'.

faithful: loyal; trustworthy.

St Paul had his own definition of faith: 'Now faith is the substance of things hoped for, the evidence of things not seen.'

The word is first recorded in the phrase 'good faith'. In those early days, it represented a solemn promise, and to 'make faith' was to give a guarantee. It is this idea of a pledge that informed the use of the word as a fundamental tenet of religious belief.

To be 'faithful', then, is to be loyal and constant in one's allegiance, whether to a sexual partner, a friend, or to accuracy (when you are 'faithful to the truth'). At its heart is the Latin *fides*, 'trust', the source of 'fidelity', confident', and 'fiancée' (from the French for 'promised'). It also inspired the name once frequently given to a pet dog – the most faithful of all companions – Fido, Latin for 'I trust; I am loyal'.

fanatical: full of zeal or fervour.

> Football, wherein is nothing but beastly fury, and extreme violence; whereof proceedeth hurt, and consequently rancour and malice do remain with them that be wounded.

Such was the view of the fifteenth-century English diplomat Thomas Elyot on the sport played in numerous forms across medieval Britain. His opinion was not shared by his monarch, Henry VIII, who was a keen fan of the game, and whose custom-made football boots survive to this day.

Over half a millennium later, football continues to inspire every emotion imaginable in its fans. That word 'fan', short for 'fanatic', has a revealing history, beginning with the Latin *fanaticus*, 'belonging to the temple' and, by extension, 'inspired by a god'. For the Romans, the term reflected the frantic and manic behaviour of someone possessed by spirits or demons. In English, 'fanatic' was applied to anyone fervently involved in any pursuit. When, a hundred years ago, a fan heading for their team's home ground announced that they were 'off to the temple', they were closer to the etymological truth than they knew.

fanfreluche [fan-freloosh]: to trifle or act wantonly.

If you find yourself regularly wasting time, why not 'fanfreluche it' instead? This glorious French word passed unchanged into English in the seventeenth century to mean either generally mucking about, or behaving in a way that may please in the moment but that never bodes well long-term. In modern French, 'fanfreluche' is used for frills and flounces on soft furnishings – a bit of trumpery-finery with not much substance behind.

fascination: the state of being spellbound.

Fascination was once a supernatural phenomenon. The word descends from the Latin *fascinare*, which was to use the power of the *fascinum*, a sacred image of a phallus symbolizing masculine power. Penis-shaped amulets abounded in ancient Rome – even cattle were given such talismans. All rested upon the belief that the virility of an erect penis would divert the gaze of the evil eye. When 'fascinate' first arrived in English in the early 1600s, these senses still prevailed – to 'fascinate' someone was to bewitch them so entirely that they fell completely under a spell.

Not that every use was malevolent: a *Medical Dispensatory* of the same period spoke of the promise to 'fascinate and cure stinking breaths'. Today, anything remotely interesting can be dubbed 'fascinating', and it is no longer the be-all and end-all of life: 'It is better to have a permanent income than to be fascinating,' concluded Oscar Wilde. Still, while we throw the adjective around with abandon, spare a thought for its priapic past.

fathom: to grasp or comprehend.

'Fathom' originally meant to 'encircle someone or something with outstretched arms'. The measurement that is a 'fathom' began as the average span of those stretching arms, which was eventually standardized to six feet, particularly when referring to the depth of water. Something 'unfathomable', therefore, cannot be grasped, either by the arms, the mind, or our emotions.

fauchle: to work lazily or listlessly.

'Fauchling', from Scots, is to go through the motions whilst achieving little or nothing at all, simply because apathy won't let you.

fauxcellarm [faux-cell-arm]: the conviction that your mobile phone is ringing.

It's the unmistakable buzz in your pocket, or the 'ping' you are convinced has just emanated from your bag or briefcase. For the Americans, this is a 'fauxcellarm', a jocular blend of 'cell phone' and 'false alarm', and a word that fills a distinct gap in our language for the conviction that your mobile is ringing when its screen remains resolutely blank. In Britain, rather more prosaically, it is known as Phantom Vibration Syndrome.

fear: a strong emotion in the face of danger.

'The only thing we have to fear is … fear itself.' This was 1933, when America was in the grip of the Great Depression, a quarter of the population was unemployed, and things felt truly desperate. Franklin D. Roosevelt had won a landslide victory the previous year with his promise of a New Deal, and millions tuned into his inaugural speech as President, in which he was to explain what it all meant. The new President's most outstanding phrase is widely believed to have been borrowed from his wife Eleanor, who had observed that everyone should 'do one thing that scares you every day'. While her real words seem to have been 'You must do the thing you think you cannot do', the message is the same: that fear can be both instructive and necessary. Linguistically, the history of this emotion charts a similar trajectory, moving from absolute terror to anxiety of a broader kind.

In Old English, *fær* meant a 'sudden or terrible event, a calamity'. For the Saxons, it had meant an 'ambush', while the Vikings used the same term to describe 'misfortune' or 'plague'. The modern sense of uneasiness caused by impending danger, or by the prospect of evil, arose in the twelfth century, when 'fear' was applied to quite violent extremes of the emotion before encompassing all degrees of it.

In religious terms, 'fear' could also describe a mixture of dread and reverence towards God, a sentiment that survives when we 'put the fear of God into' someone by terrifying them into submission.

From such powerful beginnings, the adverbs 'fearfully' and 'frightfully' slid down the scale of intensity to become hyperbolic staples of the nineteenth century, when one might be 'fearfully hungry' or 'frightfully sorry'. Similarly, when we use the formulation 'I'm afraid', we forget that word's potent beginnings in *affray*, to 'strike terror in the heart'.

feckful: full of vigour and industrious.

There are two kinds of 'feck' in common currency – one that is a verbal sidestep of 'fuck', and another that appears almost exclusively in the word 'feckless'. Meaning 'valueless', 'futile', and 'feeble', 'feckless' is one in a very long line of what are emotively known to linguists as 'orphaned negatives' – adjectives descended from positive 'parents', who then abandoned them to their sorry state. 'Kempt', 'couth', **ruth**, **gorm**, 'placable', 'ept', 'mayed', and 'ruly' are all alive and well in the corners of the historical dictionary, as is 'feckful', too.

This 'feck' is a backwards formation from 'effect'. The 'feck' of something was its greater part, the ingredient that gave it vigour and energy – to be 'feckful', therefore, was to be the embodiment of power and efficiency. The adjective survived for centuries in northern English and Scottish until, ironically, it lost its head of steam, leaving only its feeble and emasculated counterpart behind. To be 'feckless' or behave 'fecklessly' is to be without vigour, care, and any sort of pep at all.

feeling: a sensation, perception, or emotion.

English is pervaded by the language of touch. We are 'in touch', 'out of touch', 'touched' by something, and, when an emotion hits us, we 'feel' it. Yet the story of the word 'feeling' is largely a mystery, part of a cloudy picture in which we can just about make out relatives in words related to the thumb or finger, as well as a caress. In Old English, to 'feel' was to have a physical sensation, whether of heat, cold, or pain. Soon after, it took on emotional responses, too. Feeling is all about having our sensibilities aroused, for good or bad. Horace Walpole tended towards the latter: 'The world is a comedy to those that think,' he wrote, 'a tragedy to those that feel.'

feels, all the: a strong emotional reaction.

A TikTok song you can't scroll past, a bad break-up in your favourite TV series; a GIF of a wide-eyed kitten tucked up in a blanket – many of us encounter daily triggers for experiencing 'all the feels'. This expression began with an Internet meme from 2010 which featured an image of two men embracing alongside the caption 'I KNOW THAT FEEL BRO'. 'Feels' here is short for 'feelings', a typical use of playful Internet grammar that became an infectious buzz-phrase for a shared, sentimental reaction as well as empathy between strangers online. If you experience something 'right in the feels', meanwhile, the implication is you feel it in your core (and genitals).

feisty: lively, sassy, and courageous.

'Feistiness' today tends to involve the venting of anger, but originally it was more about the blowing of hot air. From its earliest incarnations in the nineteenth century, it has described general sass and spirited (if not pugnacious) confidence. Take it back a step further, however, and you get to the 'fisting hound': a small pet dog notorious for its flatulence. To 'fist', in the fifteenth century, was to 'break wind', recorded in the dictionary as 'fysting' and the frequent companion of 'shyting'. As small dogs can be touchy as well as windy, 'feisty' came to embrace ballsy pluckiness, with a touch of aggression thrown in.

fellow-feeling: empathy.

Before there was 'empathy', there was 'fellow-feel'. Recorded since the seventeenth century, the latter suggests a warm and hands-on compassion, a sense of community and shared interest that positively promotes kinship and well-being. One who displays such kinship is consequently a 'fellow-feeler'.

ferhoodled: all mixed up.

The socks in your drawer might be 'ferhoodled', your timetable might become 'ferhoodled', or you yourself might feel such a confusion of emotions that your head is 'ferhoodled' too. In all these situations the idea is of something thoroughly entangled and confused.

This expressive adjective comes from the US dialect of Pennsylvanian Dutch, a form of High German spoken by immigrants escaping religious persecution in Europe between the seventeenth and nineteenth centuries. For them the word would have been more akin to *verhuddle*, a close sibling of the German *verhudeln*, meaning to 'bungle' or 'botch'. Today, the sheer sound of 'all ferhoodled' leaves the hearer in no doubt that things are more than a little shambolic.

Fernweh [German: fairn-vay]: the yearning to be elsewhere.

If you have ever felt a longing to be far away, no matter what the destination, *Fernweh* is the word you need. It is a sensual word, full of pining and nostalgia for somewhere different. Literally meaning 'far-sickness', it was deliberately constructed during the period of German Romanticism as the opposite of *Heimweh*, 'homesickness', and is, as one writer put it, 'the travel ache you can't translate'. In fact, in order to come close you'd have to reach for another German word, *Wanderlust*, the desire to travel, only this is wanderlust with an elegiac, yearning edge.

fervour: intense and passionate feeling; zeal.

The Romans had a vivid vocabulary to describe heat. 'Ebullience' and 'effervescence' both came from Latin renditions of bubbling, boiling energy, and 'fervour' adds to this list. At its heart is *fervere*, to 'boil', and indeed 'fervent' originally described glowing heat or seething liquid, before moving on to embrace an intensity of feeling and zeal. 'Life is too short to be little,' wrote Benjamin Disraeli. 'Man is never so manly as when he feels deeply, acts boldly, and expresses himself with frankness and with fervour.'

fickle: deceitful; inconstant.

'The fickleness of the women I love is only equalled by the infernal constancy of the women who love me,' laments Leonard Charteris in George Bernard Shaw's *The Philanderer*. The word 'fickle' has proved anything but, staying true to its original meaning in the eleventh century of something 'false' and 'deceitful', as well as 'unreliable' and 'inconstant'. Throughout its history it has frequently been applied to Chance, Fortune, and Nature personified: 'O Fortune, Fortune,' we hear in *Romeo and Juliet*, 'all men call thee fickle.' Today we are just as likely to use 'fickle' to describe our weather, particularly when it's **flenched**.

finifugal: avoiding the end of something.

It's the moment we never want to arrive: the end of a compelling box set, a book we've enjoyed every moment of, or even a relationship we know is no good for us. If you find yourself avoiding the final chapter or the closing scene, you are 'finifugal', based on the Latin *finis*, 'end', and *fuga*, 'flight'.

firgun [Hebrew: fear-guhn]: unselfish pride; empathetic joy.

Firgun is as far away from self-centredness as it is possible to be. Coined in the 1970s, it describes an unselfish delight in another person's success. The term has settled in Hebrew, but its story seems to have begun with the Yiddish *farginen*, meaning to 'grant'. The infinitive form of *firgun*, *lefargen*, means to offer someone praise with a total generosity of spirit.

Each year, on 17 July, International Firgun Day promotes the idea of tipping your hat to others with no agenda other than to express joy in their success. *See also* **confelicity**.

flapdoodle: stuff and nonsense.

As dismissive verbal swipes go, 'flapdoodle' is one of the best. A fanciful coinage from the 1830s, it joins 'pish', 'twaddle', 'balderdash', 'humbug', 'flim-flam', 'fiddle-daddle', and countless other articulations of absolute rubbish.

flattering: complimentary.

When Oliver Cromwell ordered a portrait of himself from the artist Peter Lely, he apparently insisted, 'Remark all these roughnesses, pimples, warts, and everything as you see me; otherwise I never will pay a farthing.' This episode, repeated later in Horace Walpole's *Anecdotes of Painting in England*, is said to be the source of our saying 'warts and all'. Cromwell, in other words, refused to be flattered by the artist's brush.

'Flattery' was once an untarnished word for delight, particularly the kind revealed by the wagging tail of a dog. It took just a few years for insincerity – of the human kind – to creep in, and so to 'flatter' was to fawn obsequiously in order to gain favour, which is where it has largely stayed. Etymologically, it began with a word meaning to 'caress' or 'stroke with the hand', with a sense of smoothing or flattening down – something

Peter Lely must have been itching to do, had Cromwell not insisted on the bare-skinned truth.

flawsome: flawed but beautiful.

It's rare for someone to introduce two words into the lexicon, rarer still for those words to linger for a while, but the super-model Tyra Banks has achieved both. First came 'smizing', smiling with your eyes, recommended by Banks as a surefire tip on how to look good on camera. Her next creation was inspired, it's said, by her own reaction to the intense and often unkind scrutiny of those same cameras. Banks describes 'flawsome' as being awesome *because* of your flaws, not in spite of them.

fleer: to mock; to smile snidely.

The noun 'fleer' is pithily described in Samuel Johnson's *Dictionary of the English Language* as 'mockery expressed either in words or looks'. The verb, meanwhile, can involve either delivering a grimacing grin, or laughing with a sneer.

flench: to give a deceitful promise of improvement.

'Flench', from Scots, is traditionally used of weather, where it describes something that promises to improve but never actually does. Clearly it also has great potential for other areas of life.

flummoxed: greatly perplexed.

No one quite knows where 'flummox' originated, but most would agree that English would be a poorer place without it. One possible source is an old dialect word, 'flummock', meaning to 'make untidy' or 'confuse': certainly the sound of both words is, as the *Oxford English Dictionary* notes, expressive of throwing something down roughly. Whatever its story, 'flummox' was clearly too good for Charles Dickens to refuse. His character Mr Weller introduces it to us in *The Pickwick Papers*:

> 'And my 'pinion is, Sammy, that if your governor don't prove a alleybi, he'll be what the Italians call reg'larly flummoxed, and that's all about it.'

FOMO: the Fear of Missing Out.

It is the ailment of the moment, one that has permeated most corners of social media and our working lives. 'FOMO' first emerged in the early noughties and is said to be the brainchild of a business strategist rather than a collectively chosen name for a new social angst. It may have taken a decade to establish itself (and to oust a similar diagnosis: 'FOBO', Fear of a Better Option), but recent research suggests that over 70 per cent of us have experienced it, and that it disproportionately affects young people.

For a term that could easily be dismissed as another throwaway shorthand of social media, FOMO has inspired academic papers and numerous psychological studies as to its causes and cures. Some see it as the unwanted offshoot of creativity and intelligence, pointing out that Google Analytics place most 'FOMO' searches in New York City and Cambridge, home of Harvard. Those that crave stimulation, the argument goes, also fear that they aren't getting enough of it. The result can be stress, social anxiety, and mental burnout, a lesson to all of us that life is rarely the way it is presented in filtered Snapchats or Photoshopped Instagram feeds. As Shakespeare warned us centuries ago, 'Striving to be better, oft we mar what's well.'

forblissed: in a state of rapture.

English once enjoyed a love affair with the prefix *for-*. The *Oxford English Dictionary* devotes pages to the results, revealing how it was used in the formation of hundreds of descriptions. Its functions are numerous – it can convey a sense of being 'away' or 'off', as in to 'forshake', to 'shake off'; a sense of prohibition, as in 'forbid'; of 'all over', as in 'forcratch', to 'scratch yourself all over'; and of doing something wrong, as in the wonderful 'forslug', to neglect something through sluggishness. Perhaps its most useful function, however, is in a multitude of past participles, where it manages to convey in the pithiest way possible the rendering of various states that some of us find ourselves in. Why be 'weak', when you can be 'forfeebled'? Or 'very happy', when you can be 'forblissed'?

formication: the feeling of something crawling across your skin.

Unlike its close linguistic counterpart, 'formication' is not a pleasant sensation. It involves a tactile hallucination that reproduces the feeling of insects crawling all over your skin. The phantom feeling is linked with various conditions and processes, including the menopause. Its root is the Latin *formica*, 'ant'.

forswunk: worn out from too much work.

The highly expressive 'forswunk' is based on the verb 'swink', to 'toil and labour hard' (and later, in some contexts, to 'drink hard' too). In the sixteenth century, you could also call yourself 'fortoiled', but 'forswunk' has the perfect ring of someone bowed down with tiredness. Change the 'for' to 'fore', and you might easily be 'foreswunk': exhausted before you even begin.

forwallowed: hit by the exhaustion of insomnia.

Sometimes, English provides a word for something that might otherwise take several sentences to articulate. 'Forwallowed' is one. It means, quite simply, 'worn out', in this case from having spent the night tossing and turning in sleep-deprived exasperation.

fragile: easily broken or damaged.

Fragility was once as much about moral weakness as it was about vulnerability. In all its guises, 'fragile' means, of course, to be 'easily broken', hence its origins in the Latin *frangere*, to 'break'.

Many of its synonyms in the historical dictionary begin with 'b', from 'brittle' and 'brotel' to 'brisel' and 'brickly' and 'break-able'. But whilst those strike a slightly discordant note, 'fragile' retains a sense of something flimsy, insubstantial, and easily blown over: an entirely relatable description if you feel fragile of a Sunday morning.

frank: open and candid.

Whenever we talk about being 'frank' we are linking ourselves with the Germanic people who conquered Gaul around AD 500. The Franks took their name from their favourite weapon, the *franca*, 'javelin', and later gave it to modern-day France. After they took possession of Gaul, they allowed full political freedom only to ethnic Franks or to those among the conquered Celts who were invited to live under their protection. As a result, *franc* came to mean 'free' and, by extension, 'socially superior'. In English, 'frank' gradually extended its meaning of 'free' to encompass 'liberal' and 'generous', and eventually 'candid'.

The word 'frankincense' preserves those historical associations: it is from the Old French *franc encens*, 'superior incense'. To 'frank' a letter, meanwhile, is to send it off 'free' of expense, while a 'franchise' is the freedom granted by a company to sell its products or services.

Fremdscham [German: fremt-sharm]: stranger shame.

Vicarious embarrassment is not a straightforward emotion. Its effects are obvious enough: a squirming and squeamishness at the sight of someone else's humiliation. But there is also a 'there but for the grace of God go I' about it, a sense that this could so easily have been us, and a slight pride in the knowledge that it wasn't.

The German *Fremdscham*, 'stranger shame', captures all of this. The 'strange' or 'stranger' here is in the sense of someone unrelated or removed. This second-hand embarrassment can be experienced even when the other person is nowhere near us – on our TV screens, for example, or in a book. And yet distance does little to temper our embarrassment on their behalf, making stranger shame a curiously social emotion.

frobly-mobly: indifferently well.

'Frobly-mobly' is the nineteenth-century equivalent of 'meh'. It is defined in *A Glossary of Provincial and Local Words* from 1839 as 'neither well nor unwell' and 'neither good nor bad'. It joins similar formulations of the time, including 'atweesh-and-atween' and 'crawly-mawly', both of which were used for something insipid, bland, and unenthused.

frolic-hearted: full of joy and fun.

What can be better than a good 'frolic', with its notions of making merry and mischief? Think of a field of gambolling lambs, full of the joys of spring. 'Frolic's' German sister is *froh*, meaning 'glad' or 'joyous', and so to be 'frolic-hearted' is to be happy indeed. Sometimes a frolic can go too far, however. In legal judgments dating back more than 200 years, judges have used the expression a 'frolic of their own' to describe an occasion when an employee acts for their own benefit in the course of their employment, only to see things going seriously wrong.

froward: perverse and hard to please.

Any of us could be 'forward' – bold or overfamiliar, pressing ahead even when we're not welcome. But even more of us could be 'froward', if only we knew the word existed. Rather than a modern take on 'forward', it is just as old, and is a shortening of the Old English word *fromward*, meaning 'perverse' or 'counter to what is needed or expected'. A seventeenth-century essay on poetry sums it up: 'When all is done, Human Life is at the greatest and the best, but like a froward Child, that must be Play'd with and Humour'd a little, to keep ite quiet, till it falls asleep.'

fury: a feeling of extreme rage.

'Tumult of mind approaching madness; wild anger; frenzied rage.' So runs the *Oxford English Dictionary*'s definition of 'fury'. The word's beginnings are simple enough: the Latin *furere*, to 'rage' or 'be mad'. The Romans used *Furiae* as their name for the Greek *Erinyes*, the avenging deities in myth sent to punish criminals, and originally imagined as the ghosts of the murdered. The Erinyes were not to be messed with; they were popularly perceived as monstrous crones or sinister, whip-carrying women, around whom poisonous snakes writhed with menace.

This rage of mythical vengeance still informs the word 'fury'. It is only its offspring, 'furious', that has diluted a little, shifting gradually from fierce, violent passion to a multi-purpose kind of rage – or even fun, if things get 'fast and furious'.

gadzooks: an exclamation of surprise or annoyance.

'He has married a young wife,' remarks a character in a seventeenth-century drama. 'Has he gadzooks?' comes the reply. This exchange gives us the first record of the exclamation 'gadzooks', now consigned to the dusty closet that also contains 'Great Scott' and 'gorblimey'. Behind the word, however, lies a telling story of profanity in the Middle Ages. 'Gadzooks' is generally believed to be a shortening of 'God's hooks', a reference to the nails on Christ's cross. 'Gad' was a popular sidestep for 'God', and 'gadzooks' joins many minced oaths of the time, including 'Gadsbudlikins' (God's body), ''snails!' (God's nails), and ''zounds!' (God's wounds). Later, it would be ''strewth!' (God's truth) leading the way, alongside 'Jeepers Creepers' and 'Jiminy Cricket' (all stand-ins for 'Jesus Christ'), as well as 'darnation' (damnation), 'dagnabbit' (God damn it), and 'drat' (God rot it). Only much later did such use of the Lord's name in vain cede to bodily functions as the supreme taboos.

gaiety: amusement and lively cheer.

There is a thin line between 'gaiety' and 'hedonism', in language at least. What started out as an entirely neutral term for the state of being happy, carefree, and joyous was soon clouded by implications of lechery. Both 'gaiety' and 'gay' were built upon the French *gai*, borrowed from the Normans in the second half of the eleventh century. 'Gay's' sense was one of brightness and brilliance, if with a slight edge of showiness. By the fourteenth century, it was a poetic choice for describing all that was noble, beautiful, and fine. But the idea of licentious and promiscuous behaviour had been lurking for a while, and 'gay' was often used of a woman who lived by prostitution, or of men who were uninhibitedly dedicated to pleasure.

The trajectory of 'gay' shifted definitively in the first decades of the twentieth century, when it became a designator of homosexuality. For some, 'gay' expressed the joy in the freedom to choose; for others it was an uncomfortable fit, thanks to the word's links with prostitution. Nonetheless, by the 1960s 'gay' was the term of choice for many homosexual men, and the earlier meanings of 'carefree' or 'bright and showy' had largely slipped away. But not entirely – given the long struggle to achieve the freedom to be gay, it seems fitting that this is a word that began with nothing but happiness and love. As for 'gaiety', it has preserved its history of merry-making and pleasure-seeking, with only a whiff of ornamentation in the air.

gaman [Japanese: ga-man]: enduring suffering without complaint.

The sentiment of *gaman*, a Japanese term of Zen Buddhist origin, is typically linked with Japanese-American citizens held in internment camps in the USA during the Second World War, as well as to those affected by the 2011 Tōhoku earthquake and tsunami in northern Japan. The emotion has been misperceived by outsiders as a form of introverted behaviour, or as a lack of assertiveness or initiative. For the Japanese, however, *gaman* signals resilience, and a demonstration of strength in the face of difficulty or suffering – a silent form of heroism.

geck: to scoff; to flounce off.

Rather happily, there is a word for the performative act of tossing one's head and flouncing off. The verb 'geck' emerged in the seventeenth century, when it meant to deliver mocking words or gestures, before landing later upon the action of tossing the head in scorn, preferably whilst walking away. Etymologically speaking, it is a relative of the word 'geek', once used to mean a 'fool' or dupe. 'Gecks' or 'geeks' were clowns at nineteenth-century freak shows, who would commit bizarrely foolish acts on stage including biting off the heads of live snakes or chickens. Such excessive and obsessive slavishness to a cause inspired the modern use of 'geek' to describe someone overly devoted to a subject (before moving, in today's world, much closer to a badge of honour, with none of 'geck's' original mockery involved). In the meantime, 'geck' has rather faded away, along with **fleer**. Were you to geck and fleer simultaneously, that would be quite an exit.

genial: friendly and cheerful.

What links a brainbox, Aladdin, and affability? The answer is the Latin *gignere*, to 'beget', and *genus*, meaning 'birth' or 'family'. Both are the ancestors of 'genius', 'genie', and 'geniality'. A 'genius' was believed to be the attendant spirit present at birth that determined personality and natural abilities, and that eventually gave rise to the idea of exceptional ability and skill. Such skills are possessed in abundance by a 'genie', a guardian or protective spirit, whose name was adopted by the eighteenth-century French translators of *The Arabian Nights' Entertainments*, largely because of its resemblance to the Arabic *jinnī*, 'jinn'. The latter is a spirit of lower rank than the angels but with the power to possess humans.

And so to 'geniality', a condition of good humour and benevolence that was believed to be core to human nature and conducive to health and growth. In the sixteenth century, the word 'genial' related specifically to procreation, and the 'genial bed' was the nuptial kind. Clearly the view was that nothing could be more natural to human society than marriage. Two centuries later, 'genial' embraced the idea of sympathetic cheerfulness and affability – again seen as an innate human characteristic conferred at birth.

gentle: mild and kind.

One of the most important words for the ancient Romans was *gens*, a family or clan descended from a common ancestor. A citizen's *gens* was expressed in a name, or *nomen*, that determined social and legal structures – a state within a state that followed its own strictures and rituals.

English borrowed several words from those Latin beginnings, mostly via the French *gentil*, 'kind'. To be 'genteel' was to be 'dignified and well-mannered', characteristic of those occupying a high social position. 'Gentle' retained those same ideas of good breeding – a 'gentleman' was one whose good manners reflected their superior class. And with courtesy and chivalry, it seems, goes a pleasant disposition, which accounts for the latest stop on 'gentle's' path, namely the meaning of 'mild', 'kind', and 'tender'.

genuine: authentic and sincere.

Some word origins seem too good to be true. English etymology is packed with compelling myths accounting for the birth of its various words and phrases. You'd be forgiven, therefore, for dismissing the history of 'genuine' as linguistic poppycock. In this case, however, the theory might just stand up. It begins straightforwardly enough with the Latin *genuinus*, a word which appears to be linked to *genu*, 'knee'. Why should a knee have anything to do with authenticity? The link is said to be a Roman custom involving a man's formal acknowledgement of a newborn's paternity by placing the child upon his knee. As this was the 'natural' order of things, so 'genuine' came to mean both 'authentic' and 'proper'.

giddy: dizzy; excited.

'I'm feeling giddy' offers numerous interpretations – you might be feeling overcome with positive emotion, or highly vertiginous, having teetered off a ride on a Ferris wheel. Neither of these bears any relation to the word's original meaning in the eleventh century, when to be 'giddy' was to be 'possessed by a god' (or even by an evil elf). The idea was of being taken over by a malevolent force and rendered insane. For most of us, a ride on Space Mountain aside, all demonic influence has been forgotten and 'giddy' simply means 'dizzy' in all its senses. To this day, however, no one has quite figured out who the original 'giddy aunt' actually was, not to mention the 'giddy goat'.

gigglemug: one who is perpetually cheery.

You might think being a 'gigglemug' is an entirely positive thing. Victorian slang for a habitually smiling face, the word describes someone permanently optimistic and jovial. For the rest of us, however, a 'gigglemug' is frequently unwelcome, especially first thing in the morning, when, to borrow another Victorian phrase, you yourself are feeling less than 'bang up to the elephant'.

gigil [Tagalog: gig-ill]: the irresistible urge to squeeze something cute.

Gigil comes to us from Tagalog, an official language of the Philippines, where it describes overwhelming joy in the face of almost unbearable cuteness. That cuteness might come in the form of a baby's first smile, or a puppy nuzzling the camera lens. Whatever its incarnation, *gigil* is the impulse that inspires you either to utter an 'aw', 'bless', and 'ah', or to physically squeeze the object of cuteness – much as a grandparent might (painfully) squeeze a child's cheeks in an outburst of affection.

There is a different side to the word, however, for 'gigil' also conveys a lack of self-control. Together with its Indonesian namesake *gemas*, it can provoke what psychologists have called 'cute aggression', reflecting the urge not just to squeeze something cute, but also to bite it – perhaps acting out the impulse behind 'I could eat you up!' It may be unsurprising, then, that should they find something irritating or frustrating, a Filipino might also exclaim '*gigil!*' to indicate they've had enough.

glad: feeling pleasure or gratitude.

If you are 'glabrous', you are also probably bald. This very old word, meaning 'smooth-skinned', is an unlikely sibling of 'glad'. Both go back to the Latin *glaber*, 'without hair'. In its earliest outings in Old English, *glæd* meant 'bright' or 'shining' – like a smooth and hairless surface that allows for a full reflection of light. By the ninth century, it also encompassed being cheerful and merry in disposition; to 'make glad' was to 'make merry', and 'glad tidings' were happy ones indeed.

glaikit: stupid or thoughtless.

There is enough of 'glee' about the word 'glaikit' for us to get it all wrong. Far from being joyful, the adjective describes someone who is exceedingly silly or thoughtless. Largely confined to northern British dialect, it seems to be a relative of the Scots 'glaiks', meaning 'tricks' or 'pranks', suggesting that being 'glaikit' involves mischief-making or scallywaggery that, for all that it irritates others, can provide a lot of fun to the doer. In West Yorkshire, each 4 November is Mischief Night, which involves all the tricks of Halloween but none of the treats: eggs are thrown at houses and people; doorbells are rung and run away from; toilet paper is festooned from trees and much more besides. At times such as these, 'glaikit' will often be the grumpy word uttered by those trapped inside.

glee: great delight.

'Glee' is a word with an edge. At its heart is a sense not just of pleasure, but of pleasure in one's own achievements, often at the expense of others. It has never been entirely innocent. In its Old English form, *gleo*, it was a poetic description of both entertainment and mockery. 'Chamber-glee' was wanton behaviour in the bedroom, while to 'make glee of' someone was to make sport of them. Perhaps its most neutral environment was music, for 'glee' could mean musical entertainment as well as the instrument providing it. The joy created by such music was rather wonderfully called a 'glee-dream', defined in the *Oxford English Dictionary* as a 'delight of minstrelsy'. From this entertainment came the idea of mirth and merry-making, and to 'make someone good glee' was to welcome them royally.

gloppened: dumbfounded.

Being 'gloppened' is a natural consequence of being **blutter-bunged**. A legacy of the Vikings, for whom *glupna* meant to 'be downcast', it describes the act of staring at something in amazement, fear, or astonishment. Some dialects go a step further and use it to mean not just startled or stupefied, but rooted to the spot with your mouth hanging wide open.

gobemouche: a highly gullible individual.

A 'gobemouche' is frequently **gloppened**: their mouth wide open ready to catch whatever spurious information comes their way. The word is a straight borrowing from French, in which it means 'fly-swallower'. In other words, a gobemouche is gullible, credulous, and easily befooled.

gongoozle: to stare vacantly at the activity of others.

What better way to spend a stifling summer's day than 'bang-a-bonking'? This perplexingly obsolete expression is recorded in glossaries of Gloucestershire dialect as meaning, quite simply, lying on a river bank and watching the world go by.

Sitting and observing activity on the water is behind another word in English, long espoused by those who love nothing better than to sit on the edge of a canal and idly observe passing boats and their crews. These are the 'gongoozlers', who take their name from a nineteenth-century term for staring protractedly at anything uncommon. In Cumbrian dialect, to 'gawn' is to 'gaze', either vacantly or with curiosity, while to 'goozen' means to 'gawp'. Nowadays, 'gongoozling' can be extended to mean staring vacantly at anything, including a cup of tea.

good: pleasing; welcome; to be desired or approved of.

It's hard to be good – as any child lying sleepless on Christmas Eve, totting up the year's behaviour balance sheet in their head, might agree. And yet a bland 'I'm good' is today's automatic response to anyone inquiring 'how are you?' Leaving aside our declining use of adverbs, 'good' is one of the most versatile, and most frequently used, adjectives of approval we have. It is also a bit of a maverick.

Entwined as it is with human history, 'good' is predictably ancient. It is not etymologically related to 'god', even though it was spelt that way in Old English. Instead it comes from a root meaning to 'bring together' or 'unite' – the idea was that things that are united are 'good', hence the word's overwhelmingly positive meanings. It has had quite the range: in the course of its lifetime it has described soil that is fertile, gold that is pure, food that is appetizing or safe, birth that is noble, faith that is loyal, and judgement that is wise. 'Good' language, meanwhile, is the 'correct' version (as opposed to the 'bad', sweary kind).

But for all its constancy, 'good' has always had a touch of quirkiness about it. For a start, it has never had a regular comparative or superlative – 'gooder' and 'goodest' never quite made the grade. Instead, we borrowed 'better' and 'best' to do the job. Nor is this idiosyncrasy confined to English – the same pattern is repeated in many other languages, for reasons that no one can quite fathom.

gorm: care and attention.

'If a hungry cannibal cracked your head open, there wouldn't be enough inside to cover a small water biscuit.' Thus Captain Blackadder's damning if consistent verdict on the increasingly gormless Baldrick. Today, you will never find 'gorm' without a 'less', the blunt articulation of a lack of sense and good judgement and a staple put-down of the parent or military sergeant. And yet people could once be *full* of 'gorm' – or 'gaum' or 'gome', as it was variously spelt. A legacy of the Vikings, 'gaum' led a contradictory double life as a word for both 'staring vacantly' and 'taking heed'. The emphasis was firmly on the latter with the rather wonderful expression 'gaum-like', meaning to 'have an intelligent look about you'.

goshbustified: excessively pleased.

America in the 1830s was the place to be if you were a word lover. The decade saw an explosion of fancy coinages, obscure abbreviations, and all-round linguistic exuberance. Only a handful of creations from the time are with us still, however, among them the glorious 'skedaddle'. Many more fell by the wayside, including 'goshbustified', a fanciful mishmash that meant 'excessively pleased or satisfied'.

gracious: courteous, kind, and pleasant.

'Grace', a fundamental principle of many religions including Hinduism and Islam, is a divine benevolence towards humanity, seated in the soul and freely bestowed without any thought of personal advantage. In Christianity, the seven gifts of grace conferred by the Holy Ghost are wisdom, understanding, counsel, knowledge, piety, fortitude, and fear of the Lord. The Virgin Mary is perceived to be particularly 'full of grace', received from God and thus an enduring force for the good. The 'grace' said before or after a meal is conceived as a form of gratitude.

In classical times, the three sister goddesses, known in Latin as *Gratiae* and in Greek as *Charites*, were believed to be bestowers of beauty, goodness, and charm, as well as charity. Indeed charity is inherent in the understanding of grace, as can be seen in several English expressions such as to 'show grace', meaning to bestow goodness from a position of power, perhaps on the part of those displaying all manner of 'airs and graces'. Winston Churchill once remarked of the Labour Party politician Stafford Cripps, 'There, but for the grace of God, goes God.'

Today, 'grace' is still used for kindness and goodwill bestowed as a consequence of faith, but it has many other uses too, particularly in the form of the adjective 'gracious', which in its earliest uses was to be full of charm, beauty, and elegance, until 'graceful' took on that mantle. Above all, graciousness today is all about a generosity of spirit, including the kind shown in a humble acknowledgement of defeat.

grandstanding: showing off in order to impress.

Nostalgia for weekend sports round-ups aside, 'grandstanding' was once all about a performance by an athlete designed to gain the approval of spectators in a stadium's principal stand. Today it still carries that charge, but has added an extra meaning of inflated and empty rhetoric designed to misdirect. 'Grandstanding' is thus essentially 'bloviating' (blowing hot air), with a dash of 'hoodwinking' on the side.

grateful: thankful.

Why be 'grateful' when you can be 'lickerous', 'feelsome', or 'lekker'? All of these historical synonyms echo the earliest meaning of 'grateful', which comes from the Latin *gratus*, 'pleasing', and which originally meant 'satisfying to the mind or senses'. Today's 'gratitude' is more a result of such pleasure; a thankfulness for something received.

grave: concerning; serious.

'Gravity' is a weighty affair, whether it's a physical force or attached to a serious situation. It comes to us via French and the Latin *gravitas*, 'weight', now a distinct term for dignity or authority and the parent of our sombre adjective 'grave'. For all its heaviness, this is unrelated to the 'grave' in which we might one day be buried, which comes from the German *Grab* (nor is it linked in any way to 'gravy', however much it might cling 'heavily' to the spoon). It is, however, related to French's 'grave' accent, marked above syllables designed to be spoken at a comparatively low or 'heavy' pitch.

greed: an excessive and selfish desire.

'Gundyguts', 'barrel belly', 'swag-paunch', 'gourmand', 'globber': the historical thesaurus has found its voice when it comes to physical greed and its results. Yet the emotion can encompass extreme appetite in all its guises. One of the seven deadly sins, it has been reviled throughout history as the ultimate and all-consuming self-interest that will trample anything in its way. Literature and religion are littered with warnings against it: 'Happy the man who has learned the cause of things and has put under his feet all fear, inexorable fate, and the noisy strife of the hell of greed,' instructed Virgil, while St Jerome believed that 'a man who is a merchant can seldom if ever please God'.

Greed was traditionally seen as the antithesis of charity, rooting people in a world where base needs are the primary motivators. It wasn't until the eighteenth century that this binary view was tempered a little, when writers and economists debated the paradox that private vices can nonetheless yield public benefit. Towards the end of the nineteenth century the English economist Alfred Marshall decided that the love of money encompasses an infinite variety of motives, among them 'many of the highest, the most refined, and the most unselfish elements of our nature'. Some would agree with him still, including the former US President Donald Trump: 'The point is that you can't be too greedy.'

'Greed' itself comes from an ancient word meaning simply to 'like' or 'want', with little hint of the extreme liking that was to follow. Perhaps the Germans express it even better with their term *Habsucht*, which translates as 'the sickness of want'.

grief: an intense sorrow.

'Grief' is an articulation of an extreme sorrow that other words struggle to convey. It is traditionally associated with tears, from Mary Magdalene's weeping at the Crucifixion to public grieving at the death of figures such as Princess Diana in 1997. And yet the connection between tears and grief has been a complex one over the centuries, as Thomas Dixon in *Weeping Britannia* richly illustrates. In ancient and early modern cultures, tears were a sign of only moderate grief but excessive sentimentality (even, in some faiths, of blasphemy), whereas the most profound kind was expected to be tearless. Elizabeth Barrett Browning, in two sonnets entitled 'Tears' and 'Grief', suggests that those who weep from suffering should be grateful: 'That is light grieving!', whereas 'hopeless grief is passionless' and expressed only through 'deathlike silence'. Such revulsion towards excessive public grief lingers still.

Linguistically, 'grief' wasn't always so intense – in the thirteenth century, it was more about hardship than suffering, and to 'take grief' was to take offence. In this it was more like a 'grievance' than the violent pain of loss with which we associate it today, hence the angry exclamation 'good grief!' But for those who have experienced it, 'grief' amply fulfils its etymology, which began with the Latin *gravis*, 'heavy'. Shakespeare gave voice to the emotion with characteristic insight: 'Well, everyone can master a grief but he that has it.'

groak: to covet someone else's food.

The act of 'groaking' in Scots and Irish once involved 'casting a suspicious eye' over something, or alternatively 'whimpering and whining'. Combine both senses and you have something close to the word's modern meaning, which is to stare longingly at someone's food in the hope that it might be shared.

As all dog-owners know, most canines are constantly groaking. But the pang of envy at your companion's plate, and the impulse to stare at it meaningfully, is not unknown to humans either.

GRUDGE

grudge: a feeling of ill will or resentment.

The words 'grudge' and 'grouch' go together in language as in life – both hail from the Old French *grouchier*, to 'grumble' or 'murmur'. There may even be a third member of the family, 'grouse'. But however much you vent your spleen, 'begrudgement' is never going to make you feel better. As one proverbial poster puts it, 'Holding a grudge is like having someone live rent-free in your head.'

gruglede [Norwegian: groog-lay-deh]: a mixture of excitement and dread.

Mixed emotions are hard to convey in language, particularly when they seem like an oxymoron. Yet Norwegian has managed to capture the mixture of anticipation and dread that we might feel when awaiting something. It consists of the two words *grue*, 'dread', and *glede*, 'happy'; put them together and you get a verb that roughly translates as to 'dread something happily'. English too once had the verb 'grue', used for shuddering or feeling terror. It is preserved, of course, in the word 'gruesome'.

gruntled: happy; contented.

Of all the lost positives, 'gruntled' may be the one most of us would like to bring back. It is unlike many of the happy counterparts to language's 'orphaned negatives' in that this one came after: a deliberate back-formation from the original adjective 'disgruntled'. The *Oxford English Dictionary* credits P. G. Wodehouse with the first usage of 'gruntled' to mean 'pleased'. In *The Code of the Woosters*, arguably the writer's silliest and funniest adventure, we read, 'I could see that, if not actually disgruntled, he was far from being gruntled.'

Wodehouse may have been unaware of historical uses of 'gruntle' to mean both 'utter little grunts' and 'grumble'. It was from the latter, in the seventeenth century, that 'disgruntle' emerged, in which the 'dis-' is merely an intensifier – to be 'disgruntled' is to be *extremely* miffed. Clearly that wouldn't have fitted the bill at all, and the sunnier face of 'gruntled' stands a fair chance of casting off its literary moorings and becoming a natural and smiling description of being perfectly content.

guilt: the fact, or a feeling, of having committed wrong or failed.

Guilt has never been a lukewarm emotion. Its journey in English began in the tenth century, when *gylt* described a 'sin', 'moral defect', or 'failure of duty'. Its ultimate etymology is unknown, though some connect it with both the German *gieldan*, to 'pay', and *Geld*, 'money', which would make clear the equation between guilt and retribution.

Guilt is both a private emotion and a public judgement. It can be a profound state of mind or a legal status determined in a criminal court (or the court of public opinion). In many faiths, guilt is a crucial adjunct to religious conviction, an inner conflict and inevitable consequence of sin for which we need to make amends, or risk eternal damnation.

Most cultures have used special tests to determine the guilt of the accused – often with fatal consequences. In medieval Europe, trial by ordeal involving fire and water was sometimes considered a 'judgement of God', a procedure based on the premise that God would help the innocent by performing a miracle on their behalf. 'Cruentation', meanwhile, was the belief that a corpse would spontaneously bleed if in the presence of the murderer.

On an individual level, everyday guilt is all too familiar – the forgotten birthday, the wounding remark, the endless childcare juggle. As Calvin in Bill Watterson's *Calvin and Hobbes* cartoons describes it, 'There's no problem so awful that you can't add some guilt to it and make it even worse.'

guilty pleasure: something one enjoys in secret; an affection for something that is not held in high regard.

Binge-watching *Murder She Wrote*, quaffing a glass of wine in the bath, or screaming along like a banshee to Meat Loaf – the 'guilty pleasure' has settled comfortably into twenty-first-century conversation. Yet while it may be the cuddly face of guilt for most of us, the expression once had an altogether different vibe, for in the nineteenth century a 'guilty pleasure' was a brothel.

What makes a pleasure guilty is the knowledge that other people might judge you for it. It requires an outside scrutiny, which means there is something distinctly performative about such delights – as though we feel the need to signal that we are indulging in them, rather than just going ahead regardless. Put this way, 'guilty pleasure' may simply be the acceptable name for self-gratification. The Foo Fighters' Dave Grohl agrees: 'I don't believe in guilty pleasures. If you fucking like something, like it.'

gusto: enjoyment or relish.

'Why should you force wine upon us? We are not all of your gusto,' runs a line from William Wycherley's play *Love in a Wood* (1672). While today we associate 'gusto' with vigour and pleasure, in those days it was all about taste. A borrowing from Italian, its ultimate ancestor is the Latin *gustus*, the root both of 'disgust' – something that leaves a 'bad taste' – and the French *dégustation de vin*, or 'wine-tasting'. Happily, the tastes must have lingered on the sweet side, for today's 'gusto' is all about enjoyment and relish.

guts: courage; determination.

In Yiddish they are our *kishkes*, in Old English they were our *arse-ropes*. Today we are beginning to recognize that our gut or guts are our second brain, and that our everyday emotional well-being may rely on their messages. This notion of the intestines as a seat of emotions is ancient, and existed long before the heart took over.

Greek poets regarded the bowels as the home of the more violent passions such as anger and love. Two millennia later, we still might 'hate someone's guts', or even want their 'guts for garters'. For the Hebrews, on the other hand, the bowels and intestines were the home of tenderness and affection, kindness and benevolence – for a time in English, too, the word 'bowel' had a secondary meaning of 'pity' and 'compassion'. Whatever emotions are attached to them, guts have long been thought to be highly prophetic, not just of health but also of human fate. A Roman soothsayer, or *haruspex*, would use the entrails of animals to divine the future.

'Gut' itself appears in Old English as *guttas*, which came from an ancient word stem meaning to 'pour' or 'drip'. In this it was related to 'gout', a disease thought to be caused by drops of viscous humours seeping from the blood into the joints. The 'gut' was conceived as a narrow passage in a body of water, and by the eleventh century had become the standard word for the contents of the abdomen as well as the bowels. Today's 'gut feelings' have quite a history.

gwenders: a painful tingling from the cold.

If you have the misfortune to have been born **nesh**, you may also need the word 'gwenders'. This Cornish term means 'a disagreeable tingling sensation in the extremities, caused by cold'. For anyone whom the Spanish would call *friolero* (extremely susceptible to the cold), there is nothing wonderful about the 'gwenders' at all.

halcyon: idyllically happy and peaceful.

'Halcyon' is a word that will resonate with anyone who has witnessed the bright blue flash of a kingfisher swooping into a shining river, for the *alkyōn* was a fabled creature identified with that brilliant bird. The name translates as 'sea-conceiving', an idea born in the myth of the goddess Alcyone, who, upon hearing the news of her husband's drowning, casts herself into the sea in grief. Moved by her plight, the rest of the gods turn both Alcyone and Ceyx into kingfishers. Every year, Alcyone builds her nest on the surface of the sea, while her father Aeolus, divine keeper of the winds, ensures that the waters remain calm and tranquil.

Traditionally, kingfishers were said to breed during the seven days before and the seven days after the winter solstice – these were the original 'halcyon' or 'kingfisher' days, always peaceful and fair. The expression later came to embrace any period of quiet, unruffled happiness.

half-hearted: without energy or enthusiasm.

John Florio was a linguist, lexicographer, and royal language tutor at the court of James I. He contributed over a thousand words to the English language, but also wrote an Italian–English dictionary, which included the word *semicorde*, which he translated as 'a coward, halfe-hearted'. The heart was regarded as the seat not just of emotion, but of understanding and intellect, too, preserved in our notion that we can learn something 'by heart'. 'Half-hearted', therefore, can describe someone wanting in mental dedication as well as emotional effort, while to be 'wholehearted' is to act with complete dedication and sincerity – or, in the words of Spinal Tap, to 'turn it up to eleven'.

Hamsterkauf [German: hum-ster-kowf]: the urge to panic-buy.

At the start of the coronavirus pandemic, when pasta was in short supply and toilet rolls were either flying off the shelves or bringing shoppers to fisticuffs, the Germans remembered an expression for the impulse to panic-buy and hoard in times of crisis. Based on the existing verb *hamstern*, to 'hoard' (literally to 'hamster'), *Hamsterkauf*, 'hamster-buying', is the stockpiling of products in anticipation of a shortage, just as our favourite rodent stores food in its pouches for later use. But neither the word nor the act is new. In the aftermath of the Second World War, thousands of German city-dwellers flocked to farms in the countryside in search of bacon, butter, fruit, and vegetables, swapping their jewellery and clothes for food. These excursions became known as *Hamsterfahrten*, 'hamster trips'.

hangry: bad-tempered through lack of food.

'Hangry', fittingly, is very Marmite. For some it is newfangled and unpalatable, but for others it is an essential description of everyday life. The first argument is easily dismissed by a check of the historical dictionary, which shows that 'hangry' – a simple blend of 'hungry' and 'angry' – was first used by Arthur Ransome in a letter from 1918: 'The elephant is very hungry and hangry from having had no dinner.' As for the second, 'hangry' might well be indispensable for anyone whose temper flares whenever their blood sugar drops. It is challenged perhaps only by the slip of the ear that has gained traction in recent times – 'lack toast intolerant'.

happy: content and felicitous.

> We hold these truths to be self-evident, that all men are created equal, that they are endowed by their Creator with certain unalienable Rights, that among these are Life, Liberty and the pursuit of Happiness.

The word 'happiness' as used here in the American Declaration of Independence is poised on the cusp of two very different meanings: one that denotes good fortune, and one that suggests a non-specific, emotional contentment. The move from one to the other has been gradual and blurry, and is also instructive of shifts in belief over the course of a thousand years.

Before the fourteenth century you could be 'glad' or 'pleased', but not 'happy'. When the word did emerge in English, as an extension of the word 'hap', it meant something rather different, for 'hap' was all about one's lot. A likely legacy of the Vikings, it appeared in compounds such as 'goodhap' (prosperity) and 'mishap' (misfortune).

'Hap' was also just as much about luck. A 'crosshap' was an unlucky accident, while something 'haphazard' was also a matter of pure chance (indeed 'perhaps' also meant 'by chance').

Most importantly, when something 'happened', it occurred randomly rather than by design.

It was from these beginnings that 'happy' emerged, meaning 'blessed with good fortune' and 'lucky'. The expressions 'happy coincidence', 'happy accident', and 'happy position' all reflect this idea of the fortunate hand of fate. By the fifteenth century, 'happy' had taken a big stride towards contentment, while to be 'mishappy', for a while at least, meant the exact opposite.

As for 'happiness', this too has been synonymous with 'luck' for much of its history. While it has now become an umbrella term for many positive emotions, it wasn't always this way. The ancients took pains to distinguish hedonistic pleasure from happiness. For Aristotle, the latter – what he called *eudaimonia* – arose from the exercise of virtue. Devotion to a god has similarly long been posited as the only path to true happiness within many religions. In modern philosophy, the focus has turned to the individual, expressing happiness variously as the absence of pain or a wish that is satisfied. And luck has also re-entered the equation, as research shows that, by and large, people create their own. Those of us who believe that good things will happen find that, generally, they actually do. Etymologically, 'happiness' may have always favoured the lucky, but it may not be as random as its journey – and our brains – suggest.

happy as Larry: extremely satisfied and contented.

Larry and a sandboy have a lot in common when it comes to happiness. But who was the Larry we can be as happy as, and where does a sandboy fit in? The main contender for the former is Larry Foley, a renowned nineteenth-century Australian boxer who retired at thirty-two and collected a purse of £1,000 for his final fight, presumably making him very happy indeed. Etymologists tend, however, to favour another source in the word 'larrikin', English dialect for a 'mischievous youth'. Perhaps larrikins were so mischievous and carefree that they inspired the modern phrase. As for sandboys, these were the errand-runners who once delivered sand to taverns as a floor covering to soak up alcoholic spillages. They would often be rewarded with a tipple themselves, making them, to add one final metaphor, 'as happy as a clam at high tide'.

harrowing: acutely distressing.

'I could a tale unfold, whose lightest word / Would harrow up thy soul,' says Hamlet to the ghost of his father, giving the *Oxford English Dictionary* the first use of 'harrow' in the figurative sense of acute, lacerating pain. His image refers to the heavy frame with iron teeth that is dragged over ploughed land to break it up and pulverize the soil. Replace 'soil' with 'soul' and you get the full power of the metaphor.

In Christian theology, the time between Jesus' crucifixion and resurrection involved a 'harrowing of Hell', in which Christ descended triumphantly to rescue souls held captive there and to bring 'good tidings'. Here, 'harrowing' involves another meaning of the term, to 'harry or despoil', suggesting not just a triumphant descent but also a forceful liberation of the righteous.

hatred: intense dislike or loathing.

'Fiendship', 'loathness', 'bitterhead': the dictionary offers a fair number of synonyms for 'hate', which was an early entrant to English, with siblings in many languages descended from the same ancient root, *haton* – each wrapped up in sorrow and venom. Hatred is so subjective that philosophers and poets have always struggled to define it. Aristotle, for instance, viewed it as distinct from anger and rage: 'anger can be cured by time, but hatred cannot'. For Nietzsche, hatred was both constructive and destructive, while Lord Byron decided that 'hatred is by far the longest pleasure; / men love in haste but they detest in leisure'.

There is a plentiful list of hateful compounds:'hate speech' is first recorded in a translation of an Anglo-Saxon poem about Satan's revolt from 1898, in which he 'Lifted himself against his leader, sought hate-speech'. The first 'hate-list' emerged in early nineteenth-century America, followed by 'hate mail', 'hate figure', and 'hate crime'. Today, 'haters gonna hate' has become a trope of modern media dismissing criticism and expressing consolation to anyone who finds themselves in the line of fire. In the end most of us would aspire to agree with Martin Luther King Jr, who decided 'to stick to love' because 'hate is too great a burden to bear'. His words were spoken just nine months before his assassination.

heebie-jeebies: a state of nervous anxiety.

The 'heebie-jeebie' was a popular dance in the 1920s, one that a journalist of the time declared to be particularly 'rich in haunch movements'. According to a contemporary dance manual, its moves included the 'get-off', the 'stomp-off', the 'fling-off', and the 'heebie-off'. The dance was alleged to have taken its name from the incantations of an Indian witch doctor before making a human sacrifice, but the slang lexicographer Jonathon Green believes that it is more likely to have originated in a less exotic setting: the American cartoon strip *Barney Google*.

Whether it was inspired by the jumping movements of the dance or the superstitions regarding its origin, 'heebie-jeebies' entered the English slang lexicon to describe a nameless terror involving extreme jitters, discomfort, and apprehension. By extension, it was also used of an alcoholic's experience of delirium tremens, or the symptoms that accompany heroin or cocaine withdrawal.

heliophile: a lover of sunshine.

The 'heliophiles' of the natural world, such as certain aquatic algae, have evolved to attain maximum exposure to sunlight. For those of us who thrive on the sun's rays and head outside the moment the clouds break, the term is equally handy.

high muck-a-muck: a pompous, conceited, and overbearing individual.

In the 1850s slang of North America, 'high muck-a-muck' was a mocking nickname for a person of high social standing – a 'bigwig'. You might think the connection here is with 'filthy lucre' or an abundance of money, but the phrase is a mangling of an expression borrowed from the language of the Chinook people, in which *hiyu muckamuck* meant 'plenty of food'. The link seems to have been with high-status givers of 'potlatch', an opulent feast at which gifts were liberally 'handed down' to those less fortunate. Satirists quickly adopted the spurious title, often adding a 'Lord' or 'Mayor' to Muck-a-Muck (or Muckety-Muck) for good measure.

hinayang [Tagalog: heena-yung]: regret over something that might have been.

In the language of Tagalog, *hinayang* is a very specific kind of regret, felt when a person knows that they could have benefited from a particular situation but missed their chance. It is the full knowledge of a wasted opportunity, and can encompass circumstances of deep regret, such as not seeing a relative before they die, as well as more irksome ones, such as losing a winning lottery ticket.

hingum–tringum: feeble and barely presentable.

Scots offers a host of words for low spirits, from 'drowff' to 'drumoolich', 'glumsh' to 'waff'. Amongst the most evocative is surely the nineteenth-century 'hingum-tringum'. The adjective is given several definitions in the *Scottish National Dictionary*, including 'in a weak state of health', and 'barely presentable'. The two are more pithily combined in a further description that most of us can readily relate to: 'just about hanging together'. In other words, when we are hanging on by our fingernails and only just able to get moving ('noggling it', as English dialect might put it), we can say that we are truly 'hingum-tringum'.

hiraeth [Welsh: hi-ry-eth]: a deep nostalgia for home.

There is a kind of homesickness that lingers even when you return. It is a call as much to your spiritual as to your physical home, which may never quite be found. This nostalgia for the unreachable, for the loss of love and home, is known in Welsh as *hiraeth*. A word with Celtic roots, it is an ancient concept recorded as early as the sixth century, articulating both incompleteness and the longing for something now gone, or for what could have been. *See also* **desiderate** and *hwyl*.

homage: tribute or public respect.

At the heart of 'homage' is *homo*, the Latin for 'man'. Its associations with respect and honour began in feudal times, when a selected person could become a 'king's man' or vassal in a formal and carefully choreographed 'homage' ceremony, at which he would publicly announce his allegiance. The subject would kneel and place his hands between those of his lord as an affirmation of obedience. When today we pay homage to something or someone – or, more likely, pay 'ommage' (*à la française* and a return to the original pronunciation, as it happens) – we are silently and metaphorically kneeling before it in full respect and reverence.

homefulness: filled with a sense of belonging.

In July 1841, the poet John Clare escaped from High Beech asylum in Epping Forest, desperate to get home to his beloved Mary Joyce. He walked for days with broken shoes, subsisting only on grass from the verges. When, utterly exhausted, he reached the point where the road forks to Peterborough, he felt a renewed sense of vitality and later recalled, 'I felt myself in home's way.' The writer Iain Sinclair, retracing Clare's journey in his 2005 book *Edge of the Orison*, used the little-known word 'homefulness' to describe Clare's feeling at exactly this point – a moment when he became full of the feeling of home.

honest: straightforward and truthful.

'Honesty' was once first and foremost about 'honour'. The two words share the same ancestor in *honestus*, which for the Romans signified all that was respectable, decent, and fine. An honest person – usually one considered well-born – had all of those qualities in spades. Today's meaning of truthfulness is an extension of the attributes expected of chivalrous or courteous behaviour. A sense of transparency and lack of deceit also inspired the naming of the plant 'honesty', on account of its diaphanous seed pods.

honour: high respect; great esteem.

For a word that is so integral to modern preoccupations of reputation and cancellation, 'honour' is surprisingly varied in its meanings. Even Samuel Johnson, a lexicographer

particularly keen to nail language down, gave it thirteen definitions. The word has variously meant esteem or repute; a sign
of that esteem, such as a New Year's Honour; chastity or fidelity
when applied to a woman; a matter of moral righteousness
such as might be decided in a duel; a formal title of address; the
king, queen, or jack in a pack of cards; and the respect paid to
a fallen soldier at a funeral. At the heart of each are reverence
and reputation, which can be both individual and collective
(including 'Scout's honour', 'schoolboy's honour', and, famously, 'honour among thieves'.)

Etymologically, 'honour' came to us from the French *honneur*,
itself from the Latin *honor*, meaning 'privilege' as well as 'private
or public office'. American and British English are distinguished through the addition in the latter of the *u*, but this only
emerged as the standard spelling in the seventeenth century –
until then, British English had stuck firmly with the Latin
version. In Shakespeare's First Folio, 'honor' outscores 'honour'
handsomely.

horror: an intense feeling of shock or disgust.

Imagine a cat recoiling in fright at a dog, its back arched and its
hair standing stiffly on end, and you'll be able to picture the
original meaning of 'horror', which began with the Latin
horrere, meaning to 'bristle with fear'. From the same root came
'horrid', which originally meant 'hairy, prickly, and rough'.
Today, 'horror' still holds a flicker of the loathing, fear, and
shuddering of dread that characterized its physical beginnings.
It's not all bad, however, for there is a definite evolutionary
advantage to the cat's bristling fright, as it effectively makes the
animal grow in size, often scaring off its stronger predator.

horror silentii: the fear of silence.

In response to the frequent debates over modern speech characteristics, such as the use of fillers ('like', 'totally', 'you know'), the US linguist Michael Shapiro has coined the expression *horror silentii*, which he based on **horror vacui** but which describes the fear of linguistic rather than spatial emptiness. The result is continuous chatter of the kind that Shapiro calls 'a totally gratuitous percussive punctuation of one's presence'.

horror vacui: the fear of empty spaces.

Horror vacui has been a driving force of art and design for centuries, although the term itself was coined late on, by the twentieth-century art critic Mario Praz, who used it to describe the Victorian impulse to decorate every inch of space in a piece of art. The phenomenon is now ubiquitous in modern living, from menus to posters, *Where's Wally* books and website pages. *Horror vacui* is, in essence, a fear of emptiness, and the desire to leave no part of a canvas unfilled.

hostile: showing opposition or dislike.

In Latin, the word for 'host' is the same as the word for 'guest': *hospes*. It's a curious story that binds the two together, yet both descend from a central tenet in ancient society. In nomadic times, strong rules for the guest–host relationship were key to avoiding skirmishes and warfare between tribes. Mutual respect and friendship were encompassed by *ghos-ti*, a term from Proto-Indo-European, the ancient common ancestor of the Indo-European family of languages that includes English. No direct record of PIE, as it is known, exists, but the language has been reconstructed using early records of the Indo-European languages themselves. *Ghos-ti* is the hypothetical source of 'guest', 'hospice', 'host', 'hostel', and many other words that are bound up in the exchange of hospitality – including, counter-intuitively, 'hostile'. By Roman times, the code of mutual respect couldn't always be relied upon, and so a line was drawn between the known and the unknown guest. The Latin *hostis*, another descendant of *ghost-ti*, originally meant 'stranger', describing one who might be a guest at a hostel or hospice. But as strangers have long been mistrusted, so *hostis* also generated 'hostile', in case that guest turned out to be the enemy.

hot-blooded: lustful; passionate.

The polarity between cold blood and hot blood was established in the seventeenth century, a relic of ancient medical beliefs about human physiology and the influence of the bodily **humours**. Shakespeare was the first to give us the adjective 'hot-blooded', in *The Merry Wives of Windsor* ('Now the hot-blooded gods assist me') – just as he gave us its antithesis in *King John*: 'Thou cold-blooded slave, / Hast thou not spoke like thunder on my side?'

With hot blood goes lust as well as temper, while the cold kind renders us entirely emotionless. Far better, then, to be simply warm-blooded: ardent and passionate, but less prone to fly off the handle.

The notion of acting 'in hot blood' is important in criminal law too. In a concept formalized in the sixteenth and seventeenth centuries, crimes committed in hot blood were justified in having a partial defence of 'provocation', which might incur a lighter sentence – the precursor to 'voluntary manslaughter' as opposed to premeditated murder.

hot-headed: impetuous or quick-tempered.

It would be nice to know a little more about the Hothede family, who are registered in the court rolls of Henry III in 1256. We know nothing more than their names – Johannes

Hothed and Ceciliam Hothede – but given that appellations of the time frequently reflected an individual's personality, we can assume that they or their ancestors were impulsive by nature. The adjective 'hot-headed' appeared around 300 years later, and is joined in the *Oxford English Dictionary* by some impressive synonyms for being over-ready to fight, including 'ram-stam', 'scapperboiling', and 'torrentuous'.

humane: showing compassion.

Is there a greater exercise of humanity than kindness? Clearly those in the sixteenth century felt the same, for 'human' and 'humane' were one and the same thing. Each meant 'having qualities befitting of a human being', namely courtesy and compassion. By the early eighteenth century, 'human' and 'humane' had parted ways, and the latter took on most of the kindness. Today, to state that 'you're only human' is more a recognition of fallibility than benevolence.

humble: modest; deferential.

To be *humilis*, in Latin, was to be 'lowly' or 'base', for it was built upon the Romans' word for 'earth' or 'ground', *humus* (which was later to inform our word 'posthumous', after death, when we are lowered into the ground). To be 'humble' in the thirteenth century was similarly to have a 'low' sense of one's own importance or merits. By the fourteenth century, Geoffrey Chaucer was showing us how to sign off letters to those considered our superior by adding a 'Yours humbly'. From low self-esteem duly came the idea of modesty and a lack of pretension.

In a separate development, 'humble' also became a variant spelling of 'umbles' or 'numbles', words borrowed from the Norman elite for the entrails of a deer or hart and based on the Latin *lumbus*, 'loin'. In the nineteenth century, 'humble pie' became a humorous play on 'umble pie' – one cooked with inferior cuts of meat and allegedly served to the lowlier dinner guests at a gathering.

humblebrag: an apparently self-deprecating statement designed to make the speaker look good.

'What would you say is your most negative quality?': so runs one of the most feared questions in any job interview. Most respondents come up with a negative that actually suggests the opposite: 'I'm a perfectionist', for example, or 'I like to listen to *every* member of the team, which takes time.' Welcome to the 'humblebrag', the ostensibly self-critical statement that is really designed to amplify one's admirable qualities. When used as a self-referential hashtag on social media, the true home of the humblebrag, it surpasses even itself: 'I bumped into Jason Isaacs today and hadn't even brushed my hair! #humblebrag.'

humdudgeon: a fit of despondency that results in an imaginary illness.

First recorded in Francis Grose's *Classical Dictionary of the Vulgar Tongue* (1785) – an earthy collection of the slang deemed unfit for standard dictionaries, collected from tavern- and brothel-keepers, highwaymen and pickpockets – a 'humdudgeon' is an imagined illness that accompanies being down in the dumps. The word is made up of 'hum-', a shortening of 'humbug', and 'dudgeon', a state of begrudging indignation. In other words, a 'humdudgeon' is the all-overishness you feel coming on when gloom descends.

humicubation: the act of lying down in repentance.

Humicubation involves lying on the ground in extreme submission. Since the seventeenth century it has been used, admittedly rarely, in situations of religious passion, but it has also stretched to more prosaic circumstances, such as the stereotypical occasion of a drunken husband arriving home late from work and prostrating himself in front of his wife (in need perhaps of a compensation present or what the Germans misogynistically call *Drachenfutter*, 'dragon food'). The word is made up of Latin *humi*, 'on the ground', and *cubare*, to 'lie down'.

humiliation: shame; mortification; embarrassment.

There are several expressive synonyms for the act of humiliation, such as 'drawing someone's eyeteeth', 'wiping a person's eye', and 'putting someone's pipe out'. Colourful as these are, they all lack the vehemence of the original, for the verb 'humiliate' is another word with its roots in the Latin *humus*, 'ground', suggesting that the estimation we hold of our humiliated victim is rock bottom, or that the humiliated person is prostrate in submission. The word is thus a sibling of 'humble', which as an active verb – to 'humble' someone – implies the same level of abasement.

Many now-obsolete public punishments were designed to be so humiliating that they served as a deterrent to others. Some practices, such as tarring-and-feathering, became tools of unofficial mob justice. Formal traditions such as the English 'skimmington rides', in which wrongdoers (and in particular 'nagging' wives) were paraded through the streets and subjected to the noisy derision of the crowd, became regular demonstrations of collective moral disapproval: strange rituals of humiliation and celebration.

humour: the quality of being amusing; a mood or state of mind.

Having a sense of humour – and of its history – is fundamental to an understanding of emotions and how they have been perceived throughout history. 'Humorism' was a system of belief in medicine that attributed feelings and behaviours to a predominance of one or more bodily fluids. The concept was eagerly espoused by Greek and Roman medics and philosophers, but is likely to be older still, rooted in the medicine of ancient Egypt. Humorism also has parallels in other cultures such as Indian Ayurveda medicine and medical tradition in the Golden Age of Islam, but it was the Greeks who formalized the belief, deriving the name for it from the Greek *chymos*, meaning 'fluid', 'sap', or 'juice'. The Greek physician Hippocrates was among the first to nail humorism firmly to medicine, suggesting that human moods were determined by four fluids: blood, phlegm, yellow, and black bile. An excess or deficiency of any of these vital 'juices' dictated personality as well as health. The idea was further developed by Galen, one of the most accomplished and influential physicians in antiquity.

The equations between the four fluids were enshrined not just in medicine but in language too. A 'sanguine' individual (from the Latin *sanguineus*, 'bloody') is optimistic, ruddy-cheeked, and stable, while a 'melancholic' one has an excess of 'black bile' (*melas khole* in Greek). A 'phlegmatic' person, 'full of phlegm', was stolidly calm. Yellow or green bile, or 'choler', rendered someone peevish and choleric. It was Shakespeare who ascribed green to jealousy. When Iago talks of the 'green-eyed monster', he displaced the earlier twinning of green with avarice, and of jealousy with yellow. All these associations were born in the context of the bodily humours. Soon after Shakespeare, belief in humorism began to be dismantled, after some 2,000 years of dominance in medical thinking. *See also* **choleric**.

hunch: an intuition.

Having a 'hunch' is a less elegant articulation of what in the Middle Ages was known as a 'forefeeling' and in the eighteenth century as a 'presentiment'. Each expresses a perception of future events based on intuition rather than fact. The first meaning of 'hunch' was a 'push' or 'thrust', and so when we have a hunch about something it is as though a thought is 'pushing' itself into the mind. Similarly, we hunch our backs by 'pushing' our shoulders up, but one theory goes a step further, and connects 'having a hunch' to an old superstition that touching the curvature of a 'hunchback' would bring good luck. This tradition of the 'lucky' hunchback dates back centuries, when those afflicted were believed to divert the gaze of the evil eye – a hunchback talisman called a *gobbo* can still be bought in Italy today. There is no linguistic evidence to support any link, but superstition rarely listens to fact.

hungover: suffering the after-effects of alcohol.

The search for the origins of the term 'hangover' have made for some compelling stories. One of the most popular tells how the term refers to ropes once provided to drunkards for leaning or sleeping upon in return for a small fee. It is true that, in the late nineteenth and early twentieth centuries, the Salvation Army operated many homeless shelters, which charged varying amounts according to requirements. A 'penny sit-up' included food and shelter for a penny, but no provision for sleep. The 'twopenny hangover' involved placing a rope in front of a bench which the customer could then lean over. At the top end of the scale, for the kingly sum of fourpence, was a coffin-like wooden box in which the especially needy could lie flat and sleep. George Orwell's *Down and Out in Paris and London* of 1933 vividly describes such a system:

> At the Twopenny Hangover, the lodgers sit in a row on a bench; there is a rope in front of them, and they lean on

this as though leaning over a fence. A man, humorously called the valet, cuts the rope at five in the morning. I have never been there myself, but Bozo had been there often. I asked him whether anyone could possibly sleep in such an attitude, and he said that it was more comfortable than it sounded – at any rate, better than bare floor.

It's a gloomy tableau. Linguistically, however, such venues were not the inspiration for 'hungover', which from the outset has simply described something that is left or that 'hangs over' from a previous event. And few after-effects have attracted more woeful attention than those involving **crapulence**.

hungry: lacking in or desiring food.

'Spit', 'ashes', 'black' – among the words believed to date back 15,000 years are many that underscore the importance of fire, essential for both warmth and cooking food. Hunger is an eternal catalyst for human behaviour, and an unhappy determiner of human fate. John F. Kennedy proposed that 'The war against hunger is truly mankind's war of liberation.' History cannot escape hunger, and food is our common ground – it is unsurprising, therefore, that 'hunger', and being 'hungry', have come to embrace all kinds of metaphorical uses that express a strong desire or need. We can be hungry for success, fame, love, justice, or even stimulation. For Samuel Johnson, 'hungry' was a marker of something that is lacking and that is 'more disposed to draw from other substances than to impart to them' – a hungry river is one that has no fish; a hungry wine is one that is acrid or weak.

In many languages, a person will say they 'have hunger' as opposed to being 'hungry'. A French speaker will say *J'ai faim*, a German *Ich habe Hunger*, and an Italian *ho fame*, while Turkish *acikmak* means 'I hunger'. Each conveys a more forceful, tangible expression of need.

hwyl [Welsh: hoo-eel]: emotional fervour.

Hwyl is defined in the *Oxford English Dictionary* as 'an emotional quality that inspires and sustains impassioned eloquence', and as 'the fervour of emotion characteristic of gatherings of Welsh people'. *Hwyl* represents fun, energy, and zest, but it is also used to express stirring emotions: fervour, motivation, and enthusiasm, as well as something more elusive, namely a sense of belonging and home, akin to **hiraeth**. Its story is telling: *hwyl* originally denoted the sail of a ship, which might explain how it became a metaphor for the course we sail in life, and for the moorings of home.

hygge [Danish: hoo-guh]: cosiness and conviviality.

Entire books have been devoted to it, blankets and socks pay homage to it, steaming hot chocolate or *glögg* seem born for it. Rooted in the Old Norse *hygga*, to 'comfort', and a sibling of 'hug', the Danish *hygge* defines a lifestyle based on cosiness and conviviality. *Hygge* comes with wood fires, scented candles, and fleece-lined slippers – anything, in fact, that hugs the senses. Above all, *hygge* is about being soothed and unruffled by the outside world. Those that subscribe to it can be described in terms of the bouncier and even more delightful *hyggelige*.

hyperbole: exaggeration or inflation.

When is any agreement not a 'landmark' one, an interview not 'exclusive', a clever idea not 'genius'? Even 'literally' has gained a secondary sense in our dictionaries, meaning of course anything but. 'Unbelievable' is now all-too-believable, while 'average' and 'mediocre' have lost their happy middle-of-the-road status to become plodding markers of inferiority. Never call someone's work or appearance 'fine' or 'nice', unless you're 'dying' for semantic fisticuffs.

We are well accustomed to linguistic inflation, whereby 'heroes' now need to be 'superheroes' and takeaway coffees are religiously classed as a 'Tall' or 'Grande', never 'Small'. Apart from wanting more linguistic bang for our buck, why exactly do we do it? Psychologists now conclude that extroverts require more cortical stimulation from their language than introverts in order to feel any impact, opting for extreme vocabulary such as 'sweltering' over 'hot', or 'tragic' over 'sad'. And it appears we *feel* what we say: we are likely to feel hotter or more tired if we choose the language with the biggest hit. Much of this super-sizing is a modern phenomenon, a means of being heard above the cacophony of noise. But the human instinct to overdrama-tize is nothing new – the ancient Greeks knew all about it, bequeathing us their word *hyperbole*, meaning 'excess'.

hypnopompic: accompanying the process of waking up.

In 1901, F. W. H. Meyers wrote, 'To … illusions accompanying the departure of sleep, as when a dream-figure persists for a few moments into waking life, I have given the name *hypnopompic*.' Meyers coined this as the counterpoint to 'hypnagogic', which describes the companion processes to falling asleep (including the bumpy shock of 'night jerks'). To be 'hypnopompic', however, is much more than hovering in a limbo state between sleep and wakefulness. For it is most often to be trapped in a dream state that you really don't want to be in. These are hallu-cinations, often unpleasant ones, that occur on the borders of sleep. Unlike nightmares, which often feature a complex storyline, these are usually simple images, sounds, and sensa-tions. Ultimately, we return to reality, a shift embodied in the origins of 'hypnopompic' itself: the Greek *hypnos*, 'sleep', and *pompē*, a 'sending away'.

hypocritical: acting in contradiction to one's stated beliefs or feelings.

Theatrical metaphors have percolated through English for centuries. Even as fundamental a word as 'person' comes from the Latin *persona*, a 'mask' of the type worn by Roman actors. 'Hypocrisy' is equally rooted in acting, fittingly enough, and comes this time from Greek, where *hypokrinesthai* meant to 'play a part' and thus 'pretend'. A 'hypocrite' is one who dissembles by pretending to have higher qualities or more noble beliefs than is actually the case. The Greek term comes in turn from *hypo*, 'under', and *krinein*, to 'sift' or 'decide', implying the inability to sort out one's moral convictions.

Carl Jung attributed hypocrisy to those who are not aware of the dark side of their nature, which he called the 'shadow side'. This might, in the end, apply to most of us: the author Robert Wright decided that 'human beings are a species splendid in their array of moral equipment, tragic in their propensity to misuse it, and pathetic in their constitutional ignorance of the misuse.' That array of moral equipment brings us right back to the stage, and the masked 'persons' who populate it.

hyppytyynytyydytys [Finnish: hoop-uh-tu-nuh-tu-duh-tis]: the pleasure of dropping into an armchair.

At the end of a hard day you might find yourself 'sossing' into the nearest soft furnishings. 'Soss', as a verb, means to 'fall with a heavy impact', while the noun is made a little more expressive, representing the sound of a soft body flopping down heavily. This sensation of letting oneself drop with a sigh has been given the Finnish name *hyppytyynytyydytys*, a vowel-less confection that is probably known nowhere beyond the confines of the Internet and that has been joyously translated as 'bouncy cushion satisfaction'. In other words, this is both the feeling and sound of plopping down into a comfortable chair.

hysteria: overwrought; excessively emotional.

'Hysteria' is defined in the *Oxford English Dictionary* as a 'morbidly excited condition'. There may be more to this than meets the eye, for even today, the majority of those described as 'excited' and 'excitable' are women.

For centuries, the belief persisted that hysteria was caused by a disturbance of the uterus or womb. The 'complaint' was given its name by male pathologists in the nineteenth century, who based it on the Greek for 'womb', *hystera* (hence 'hysterectomy'). The ancients believed that a woman's uterus was untethered and could migrate around her body, causing not only ailments but irrational behaviour too (murder wasn't out of the question). 'Cures' included coaxing the uterus into its rightful place by bringing good smells near the vagina, and bad smells near the mouth. Hysteria was also known as 'the vapours', thanks to the idea that the womb and stomach let off noxious exhalations that disturbed a woman's mind as well as body.

Sigmund Freud marked a significant departure in the understanding of hysteria by seeing the condition as a disease of the mind rather than the body, rooted in the repression of unpleasant emotions and a woman's 'Oedipal' moment of recognition that she has no penis. His early book *Studies on Hysteria*, written with the physician Josef Breuer, became one of the cornerstones of his career.

Even today, few men are ever described as being 'hysterical', unless of course they are funny. The footprint of an erroneous belief dating back some two millennia lingers still.

iarmhaireacht [Irish: eea-wire-acht]: the loneliness felt at dawn.

In *Thirty-Two Words for Field*, the documentary-maker Manchán Magan writes of his love for the vanishing vocabulary of his native Ireland, and for the lore wrapped around it. He laments the loss of such terms as *ceap*, originally a simple description of a tree stump but also, by extension, the place where one feels nurtured and rooted. Here too is the exquisite *iarmhaireacht*, which Magan defines as 'the loneliness you feel at cockcrow, when you are the only person awake and experience that existential pang of disconnection, of not belonging'.

idiorepulsive: self-repellent.

Technically, this adjective from the nineteenth century has always been confined to science, used of heat that, according to an early theory of thermodynamics involving the cooling of liquids, is 'self-repulsive' or expansive. It might have been left there, had English not had a gap for the feeling that engulfs you as you look in the mirror first thing in the morning (or last thing at night, depending on your drinking habits). Given that gap, 'idiorepulsive' does the job because, quite simply, we sometimes disgust ourselves.

idle: lazy; ineffectual.

The original sense of 'idle' was 'empty': it is related to the German *eitel*, meaning 'bare'. The adjective has inspired several useful expressions in English, most of them long forgotten. 'Idle yelp' was once a synonym for boasting, 'idle bellies' were lazy sluggards or gluttons, and to be 'sick of the idles' was to be bored or apathetic. In South Africa, a grass-bird so sluggish that it is easily caught is known as an 'idle Dick'.

idle worms: laziness and indolence.

'A round little worm / Pricked from the lazy finger of a maid.' In these lines from *Romeo and Juliet*, Shakespeare invoked the superstition that worms like to breed in the fingertips of lazy women. These were the 'idle worms', summoned proverbially to warn against indolence and to promote female productivity.

iktsuarpok [Inuktitut: eet-so-ahr-pohk]: the anticipation of waiting for someone to arrive.

When it comes to visitors, English does its job pretty well. It has given us a word, for example, for rushing around the house, desperately tidying up just before guests arrive: this is 'scurryfunging'. There is even a term for a dinner at which the host gets drunk before the guests, namely a 'Dutch feast'. Yet the act of waiting for your guest to arrive – the eager anticipation of their footsteps along your path – has yet to find expression. And so we can turn to *iktsuarpok*, a word from the Inuit language of Inuktitut which for all its unpronounceability packs in a lot of emotions. This is the restlessness of expecting someone and the repeated process of going outside to check for their approach. Above all, *iktsuarpok* is the mix of inner anguish and excitement that defines the act of waiting.

ilinx: a perception-altering vertigo.

Roger Caillois, a twentieth-century French sociologist and major figure in game studies, defined four types of game play. These were *agon* (competition), *alea* (chance), *mimicry* (simulation), and *ilinx*. From the Greek for 'whirlpool', 'ilinx' was described by Caillois as the operation of 'voluptuous panic upon an otherwise lucid mind'. This is the sensation of spinning out of control, as when children spin round and round or dervishes furiously whirl. Thus 'ilinx' has been extended to other experiences far beyond the world of gaming, as in the intentional smashing of china plates, or the casual destruction of a lovingly crafted cake. In other words, to experience 'ilinx' is to be wilfully, and satisfyingly, out of control.

ill-snored: ill-tempered; crusty.

Derived from an old Norwegian word meaning 'offended' or 'displeased', 'ill-snored' describes someone who is decidedly crotchety and **mumpish**. Such people are also known in Orkney as being 'ill-snorted'. Either way, the distinct suggestion is that you should keep out of their way until the clouds have cleared.

ill–willy: malevolent; wishing bad luck upon others.

We are all happily familiar with 'goodwill', and a little too aware of 'ill will', but you may not have guessed that these were once accompanied by some very useful adjectives. To be 'good-willy' or 'well-willy', in the fifteenth century, was to be full of goodwill and benevolence, while it was best to swerve anyone feeling 'ill-willy'. And then there was 'evil-willy', the most extreme of the willies, reserved for one who harboured malevolence and spite. *See also* **well–woulder**.

impetuous: impulsive and rash.

'Impetuous' was borrowed by English in the late fourteenth century, where it described people or objects that moved with force or violence – an impetuous sea, for example, was a roiling and turbulent one. This sense reflects the word's origin in the Latin *impetus*, 'assault' or 'force', which of course entered English separately as a word itself.

Today, impetuosity embraces a more human passion and impulsiveness, with little trace of its early violence. The dictionary doesn't yet offer 'petuous' for the sensible character who is measured and risk-averse, but it may just be a matter of time.

Impostor Syndrome: the perception of being a fraud.

> I have written eleven books but each time I think, 'Uh-oh, they're going to find out now. I've run a game on everybody, and they're going to find me out.'

Even the enormously accomplished, Pulitzer Prize-winning poet Maya Angelou had doubts that she was worthy of her accolades. It is estimated that at some point in our lives nearly three-quarters of us have experienced Impostor Syndrome, when we feel undeserving of the success or credit we have achieved, and are confident we will, at some point, be horribly exposed.

The condition was named in 1978 in a paper by the psychologists Suzanne Imes and Pauline Rose Clance, who speculated that those most likely to suffer from the persistent feeling of unmerited success are women. Subsequent research has shown that, in fact, we are all susceptible to the dread of being found out. Albert Einstein perhaps put it best, long before the term itself was coined:

> The exaggerated esteem in which my lifework is held makes me very ill at ease. I feel compelled to think of myself as an involuntary swindler.

imprescience: lack of foresight and foreknowledge.

'Improvidence, imprescience, and selfish ease': such was a damning comment on the times delivered by the nineteenth-century essayist Thomas De Quincey, who could just as easily have been talking about today. 'Imprescience', quite simply, is a careless lack of foresight that is bound to lead to trouble. 'Science', from Latin, means 'knowledge'. 'Prescience', therefore, is foreknowledge: a kind of second sight.

impulsive: impetuous; spontaneous.

Anything described as 'impulsive' in the seventeenth century had been 'impelled' or 'set in motion'. By the middle of the nineteenth century, the word had shifted from mostly scientific contexts to describe a distinct personality type: one moved by sudden impulse or easily swayed by emotion. *See* **impetuous**.

indifferent: unconcerned; commonplace.

The 'different' bit of 'indifference' might seem a little curious until you realize that an indifferent individual has no difference of opinion between one thing and another – they are so neutral that they make no distinction. This sense of 'unbiased' gradually shifted to mean 'disinterested', as well as 'insipid'. An 'indifferent' piece of art is simply mediocre, and 'indifferent' weather is neither one thing nor the other. Whether used in the sense of unbiased, apathetic, lukewarm, or mediocre, this is never a quality to aspire to. As the writer Kahlil Gibran put it: 'Desire is half of life; indifference is half of death.'

indignant: aggrieved and resentful.

If you are 'indignant' – aka 'stomachate' (sixteenth century), 'dudgeoned' (eighteenth century), or 'ear-sore' (nineteenth century) – you are convinced you are owed better. In other words, you consider yourself entirely undeserving of an adverse situation. The adjective originated with the Latin *indignari*, to 'regard as unworthy'.

infallible: incapable of error or failure.

These days we are more likely to hear about infallible make-up than an infallible pope. But in the nineteenth century, papal infallibility became the official position of the Roman Catholic Church, decreeing that certain solemn statements about faith or morals made by a pope, the direct representative of God, could never be questioned. Such insistence has since faded and, mascaras and lipsticks aside, 'infallible' today is usually prefaced by the word 'not'.

inkleth: a faint notion.

You'd be forgiven for thinking that an 'inkling' is a little 'inkle' and, linguistically at least, you wouldn't be far wrong. The verb to 'inkle' in the fourteenth century meant to 'have a vague idea' about something, although it is thought to be a back-formation from 'inkling' rather than the other way round. Both words were offshoots of the Middle English *nyngkiling*, meaning a 'whisper' or 'undertone', and the first uses of 'inkling' conveyed a faint or slight intimation. As for a little 'inkle', that role is played by 'inkleth' – the slightest idea or notion.

insensible: bereft of sensation.

It seems odd that describing someone as 'insensible' is not to label them irrational or idiotic, but rather without feeling. The clue lies in the original meaning of 'sensible': 'capable of being felt or perceived'. In other words, 'sensibility' is all about the senses, and to be 'sensible' was thus to feel or possess the 'good' kind. To be '*in*sensible', however, stays with that earlier meaning of being 'incapable of feeling' or, *in extremis*, 'barely conscious at all'.

insensitive: lacking in feeling or tact.

If you are 'sensitive', you are receptive to things that impress your senses. Today's uses have upped the ante a little and suggest you are acutely receptive to those outside influences, and therefore easily hurt and vulnerable. Add an 'in-' to the mix, and you have little response at all, and scant regard for the feelings of anyone else.

insipid: lacking taste or flavour.

In the fifteenth century, physicians coined the term 'diabetes' for a disease that was characterized by the passage of large quantities of urine: they based it on the Greek for 'passing through'. Medicine distinguished between two forms of the disease: diabetes mellitus and diabetes insipidus. The former, which causes high sugar in the blood and urine, is based on the Latin for 'honey', while diabetes insipidus, from the Latin for 'tasteless', causes no detectible glucose. These same doctors would differentiate their diagnosis by tasting the urine in question: the diabetes mellitus kind was sweet to the taste, while the insipidus kind was lacking in taste altogether. Unsurprisingly, those doctors who used urine-testing as their sole means of diagnosis came to be called 'piss-prophets', a term that might have an entirely different meaning today. 'Insipid', meanwhile, survives in English to describe anything lacking in flavour.

insouciant: nonchalant; unconcerned.

There is enough of a casual attitude about 'insouciance' to nudge it into the negative family of emotions. For to be 'insouciant', from the French 'not worrying', means not just to be carefree and nonchalant, but to demonstrate a distinct touch of carelessness too. *See* **nonchalant**.

inspire: to fill with the urge or ability to do and feel something.

Breathing has inspired countless words in English, most of which began with the Latin *spirare*, to 'breathe'. The 'spirit', the vital principle in man and animals, was first seen as the 'breath' of God, and therefore of life itself. To 'aspire' to something was to 'breathe towards' it; to 'respire' to 'breathe again and again'; to 'perspire' to 'breathe moisture through the skin'; and to 'conspire' was to huddle or 'breathe together' whilst plotting intrigue. To 'inspire' someone, finally, was to 'breathe' a thought or idea 'into' their heart and mind. *See also* **suspire**.

integrity: the quality of being moral and honest.

An 'integer' is a whole number – neither a fraction, nor broken down in any way. 'Integrity', in the same way, means to be 'unified and undivided', and therefore, when it comes to morals, honest, principled, and 'whole'.

interdespise: to hate someone as much as they hate you.

Not much more can be said of this rare nineteenth-century term that expresses a mutual contempt. The essayist Thomas De Quincey left us a fair illustration of its usefulness in his description of an encounter: 'They met, they saw, they interdespised.'

interrobang: a punctuation mark combining an exclamation mark and a question mark, used to indicate a rhetorical question.

Dictionary-makers credit Martin K. Speckter with coming up with a brand-new punctuation mark in 1962. As the retired head of an advertising agency, Speckter believed that ads would look better if copywriters conveyed rhetorical questions more simply. In an article in the magazine *Type Talks*, he proposed a new design, for which he solicited potential names from readers. Contenders included 'exclamaquest', 'QuizDing', 'rhet', and 'exclarogative', but he finally settled upon 'interrobang', because it had echoes of the punctuation marks that inspired it: the question mark was once called a 'mark of interrogation', while 'bang' was one of many slang terms among printers for the exclamation mark (along with 'screamer', 'pling', 'boing', 'shriek', and 'gasper').

intimate: familiar; closely acquainted.

A Roman's *intimus* was their best friend – one with whom they shared a profound affinity. When English adopted 'intimate' in the seventeenth century, it was used for something equally deep-seated or close. The word was applied particularly to one's innermost thoughts and feelings. This sense of getting up close and personal still resides in 'intimate' and 'intimacy' – with the latter becoming a euphemism for sex as early as the nineteenth century.

intuition: a feeling that arises from instinct rather than reasoning.

It is the sense that took John Lennon 'there' and 'everywhere', that is prized above all in the Myers–Briggs personality test, and that Carl Jung defined as 'perception via the unconscious'. Intuition – what today we might otherwise call our 'gut feeling' – has been guiding our actions since antiquity. Its root is the Latin *intuitus*, which in turn is based upon *in*, 'into', and *tueri*, to 'look'. That explains 'intuition's' very first meaning of introspection: a 'looking inwards' as a way of tapping into our instincts.

While intuition has always been a focus of intense interest in psychology and philosophy, Artificial Intelligence is now also embracing its value, and researchers are attempting to add intuition to algorithms. 'Artificial intuition' may sound like an oxymoron, but the endeavour to give AI the capacity to tap into this aspect of human consciousness seeks to unite unconscious impulses with all the certainty of programming. Science fiction has already taken us there. Do the machines in *The Terminator* or the replicants in *Blade Runner* act out of intuition, or are they programmed to simulate it? If the fourth generation of AI is successful, we may be about to find out.

ipsedixitism: the assertion that something is 'fact' based on one person's opinion.

Ipse dixit is used in law to refute an argument based solely on the word of one individual. It is based on a saying, translated into Latin from Greek by the Roman orator Cicero, that means 'he said so himself', used by followers of Pythagoras to insist that if the great man said it, it must be true. In the late eighteenth century, the English social reformer Jeremy Bentham adapted *ipse dixit* into the word 'ipse-dixitism' to describe any gratuitous political argument. By extension, it is the act of making a dogmatic statement of 'fact' because someone, somewhere said so, and without offering any accompanying proof whatsoever. Those who dogmatically assert such facts are of course 'ipsedixitists'.

irritating: causing annoyance or impatience.

'Pricking', 'proking', 'baiting', 'stinging', 'trinkling': all words from the past and present for the act of provoking someone, or of stirring up turmoil. 'Irritating' is fairly tame by comparison, although it is one of the oldest, rooted in an ancient word meaning 'whirled' or 'stirred'.

jamais vu: the feeling that you have never experienced something familiar.

Jamais vu, 'never seen', is used in explicit contrast to the much more common *déjà vu*, 'already seen'. Both represent a mismatch between illusion and reality. In the case of *jamais vu*, it is a sense of the familiar being encountered for the first time, a form of experience blindness – such as walking into your old home and feeling as though you have never been there before.

jaunty: lively, cheerful, and self-confident.

Picture a hat tilted at a 'jaunty' angle and you might imagine someone fashionably 'genteel'. As it turns out, those two words are very much from the same stable. Their shared ancestor is the French *gentil*, 'kind' and 'noble', for jauntiness was originally all about good breeding. As a gentleman was expected to be stylish and smart, so 'jaunty' took on the idea of elegance and easy sprightliness, as well as an airy sense of satisfaction or unconcern. A 'jaunting' or 'jaunty car' became in the nineteenth century a highly popular light carriage for a single horse: one that was lively and brisk and perfect for going 'on a jaunt', an expression dating back to the seventeenth century for an excursion taken entirely for pleasure.

jealousy: a feeling of resentful envy or suspicion.

According to Jay-Z, 'jealousy is a weak emotion.' Yet while it may reflect a weakness in those who harbour it, jealousy is surely one of the most potent emotions of all. Its thrall has inspired literature, art, drama, film, opera, and every branch of creative endeavour, in which it is often polarized as the counterpart to all-consuming romantic love. Shakespeare was fascinated by jealousy, famously breathing life into its bones as 'the green-eyed monster'. It is so central to his tragedy *Othello* that it should be listed in the dramatis personae.

Linguistically, 'jealousy' came to us via the French *jalousie*, which ultimately derives from the Greek *zēlos*, 'zeal'. Historically, the emotion is distinguished from 'envy': whereas jealousy usually involves a rival, envy is essentially acquisitive. The philosopher John Rawls (as well as Homer Simpson) distinguishes between jealousy and envy on the grounds that jealousy involves the wish to keep what one has, while envy is the wish to get what one does not have. In reality, the difference between the two – even in dictionary definitions – has become increasingly blurred, and each can now mean both 'covetous' and 'possessively suspicious'. Only in love can 'jealousy' never be replaced.

As for its effects, the seventeenth-century English religious reformer William Penn advised that 'the jealous are troublesome to others, but a torment to themselves . . . Nothing stands safe in [jealousy's] way: nature, interest, religion, must yield to its fury.' A monster indeed.

jejune: naive and simplistic.

If you consider yourself starved of satisfaction, the word 'jejune' might come in handy. It is based on the Latin *jejunus*, meaning 'empty of food', which also produced the French for 'lunch', *déjeuner*, and breakfast, *petit déjeuner*, both inspired by the exact same idea of 'breaking one's fast' that produced our English 'breakfast'. It was the sense of 'lacking in food' that gave rise to 'jejune's' earliest uses for anything 'insubstantial' and 'unsatisfying'. Today's modern meaning of 'naive' and 'childish' are a little different, influenced perhaps by association with the French *jeune*, 'young'. Meanwhile the choice of the name 'jejunum' for part of the small intestine is said to have been inspired by the observation made by ancient medics that, at death, the jejunum is always empty of food.

jeremiad: a complaining tirade.

> She weepeth sore in the night, and her tears are on her cheeks: among all her lovers she hath none to comfort her: all her friends have dealt treacherously with her, they are become her enemies.

Some of the opening lines from the Old Testament book of Lamentations, in which Jeremiah laments the fall of Jerusalem at great length. A 'jeremiad' consequently came to mean a long and serious literary work in which the author bitterly laments the state of society and its morals, and which always contains a prophecy of society's imminent downfall. The Puritan Fathers were particularly fond of them.

In 1780, the memoirs of the philanthropist Mrs Hannah More noted, 'It has been long the fashion to make the most lamentable *Jeremiades* on the badness of the times.' By this period a 'jeremiad' had come to describe any litany of complaints or grievances. It is not to be confused with the large wine bottle that is a 'jeroboam', although some might seek comfort there from their troubles and complaints.

jobation: a lecture of rebuke.

An altogether different biblical character is involved in the story of a 'jobation'. Its inspiration was Job, who was famously subjected to lengthy and painful trials by Satan as a means of testing his faith. These involved the deaths of his livestock, servants, and ten children in a single day, and finally the affliction of terrible boils. When Job complains to his friends, wishing he was dead, God angrily appears inside a whirlwind and rebukes him at great length, making detailed digressions about aspects of his creation. A 'jobation' thus came to mean a long and drawn-out rebuke, later often adjusted to 'jawbation' – understandably, given the amount of talking involved.

joblijock: any kind of domestic disturbance.

Builders drilling at dawn, small children jumping up and down on the bed at 4 a.m. on Christmas Day, neighbours sharing their dubious music choices with the whole street – such are the 'joblijocks' of modern life. This centuries-old Yorkshire dialect term was once reserved for cockerels whose insistent crowing at sunrise cut through any chance of peace.

jocoserious: half-joking.

The Latin *jocus*, 'jest', produced a large family of words in English, including 'joke', 'jocular', and 'jocund', meaning 'pleasant, cheery, and light-hearted'. It also yielded the pithy adjective 'jocoserious', used to describe a statement or action that is partly in jest, but also partly in earnest.

joie de vivre [French: zhwah-duh-veevre]: exuberance and high spirits.

English understandably borrowed this effusive French expression for the 'joy of living' to describe a healthy enjoyment of life or a sense of carefree happiness. Thanks to its air of Gallic glamour it has proved much more popular than another foreign borrowing, *Lebenslust* – German for very much the same thing.

jolly: bright; lively; joyous.

First cited as a surname in the thirteenth century and as a dog's name in the fourteenth, no one quite knows the origin of 'jolly', save that it came into English via the French *jolif*, a descriptor of everything merry, bright, and somewhat remarkable (hence its use as a now rather old-fashioned intensifier: 'that's jolly interesting'). Traditionally, the word is thought to be a sibling of 'Yule', a legacy of the Vikings for whom *jol* was a pagan festival at the winter solstice, which eventually became the Christian Christmas. An alternative theory involves *gaudere*, the Latin verb for 'rejoice'. Whatever its story, 'jolly' remains a word full of heart and shoulder-shaking merriment. As a noun, it has also become shorthand for an (often illicit) excursion in search of fun.

jouissance [French: szh-wee-sonse]: delight; ecstasy.

There is enjoyment, and there is *jouissance*. The former certainly fits within the latter, but the French word has a far greater breadth than simple 'enjoyment' suggests. *Jouissance* is both physical and intellectual pleasure; it can be the delight of learning something new, or the total ecstasy of orgasm. The French psychoanalyst Jacques Lacan, with characteristic vividness, described the emotion as one that 'begins with a tickle and ends with a blaze of petrol'.

jovial: jolly and convivial.

Jupiter, for whom another name was 'Jove' ('by Jove!'), was the king of the Roman gods, believed to be the source of joy and happiness. Anyone born under his influence was said to have inherited his 'jovial' nature.

joy: a feeling of intense happiness.

John Keats found it in 'a thing of beauty'; Emily Dickinson experienced it in 'the mere sense of living'; Stephen Hawking sought it in 'discovering something no one knew before', and Bono sources his from Abba. Joy, and where we look for it, is as individual as it is powerful.

The name for this most vivid of emotions came to us, via the French *joie*, from the Latin *gaudere*, to 'rejoice'. Its definition, of a vivid sense of elation and an exultation of spirit, has changed little since it first entered English in the thirteenth century. Like 'bliss' and other terms for happiness, 'joy' attracted both secular and religious meanings, encompassing both earthly pleasures and the beatitude of heaven. The *Book of Common Prayer* from 1552 expresses the hope that 'at the last, we may come to hys eternal ioye'.

Wherever we find it, this is an emotion whose infrequency makes it all the more exquisite. W. B. Yeats is said to have observed of a fellow countryman that 'Being Irish, he had an abiding sense of tragedy, which sustained him through temporary periods of joy.'

jubilate: to rejoice.

We love to be 'jubilant', and welcome any occasion to offer 'jubilations' of exultant joy, but there is a third relative in this happy family derived from the Latin *jubilare*, to 'call out', namely the verb 'jubilate', which means to 'halloo', 'huzza', and generally 'shout for joy'. 'Jubilate' is not directly related to 'jubilee', which comes from the Hebrew *yobel*, 'ram's horn' – a reference to the trumpeting that proclaimed each Jewish year of jubilee throughout the land – but the association with rejoicing must have been too good to miss, and the two words ended up looking very similar.

kalopsia: when everyone and everything looks beautiful.

Most new words are blends of the old – mash-ups of existing words in order to create something fanciful or useful. 'Kalopsia' is one of these. It describes a level of intoxication that makes the world and its inhabitants look a lot better than they did before – or, crucially, than they actually are. A more inspiring alternative to the more prosaic 'beer goggles', the word is a recent blend of the Greek *kalos*, 'beautiful', and *opsis*, 'sight'. *See also* **callomania**.

kayfabe: the presentation of something fake as real or authentic.

'Kayfabe' is the presentation of staged events within the professional wrestling industry as 'real' or 'true', specifically in the portrayal of competition, rivalries, and relationships between fighters. In the US, 'kayfabe' is more often the suspension of disbelief used to create the non-wrestling aspects of promotions, such as feuds, angles, and gimmicks that bring it closer to fictional entertainment – a wrestler breaking 'kayfabe' during a show would be akin to an actor breaking the fourth wall.

The story of the word remains elusive. One theory suggests that it was derived from a deliberate mangling of the term 'be fake' (à la pig Latin), designed to conceal its true meaning. Another claims that there actually was a wrestler called 'Kay Fabian' who was mute. Neither claim has ever been substantiated.

kerfuffle: a commotion or fuss.

'Kerfuffle' has such a cuddly, fluffy sound that it is hard to take it very seriously. Nevertheless, this word is all about discordancy, and a commotion borne out of conflicting views. It sounds Scottish, and it probably is, based on the Scots 'curfuffle' in which *fuffle* means 'disorder'. *Ker-* would have been a later add-on that is found frequently in onomatopoeic formations such as 'kerching', 'kerplunk', 'kerthump', and 'kerwhop'.

kind: generous; considerate.

'Kind' is a word with many meanings, but running through all of them are the ideas of family and of shared characteristics. In Old English, the original senses of 'kind' related to 'the natural order' and 'innate character' of people and objects. The word is of Germanic origin, and is related to the 'kin' that is our family or relations, and to 'kindred', meaning 'similar in kind'. (Unexpectedly, those same origins also gave us 'king', as the first kings in England were the heads of tribes or 'kins' of invading Angles and Saxons who established their own small territories.)

In medieval times, 'kind' came to mean 'well-born', and because nobility was associated with good manners (*see* **gentle**), it later shifted to mean 'generous' and 'considerate'. But within its story linger two suggestions: first, that we owe most of our generosity and compassion to our own kin or kind, and, secondly, the happier notion that it is within our core human nature to be kind.

Kopfkino [German: kopf-keeno]: intense daydreaming, often of something unpleasant.

The reflexive question 'what did I do?' when your friend doesn't text you back, the panicked assumption of bad news written on a doctor's face, the 'knowledge' that you have failed an exam before you open the envelope – all of these are examples of *Kopfkino*, a German word for the involuntary thoughts and wild imaginings that beset you when things don't quite go to plan. Literally translated, your *Kopfkino* is your 'mind cinema', where things (almost always bad ones) are played out in your head with the vividness and verisimilitude of a movie.

kuchisabishii [Japanese: koo-chi-sa-bi-shee]: 'lonely mouth'.

'Comfort eating' is a loaded term. So many of us in recent years have turned to food for solace, deriving pleasure from preparing, cooking, and enjoying it as a necessary antidote to gloom and anxiety. And yet eating for comfort has assumed an unrelentingly negative reputation, associated invariably with obesity and excess.

We are not alone. German has *Kummerspeck*, literally 'grief bacon', a semi-affectionate description of the excess fat we accumulate when times are hard. In French, there is *manger ses émotions*, 'eating one's emotions'. But of all the efforts in language to convey the feeling that leads you again and again to the fridge, the Japanese *kuchisabishii* is surely one of the most evocative, for it simply means 'eating because your mouth is lonely'.

kvell: to feel pride and joy in someone else's accomplishment.

Parents and grandparents know all about 'kvelling'. It essentially involves a swelling of pride over the achievement of someone you love, rendering you incapable of restraining yourself from revelling in their success.

The word is recorded in the 1952 *Handbook of Familiar Jewish Words and Expressions* (a short glossary 'for making friends with Jewish Merchants'), and is based on the Yiddish *kveln*, to 'be delighted', itself an alteration of the German *quellen*, to 'swell'. Its uses are manifold. If your grandfather calls every friend and neighbour to announce that you have passed your driving test first time, he is 'kvelling', as is your mother in her round-robin Christmas bulletin featuring every detail of your latest promotion.

Yet mavens of Yiddish will tell you that to 'kvell' is not nearly as brash as boasting; it is less calculated and more instinctive, rooted in genuine pride and joy. As such, it goes hand in hand with the emotions of *naches* and **confelicity**.

lackadaisical: lethargic and indifferent.

Anyone who is 'lackadaisical' today is both lazy and wearily unenthusiastic. The chirpy word's earliest incarnation, however, was far more bothersome. 'Lackaday!', short for 'alack-a-day!', was a dramatic expression of sorrow and disappointment, one you might expect from an attention-seeking, mawkish individual who throws themselves on the floor in exaggerated misery. It was this idea of feebleness and languishing that inspired the modern sense of lazy lethargy, and 'lackaday' was later given a flowery embellishment in 'lackadaisy' and eventually 'lackadaisical'. In much the same way, when we utter 'whoopsadaisy!' to jolly along a child who has fallen over, we are echoing an earlier expression, 'upaday!' – once again, the flowery note was a happy afterthought.

lacrimae rerum: tears shed for human sorrows.

'There are tears for things, and mortal matters touch the mind': so reads one translation of words spoken by the Trojan hero

Aeneas in Virgil's epic poem, the *Aeneid*. Here Aeneas is look-ing at a mural, found in a Carthaginian temple, that represents the Battle of Troy. As he mourns the loss of his ancestors and compatriots, he utters the phrase *sunt lacrimae rerum et mentem mortalia tangunt*. Two of those words, *lacrimae rerum*, have been variously interpreted as 'the tears for things' and the 'tears of things' (the poet Seamus Heaney added a third version: 'tears at the heart of things'). Proponents of the *of* version argue for a physical world that feels its own sorrow. 'Tears for things', on the other hand, emphasizes the pathos of life as observed by humanity. Either way, *lacrimae rerum* offers an exquisitely melancholy comment on how we – and perhaps the universe – experience life and sorrow.

lagom [Swedish: laah-gom]: just right.

Such is our love of linguistic inflation that if someone tells you that your work is 'sufficient' or 'satisfactory' you'll end up a little disappointed. 'Sufficient' belongs in the same category as 'adequate', 'nice', and 'interesting', which almost always need additional bigging up. There is very little upbeatness about any of them, which is what makes the Swedish *lagom* all the harder to translate. The best we can probably do is to define it as 'not too little, not too much, but just right'. It is, in other words, a Goldilocks word. This is not about perfection, but the adequacy of moderation, when less is definitely more. *Lagom* is the happi-ness of standing still, rather than the stress of striving for more.

Its roots lie in the Swedish *lag*, meaning 'law' or 'custom'. Legend, however, puts its etymology elsewhere: in *laget om*, 'around the team', referring to the Viking tradition of taking just the right amount of mead as a cup was passed round. Although apocryphal, the story fits nicely with the idea of consensus and democracy. Above all, *lagom* is about taking time to appreciate what we already have.

lalochezia: the relief of stress and pain through swearing.

If you are someone who experiences an overwhelming urge to scream 'Fuck!' at the bed that just stubbed your toe, or 'Bugger off!' at the unexpected kerb that made you spill your coffee, there is at least a name for it. This is 'lalochezia': the use of vulgar language to relieve oneself of stress, pain, or frustration.

It began simply enough. A modern neologism based on classical elements, the word is made up of the Greek *lalon*, meaning 'talking', 'chat', or 'babble', and *chezia*, the 'act of defecation'. Put the two together and you have the figurative idea of relieving yourself through words – or in blunter terms, dumping your verbal shit.

'Lalochezia' has found much favour in recent years, as studies have proved the benefits of letting it all out by turning the air blue. Serotonin levels soar, and cortisol levels plummet when we shout our favourite expletives. For many of us, it is the cheapest and safest analgesic there is. It turns out that a bout of extreme effing and jeffing helps us more than we might think.

languorous: characterized by pleasurable inactivity.

It's a strange word that combines a total lack of energy with passionate longing, but that is what 'languorous' does. It is built, of course, upon 'languor', which came over to English from the French *languir* in the late fourteenth century. Its earliest outings in English described mental distress or grief. Over the following centuries it took on a sense of torpor or lethargy, as well as a woeful pining for another person. The adjective 'languorous' pushed this a stage further, so that by the middle of the eighteenth century the idea of love-sickness had taken over: a *Dictionary of Love* noted, 'They are very tiresome ... when a languorous lover "Vents only in deep sighs his am'rous flame"'– an older version of coming on too strong.

lassitude: weariness.

In the fourteenth century it was known as 'werihede' ('weary-head'), in the seventeenth as 'languishment', and in the twenty-first as 'exhaustion' or, more probably, the state of being 'knackered'. Perhaps the most poetic of the collection, emerging in the sixteenth century, is 'lassitude', a flagging of the body or spirit that Francis Bacon, in a book of experiments, reckoned might require 'bathing or anointing with oil and warm water'. The word comes via the French *las*, 'weary', from Latin *lassus*, 'faint', the inspiration for probably the ultimate expression of palm-to-forehead lament, 'Alas!' – literally 'Oh weariness!'

latibulate: to hide in a corner.

The verb 'latibulate' is defined in an early dictionary from 1623 as 'privily to hide ones selfe in a corner'. Long since obsolete, it is surely forgivable to broaden its scope to the intense urge to retreat. For those times when we just want to shrink away from everything and everyone, 'latibulate' covers it perfectly.

laughter: the act of laughing.

In a much-loved sketch from *Monty Python's Flying Circus* set during the Second World War, a joke is created that is so hilarious that anybody who hears it instantly dies. The Funniest Joke in the World becomes an unstoppable British weapon against the German army, so dangerous that its individual words have to be translated by separate people. British soldiers march through a battlefield, leadenly chanting a string of German words at Nazi soldiers, who burst out laughing and promptly drop dead. After the war, a joke warfare ban is agreed at the Geneva Convention and, in 1950, the last copy is sealed under a monument in the Berkshire countryside, bearing the inscription 'To the Unknown Joke'.

The real joke here, of course, is that the very idea is impossible, for there is no such thing as something that can make everyone laugh. 'The funniest thing about comedy,' said the US humorist W. C. Fields, 'is that you never know why people laugh. I know *what* makes them laugh but trying to get your hands on the *why* of it is like trying to pick an eel out of a tub of water.'

If the anatomy of laughter is a slippery beast, we can at least grasp it linguistically, where it is a relative of the modern German *Gelächter*. We are lucky to have it, for if you look up 'laugh' in the dictionary you'll find an inordinately complex definition: 'to make the spontaneous sounds and movements of the face and body that are the instinctive expressions of lively amusement and sometimes also of derision'. Like the killer joke, it's probably best not to analyse things.

lazy: unwilling to work or move.

The origins of 'lazy' have proved a bit of a mystery. It may be related to an old German word, *lasich*, meaning 'languid' or 'idle', but the jury is still out. Less in doubt is the sheer number of synonyms for those who prefer to loll about rather than apply themselves. They may take their pick from a lexicon that includes 'lurdan', 'lusking', 'bumbard', 'slottery', 'litherly', 'sluggardish', and **pigritious**.

letabund: full of joy.

'Letabund' is one of those words whose sound and appearance suggest the very opposite of its actual meaning. It has, after all, some rather gloomy siblings, including 'moribund' (on the point of death) and 'pudibund' (prudish). But while its ponderous, dragging final syllable suggests moroseness and solemnity, to be 'letabund' is to be 'filled with happiness'. The root of this rare Scottish word is the Latin *laetabundus*, from *laetari*, to 'be joyful'.

All of which puts 'letabund' up there with 'pulchritudinous' as one of language's unexpectedly pleasant surprises.

lethargic: without energy or enthusiasm.

The letter 'L' definitely favours the lazy and the lackadaisical. 'Lethargy' adds to the list, and was once a much more serious affair than the inability to rouse oneself from the sofa. In the fourteenth century, 'lethargy' was a medical diagnosis – a disorder characterized by 'morbid drowsiness' and an unnatural amount of sleep. One surgeon's manual from 1400 suggests cauterization of the brain as a potential cure. Look back to ancient Greece, however, and you'll see that lethargy once *was* the cure, a panacea for the ills of anxiety and care. The Greek *lēthargos* means 'forgetful', a reference to Lethe, a river in Hades which could make any soul of the dead who drank from it forget their time on earth. Lethe's waters were ones of oblivion, a means of forgetting sorrow and an adjunct to **nepenthe**, a potion that liberated the mind from grief. *See also* **resipiscence**.

lickspittle: a parasite or sycophant.

'It is only in England,' wrote the writer and traveller George Henry Borrow in 1851, 'that literary men are invariably lickspittles.' He could scarcely have been more damning, for a 'lickspittle' is defined in the *Oxford English Dictionary* as 'an abject parasite or sycophant' – namely one that would lick a master's spittle from the ground if it proved advantageous.

liget [Ilongot: li–get]: the rage of grief; the spur of energy.

Liget belongs intimately to the Philippines. It is an intense emotion that only a few have managed to describe, among them the anthropologist Renato Rosaldo, who with his wife lived in the rainforest among the Ilongot tribe. He understood their word vaguely to mean 'energy' – both negative and positive, for the tribe were headhunters – but confessed to not grasping it entirely, comparing it to 'trying to describe the colour blue without seeing it'. Tragically, he only appreciated the full emotional power of *liget* when his wife was killed in an accident. At that moment he believes he finally understood, experiencing *liget* as a 'cosmic heaving' that overtook his entire body.

There is not even an approximate equivalent of *liget* in English, and it remains an obscure word for a high-voltage sensation – be it the rage of grief or the intense desire to *do*. This is a term with an explosive complexity that, in all likelihood, only the Ilongot can truly comprehend.

like: similar to; to find agreeable or enjoyable.

'Like' has multiple personalities – some pragmatic, others highly pleasing, and one that is fast becoming the number one language bugbear for many. Its story in all these guises began with the Old English *gelich*, which carried the literal meaning of 'having the same body' – in other words, it described something similar to something else, just as it does today. That *gelich*, 'body', is at the heart of the roofed 'lich-gate' in a churchyard, where a coffin and its corpse are rested to await the minister, and of the 'lich-owl', so-called because it was believed to portend death. It seems a far cry, then, from these senses to the happier uses of the verb 'like' – meaning to 'find enjoyable or pleasing' – but the idea seems to be that if something has the same 'body' as another, by conforming to a norm, then it is suitable and therefore pleasing.

Up until the early thirteenth century, it was just as usual to use **queem** instead of 'like' if you were pleased by something. But as that word slipped away so 'like' took hold, and has extended its journey by becoming a multi-purpose filler with which we like to pepper our conversation: 'are you, like, for real?' For all that it grates on modern nerves, like-bashers might appreciate that this use is recorded as far back as 1778.

lily-livered: cowardly.

The Middle Ages were full of livery conditions, including being 'liverish' itself, implying a personality prone to anger and biliousness. The reason for such linguistic abundance was straightforward to the medieval mind. The liver was believed to be the seat of love as well as other passionate emotions such as anger and bitterness. If it was dysfunctional, the result was the antithesis of passion, namely bodily and mental weakness. To be 'liver-faced' was to have a 'pallid complexion' or a 'mean spirit', while any 'lily-livered' individual was held to have such a bloodless liver that it contained no courage at all.

limerence: the state of being romantically infatuated or obsessed with another person.

The smooth notes of 'limerence' were coined by the twentieth-century American psychologist Dorothy Tennov, filling a gap in the language that until then had been serviced only by 'infatuation'. Tennov was inspired by the concept of crystallization, which the French writer Stendhal explores in his long essay *On Love*. Here he describes the mental gymnastics that occur spontaneously when we fall in love, when even the most unattractive characteristics become like scintillating and dazzling crystals. Tennov's 'limerence' describes not just an obsessive adoration, but the euphoria that comes with that adoration, and the intense desire to have it reciprocated.

limpsy: limp and floppy.

Not much needs to be said about 'limpsy' other than it is defined with a single word in the dictionary: 'flaccid'. It was originally, in the nineteenth century, used of someone just before they faint. Heralding from the easternmost counties of England, it travelled to the US in the 1800s. Harriet Beecher Stowe, author of *Uncle Tom's Cabin*, provided a helpful example: 'She . . . looked sort o' limpsy, as if there wa'n't no starch left in her.'

ling di long [Welsh]: lethargic and without purpose.

You might be 'lackadaisical', and you might feel 'languorous', but if you wanted to turn to a rarer beauty, you could declare yourself to be *ling di long*. The very sound of this Welsh expression suggests a casual contentment and an amble with no destination in mind.

lion drunke: aggressively drunk.

Any town or city centre at night has its displays of people behaving strangely. It has been half a millennium since Thomas Nashe, the Elizabethan playwright whose boisterous barbs pricked many a sixteenth-century ego, described his eight different kinds of drunkards, but he would be able to recognize the same types today. Here you will find one who is 'swine drunke', for example, who is 'heavy, lumpish, and sleepie, and cries for a little more drinke'. He who becomes 'goate drunk', meanwhile, 'hath no minde but on Lechery'. And then there is the type we still know to avoid, who becomes 'lion drunke' and 'flings the pots about the house . . . breakes the glasse windowes with his dagger, and is apt to quarrell with any man that speaks to him.'

listless: lacking in energy or spirit.

What is this 'list' that we can be without? It is not the one we know, but rather a relative of the Icelandic *lyst*, the appetite for food. To 'have list', in the thirteenth century, was to feel pleasure, joy, and delight, as well as an appetite or **lust** for life. It follows that to be 'listless' was to be devoid of any desire or relish whatsoever.

litost [Czech: lee-tost]: regret.

Litost is usually translated into English as 'regret', but it comes as a bundle of other, less tangible feelings, an amalgam of the shame, resentment, and frustration we experience when another person, however unknowingly, makes us feel wretched.

In his *Book of Laughter and Forgetting*, Milan Kundera gives a compelling example of the emotion, which he once described as a torment that is accompanied by the desire to make another person as miserable as oneself. In the story, a child plays a wrong note on his violin over and over again until his maddened teacher throws him out of the window. As he falls, the child delights in the thought that the nasty teacher will be charged with murder. Put this way, *litost* is as pointless as it is irresistible.

Kundera searched in vain for an English equivalent. Yet so convinced was he of its importance that he declared, 'I find it difficult to imagine how anyone can understand the human soul without it.'

loathe: to dislike with intensity.

'Hate', 'detest', 'abhor', 'abominate' – such are the words used to define the act of 'loathing'. It has never had a softer edge, originating as it does with the Old English *lathian*, to 'be hateful'. Chaucer's 'Wife of Bath's Tale' tells the story of the Loathly

Lady ('loathly' here meaning 'repulsively ugly') who is freed from the spell she is under and becomes 'unloathly' only when her new husband can correctly answer the question 'What do women most desire?' (The answer, it seems, is 'sovereignty'.)

lollygag: to spend time aimlessly.

'Lovemaking and lollygagging are hereby strictly forbidden ... The holding of hands, osculation and constant embracing of WAVES [Women Accepted for Volunteer Emergency Service], corpsmen or civilians and sailors or any combination of male and female personnel is a violation of naval discipline.' This stern warning was issued by a US Navy captain in 1946, when 'lollygagging', or alternatively 'lallygagging', was more about public displays of affection than the dawdling and dallying it describes today. Its origin is sadly unknown, but there is in its sound a distinct sense of idleness and a snoozy, lolling head.

lonely: sad from a lack of company.

We are, according to many, experiencing an epidemic of loneliness: the effects of both a global pandemic and a fundamental shift in social interaction whereby we spend our days talking with our fingers, tapping out conversations remotely on our screens even as we experience the dread of **FOMO**.

The existentialist school of thought views loneliness somewhat bleakly as the essence of being human. Each of us comes into the world alone, travels through life as a separate person, and ultimately dies alone. Coping with this, accepting it, and learning how to direct our own lives with some degree of grace and satisfaction is part of the human condition.

Some historians of emotions believe that loneliness didn't exist prior to 1800, or at least that it only became a negative emotion at around that time. Before then, the lines between loneliness and solitude – the negative and positive faces of aloneness – were blurred. Linguistically, the picture is less complicated. Before Shakespeare, 'alone' was, fittingly enough, written as two separate words. To be 'all one' was to be without companionship. In Old English, *ān*, 'one', was pronounced much like our modern English 'own', and so to be 'all one' became, over time, 'alone'. From a simple sense of physical removal, the word took on an emotional state of withdrawal and loss, and 'lonely' soon followed in its wake.

Whether or not being alone is inextricable from being human – 'we live, as we dream – alone,' wrote Joseph Conrad – what seems certain is that while solitude is a privilege available to those who have the money and space to find it, loneliness is not.

lonesome-fret: boredom and disquiet borne of loneliness.

A useful word for times of lockdown and isolation, 'lonesome-fret' describes a feeling of restless unease that comes from being on your own too long. Defined in the *English Dialect Dictionary* as 'ennui from loneliness', it comes to us from nineteenth-century Devon, and its resonance has surely returned.

love: deep affection.

According to the ancient Greeks, there were six different states of love:

  storgē: natural affection, the love you share with your family.
  philia: the love that you have for friends.
  erōs: sexual love.
  agapē: unconditional or divine love.
  xenia: hospitality, the love you have for your guests.
  philautia: the love of the self.

These are clearly six very different feelings. Our love for a partner is not the same as the love we feel for our mother. And both kinds change over time. The spectrum of love is vast, and yet in English we use just one word to cover all of it. But it wasn't always that way.

The term 'love' is suitably ancient. Its roots lie in *leubh*, found in the ancestor to Indo-European languages known as PIE (Proto-Indo-European), believed to belong to the Neolithic and Bronze ages. When 'love' entered Old English as *lufu*, it was used both as a noun meaning 'deep attachment' and as a verb meaning to 'hold dear'. Distinctions between different kinds of love were once as carefully drawn in English as they were in Greek. *Bearn-lufe* was a 'mother's love for her child'; *sib-lufu* was 'kin-love' for one's relatives; *freond-lufu* was 'friend-love', the platonic kind; and *sorh-lufu* was a 'sorrow-love' – one that brings heartbreak and a consequence perhaps of *ofer-lufu*, 'excessive love'. Today, we rely on that single word 'love' to express them all, yet rather than weakening in power, it remains one of the most meaningful descriptions of emotion available to us.

love–light: a look of adoration in another person's eyes.

Sickly for some, glorious for others, 'love–light' emerged from nineteenth-century poetry to describe the radiance in our eyes that comes from looking at someone we love.

loyal: faithful and true.

Personal loyalty and strictures of the law might seem strange bedmates, but 'loyal' and 'legal' originally meant one and the same thing. The laws in this case were those demanding allegiance, decreed by sovereigns and central to a code of honour. To be faithful to these laws was to be 'loyal', a word that – along with 'legitimate', 'legacy', and 'legitimate' – descends from the Romans' *lex*, 'law'.

lucky: favoured by good fortune.

When it comes to luck, the eyes have it, and have done so for millennia. One of the most popular amulets in ancient Egypt was the *wedjat*, a symbol that combined the features of a human and a falcon's eye to represent the god Horus. In Egyptian mythology, the conflict between Horus and his rival Set resulted in Set tearing out one of his enemy's eyes, which was then restored by another deity, Thoth. This event was commemorated in the *wedjat*, whose name meant 'the one that is sound' and which was thought to protect its wearer through its power of regeneration and healing. It is just one of a multitude of amulets and talismans believed to ward off bad luck across a host of religions and cultures, from travellers' St Christopher charms and the phalluses designed to divert the gaze of the evil eye (*see* **fascinate**), to bags of mojo worn in Africa and four-leaved clovers in Britain. The desire to invest inanimate objects with magical powers is universal.

But what exactly is 'luck', and how did it begin? Linguistically speaking, it didn't really emerge until the late fifteenth century, when the term described the sum of chance events that affected (favourably or unfavourably) a person's interests or circumstances. Until then, the more common word was **hap**. 'Luck' is a direct borrowing from German, but its ultimate ancestry is unknown. Many of its earliest outings in English were in the context of gambling, and in many ways the metaphorical sense of a random throw of a dice has lingered ever since. Our superstitious investment in amulets and charms has abated little too, even if they are today described more usually as 'mascots'. Here, again, is a word with the same magical potency as the *wedjat* eyes tucked into tombs and mummies. From the French *mascotte*, a 'sorcerer's charm', 'mascot' ultimately goes back to the Latin for 'witch'.

lukewarm: moderately warm.

Who or what is the 'Luke' that makes things and emotions a little tepid? The answer has nothing to do with any individual, but rather an old dialect word, *lew,* meaning ... 'lukewarm'. Which means that 'lukewarm' is essentially a tautology meaning 'warm warm', and a simple 'luke' would have been fine all along.

lulled: calmed and soothed, sometimes deceptively.

The word 'lull', imitative of the sound used to soothe a child, belongs in the same family as the Romans' *lallare*, to 'sing to sleep', as well as the Swedish *lulla*, to 'hum a lullaby', and the Dutch *lullen*, to 'talk nonsense'. It also, of course, includes 'lullaby' itself. All suggest a sense of peace and sleepiness, although English has added a more grown-up edge, when we are 'lulled' into a false sense of security without realizing the peril ahead.

lust: strong physical or sexual desire.

'Lust's winter comes ere summer half be done,' wrote Shakespeare in his poem *Venus and Adonis*. In literature and life, love and lust occupy very distinct spaces on the spectrum of human emotion.

'Lust' is a borrowing from the German *Lust*, meaning 'desire'. In its earliest appearances in Old English, around the ninth century, it meant simply 'pleasure' or 'delight', and it continued in this restrained manner right up until the sixteenth century, when it could also mean a 'friendly inclination' towards some-one as well as wholesome desires, such as the 'lust for life'. In German still, the word makes little hint at bodily pleasures, other perhaps than in such sentences as '*Ich habe Lust auf einen vollmundigen Rotwein*' – 'I fancy a full-bodied red wine' (an echo of a remark once made by C. S. Lewis: 'He that but looketh on a plate of ham and eggs to lust after it, hath already committed breakfast with it in his heart.')

The implications of appetite were nonetheless there from the start, running in parallel to 'lust's' more innocent incarnations. To follow 'after one's lust' was to indulge one's personal pleasures, while seduction by the 'lusts of the flesh' led inexorably to sin and a trampling of morality. So it was that 'licentiousness' and 'lust' joined in meaning, and lust was chosen as one of the seven deadly sins.

Dante was fascinated by the emotion. In the first canticle of the *Divine Comedy*, the lustful are punished by being continuously swept around in a whirlwind that symbolizes their passions. Like the two famous lovers in Dante's *Inferno*, Paolo and Francesca, the lustful receive what they desire in their mortal lives, but are condemned to be subservient to their passions for all eternity.

Shakespeare built upon this not just in his plays but also in his famous sequence of sonnets, detailing the tempestuous course of a love affair. In Sonnet 129, he gives us a world of descriptions for the complexity of emotion that lust involves:

> lust
> Is perjured, murd'rous, bloody, full of blame,
> Savage, extreme, rude, cruel, not to trust ...
> A bliss in proof and proved, a very woe.

malarkey: nonsense; a palaver.

'Humbug', 'bunkum', 'stuff and nonsense'. Such were the earliest meanings of 'malarkey' when it emerged in the 1920s. Today the term is more about meaningless chatter or silly behaviour, and most would guess at an Irish origin. But although there is certainly an Irish surname Mullarkey that might account for it, the true story has yet to be unearthed. When it comes to dismissive words for utter piffle or foolish antics, however, 'malarkey' certainly does the business.

maleficent: productive of harm or evil.

'Maleficent' is not just the name of a Disney character. It is also an adjective that has described 'evil-doing' for over 400 years. The Latin *malus*, 'bad' or 'evil', has given rise to a wide range of English words dealing with objectionable conduct and its results, from 'malcontent' to 'malnourished'. Others, while not quite so well known, are no less useful. They include 'maleficiate': to 'place under an evil spell', and 'maledicent':

'addicted to speaking evil' (potentially useful for any online trolls).

malice: ill will and the desire to hurt.

'Malice' keeps evil company. It walks out with 'malign', 'malaise', and 'malevolent', all of which also derive from the Latin *malus*, 'bad'. Since the fifteenth century, 'malice' has also had legal status, particularly as part of 'malice aforethought', which distinguishes murder from manslaughter and shows a distinct intention to harm.

malverse: to act corruptly in a position of trust.

'We hang the petty thieves and appoint the great ones to public office': words attributed to the Greek fabulist and storyteller Aesop. In the fourteenth century, those exhibiting fraudulent behaviour in public life would have been called 'corrumpent', from the Latin *cor*, 'altogether', and *rumpere*, to 'break', 'violate', or 'destroy'. These were the breakers of laws that they themselves helped to install, rendering them meaningless. To 'corrump' was to 'spread corruption' or, as the *Oxford English Dictionary* puts it, to 'cause to rot or decay'; it was eventually succeeded by 'corrupt', the earliest meaning of which was also to 'make rotten', as of spoiled fruit. A potent word, it was equally applied to anyone so debased in character that they were believed to have been spoiled or infected with evil.

The *OED* also gives us a specific term for corruption in employment, office, or a position of trust. This is the sixteenth-century 'malversation', from the Latin *maleversari*, to 'act wrongly'. To 'malverse' is thus not only to neglect one's duty, but to go out of one's way to betray it.

mamihlapinatapai [Yaghan: ma–mi–la–pee–na–ta–pay]: to look at another person hoping they will make the first move.

Included in the 1994 *Guinness Book of Records* as the world's 'most succinct word', *mamihlapinatapai* stems from the language of the Yaghan tribe of Tierra del Fuego, an archipelago at the southern tip of South America. One of the earliest records of its use comes from an essay written by the nineteenth-century British missionary and linguist Thomas Bridges, who spent two decades living among the Yaghans and who put together a glossary containing around 32,000 of their words. In his essay, he defines *mamihlapinatapai* as 'To look at each other, hoping that either will offer to do something which both parties much desire done, but are unwilling to do'.

In recent times the word has been eagerly picked up as one of the many 'untranslatables'. It captures our imagination not just because of its pithiness, but thanks to its range of potential applications in our own lives, which might be anything from a reticence to speak of love, to a hesitation over who should be the first to tell the boss there's a problem.

matutolypea: irritability in the morning.

Those of us who struggle with early mornings should be thankful for the word 'matutolypea'. In modern terms, it describes the state of being particularly bad-tempered when we wake up. This is an everyday occurrence for some, but the word's origins are more poetic. A mixture of Latin and Greek, it pays homage to the Roman goddess of the morning, Mater Matuta, whose name is combined with the Greek *lypē*, 'grief', making the literal translation of 'matutolypea' 'sorrow of the dawn'. But rather than providing an ancient equivalent to the *uhtcearu* that has us lie awake in the darkness, 'matutolypea' more exactly denotes the effects of 'morning grief' in the form of extreme irritability.

For all its classical resonances, the word is a modern invention, not yet recognized in standard dictionaries and observed more as a curiosity than as a term for regular use. Nonetheless, for those who are particularly **crumpsy** upon waking, this is one word to have in your arsenal.

maudlin: self-indulgently sentimental or gloomy.

'It is but a maudlin and indecent verity that comes out through the strength of wine.' Most of us would agree with Joseph Conrad's association of the adjective 'maudlin' with a fair amount of alcohol. But the word was born not in a tavern, but in the Bible, where it is associated with Mary Magdalene, the weeping sinner who washed the feet of Jesus with her tears, and who wept again at his tomb on Resurrection morning. It was this connection with tears that is said to have inspired the use of 'maudlin' to mean 'sentimental' and 'weepy', pronounced as Mary Magdalene's name would have been at the time (hence also its pronunciation in college names at Oxford and Cambridge). Even in its earliest uses, however, 'maudlin' implied excessive or mawkish sentimentality. The associations with alcohol began to emerge in 1592, when the playwright Thomas Nashe included 'maudlin drunk' in his list of drunken 'types': 'a fellow who will weepe for kindnes in the midst of his Ale, and kisse you'. *See also* **lion drunke**.

maverick: an unorthodox or independent-minded person.

A maverick refuses to follow the traditional path, opting to go their own way. The inspiration for the term was a man who did exactly that, and whom history tends to regard as either an obnoxiously, stubborn individual or one who thought outside the box. No matter which of these was true, he was certainly unconventional.

Samuel Augustus Maverick was a land baron in nineteenth-century Texas, and the owner of a large herd of cattle that he left largely unbranded. Some say this was out of compassion for the animals, but he may have just been too busy, for besides being a rancher, Maverick also served as a practising lawyer and a member of the Texas Congress. He is seen by many as a hero of the Texan Revolution that established independence from Mexico.

Nevertheless, it is Maverick's failure to brand his cattle that has proved his most lasting legacy. It is said that his neighbours, upon spotting one of his calves mixing with their own, would regularly mutter the refrain, 'There goes another Maverick.' It is for this that his name came to signify not quite a rogue cow, but certainly a lone wolf.

mawkish: sentimental in an exaggerated way.

We might not think of a soppy novel or piece of purple prose as being 'maggoty', but that is essentially what we are doing by calling it 'mawkish'. 'Mawk' is an obsolete dialect word for a maggot or grub, and the first meaning of 'mawkish' was 'sickly', 'queasy', or 'faint', as well as 'having a nauseating taste or smell'. It is this last meaning that we eventually went to town with, so that anything 'mawkish' today is full of sickly and fake sentiment.

mazy: giddy; dizzy; confused.

To be 'mazy' or 'mazed' is to be in a state of mental confusion. Muddle-headedness was also the first meaning of the word 'maze', at the beginning of the fourteenth century. By Chaucer's time, a 'maze' could also be a trick or deception: a delusive fantasy that might stun or 'amaze' – indeed, 'amaze' and 'maze' are likely siblings. The first record of the 'maze' that is a labyrinth for amusement comes from 1422, when The Mase was the name given to the gardens and winding walks of the Abbot of Battle's riverside inn in London's Southwark – presumably it made its visitors both 'mazy' and 'amazed'.

mean: ungenerous; unkind.

'Meanness demeans the demeaner far more than the demeaned,' decided the entrepreneur Malcolm Forbes who, for all the enviable glamour of his own lifestyle, saw the ultimate purpose of business as producing happiness.

The original uses of 'mean' as an adjective were entirely neutral. The word shares a common ancestor with the Latin *communis*, 'common', and described something that was 'common to two or more people'. Both 'mean' and 'common' systematically took on negative associations because such sharing was usually found within working communities rather than the nobility or gentry, and so 'low on the social scale' took on the additional senses of 'inferior', and ultimately 'disagreeable' and 'unkind'.

In the late nineteenth century, 'mean' took a different dive, this time into slang, where it flipped and became a term of total approval, with the suggestion that something was 'so good it's unfair'. To be a 'pretty mean dancer', for example, as Ernest Hemingway described an acquaintance in a letter of 1919, is high praise indeed.

meek: humble; submissive.

Meekness was once a quality to be proud of. Rather than describing timidity, it signified a blend of courtesy and kindness. It was used particularly for the gentleness expected from Christians towards the weak and the humble, and developed to mean a quality of heart that makes a person willing to submit to the will of another, including God. The Bible famously teaches that 'the meek shall inherit the earth, and shall delight themselves in the abundance of peace.' But what is considered laudable in some contexts is seen as weak in others, and in the end, the weakness won.

'Meek' doesn't appear in English until the twelfth century. Rather than descending from Latin, as its biblical use might suggest, it is instead an unlikely borrowing from Viking warriors and their language of Old Norse, for whom *mjúkr* meant 'soft' and 'gentle'.

meh: uninspiring and unexceptional.

'Meh' has become the modern articulation of a shrug. We utter it when we feel neither one thing nor the other, and neither enthusiastic nor highly critical – just indifferent. Used as both an adjective and an exclamation, 'meh' may have begun with the Yiddish *me*, 'be it as it may' or 'so so', but it was popularized by *The Simpsons* (a show responsible for introducing another three-letter interjection to our language in the form of 'doh!'). It took off after an episode in which Lisa spells it out for emphasis – M-E-H – after Homer fails to interest her in going to a theme park.

melancholy: sadness and despondency.

The epitaph on the tomb in Christ Church, Oxford, of Robert Burton, author of *The Anatomy of Melancholy*, ends with the puzzling Latin words *cui vitam dedit et mortem Melancholia*: 'to whom Melancholy gave life and death.' According to a rumour perpetuated by Burton's contemporary and Oxford gossip Antony Wood, the words were a grim reference to Burton's reading of an astrological chart that had predicted his death in 1640. The implication was that the depressive clergyman had, on 25 January of that same year, hanged himself, thereby validating the astrologer's prediction. Thus melancholy, a premodern form of depression that Burton had devoted so much of his life to understanding, may also have brought about his death.

First published in 1621, *The Anatomy of Melancholy* was dedicated to the causes and treatment of the complaint Burton considered to be an 'inbred malady' in all of us. He was driven to write about it as a form of self-therapy: 'One must scratch where it itcheth.' Part treatise, part encyclopedia, part self-help book, and part classical anthology, the impact of his thousand-page book was such that, 400 years on, it remains in print. It explores both the nature of the disease and its causes (including witches, devils, and the 'overmuch use of hot wines') in great and discursive detail. Burton believed melancholy was connected to the imagination and could frequently bring delusions, citing the story of a melancholic baker in the Italian city of Ferrara who became so convinced that he was made of butter that he dared not go near his oven or sit in the sun lest he melted. His proposed cures included blood-letting and exercise; he himself found solace watching the bargemen at Oxford's Folly Bridge, 'who scold and storm and swear at one another [. . .] and laugh most profusely'.

For the frequently gloomy Samuel Johnson, *The Anatomy of Melancholy* was the only work that on bad days could tempt him out of bed. Inspired by Burton, he offered his own advice on the 'management of the mind' to his biographer James Boswell: 'Let him take a course of chymistry, or a course of rope-dancing, or a course of any thing to which he is inclined at the time. Let him contrive to have as many retreats for his mind as he can, as many things to which it can fly from itself.'

Today, 'melancholy' is defined in the dictionary as 'a feeling of pensive sadness, typically with no obvious cause'. Linguistically, it comes from the ancient belief that human health was governed by the bodily **humours**, for melancholy was believed to emanate from an excess of 'black bile': a direct translation of the word itself, which is based upon the Greek *melas*, 'black', and *cholē*, 'bile' (*see* **choleric**). An imbalance was believed to provoke sullenness, ill temper, brooding, unprovoked anger, and unsociability, before becoming inextricably associated with despondency.

Together with spleen and 'the vapours', 'melancholy' was one of the standard words for such feelings before the clinical term 'depression' took over in the nineteenth century. The latter was far from a perfect match, since melancholy was at that time also viewed as a positive emotion, and a necessary adjunct to creativity. The 'cult' of melancholy, which began in the fifteenth century, offered the appeal of a gloomy but dignified solitude as a wellspring for poetry and art. For the Elizabethan gentleman of leisure, to be painted in the pose of the melancholy man – reclining alone, dressed in black and holding a distracted gaze – was how things should be. But as Burton (and his fate) vividly showed, it was a slippery slope: 'A most incomparable delight it is so to melancholise, and build castles in the air ... [until] these fantastical and bewitching thoughts so covertly, so feelingly, so urgently, so continually set upon, creep in, insinuate, possess, overcome, distract, and detain [that we] cannot go about more necessary business, stave off or extricate ourselves, but are ever musing, melancholising, and carried along.'

Today, scientists have still not fully agreed what stuff melancholy is made of. As its early biographer realized, it is an endlessly varied disease. *See also* **black dog**.

memento mori: an object kept as a reminder of death.

A reminder that death is inevitable doesn't sound like the most motivational of rallying cries. And yet *memento mori* takes us back to the 'triumphs' of ancient Rome – ceremonies marking the grand entry into the city of a victorious general, whose ears would ring with the roars of adulation from the crowds. But beneath the clamour the general might also pick up the voice of a slave, whose sole duty was to attend him and whisper, '*Respice post te. Hominem te esse memento. Memento mori*' – 'Look behind. Remember thou art mortal. Remember you must die.' This was an admonition that, no matter how great the adoration of the people, celebrity will eventually fade, while death is assured.

Even by this time the message behind *memento mori* was well established. The Greek thinker Socrates believed that, fundamentally, philosophy was 'about nothing else but dying and being dead'. In ancient Egypt, the mummification of bodies was a way not just of attending to death but also of celebrating life. During times of festivities, it was traditional to parade a skeleton, to which the audience would cheer, 'Drink and be merry, for when you're dead you will look like this.'

Memento mori, and its embodiment in physical objects, has inspired art and literature ever since. Portraits and still lifes from the sixteenth and seventeenth centuries regularly feature skulls and snuffed-out lamps as reminders of mortality. But it was in the Middle Ages that the preoccupation with death was arguably at its most acute. Manuals on how to die were distributed widely, and many nursery rhymes of the period are dark tales full of death and blood. Out of the grimness and horror of the Black Death grew the *Danse Macabre*, or Dance of Death, a genre of allegory in which a personification of Death calls people from all walks of life to their grave.

If *memento mori* are less visible today, their message still inspires creativity and artistry. Apple's Steve Jobs once famously said, 'Remembering that you are going to die is the best way I know to avoid the trap of thinking you have something to lose. You are already naked. There is no reason not to follow your heart.'

mercurial: unpredictable or moody.

For centuries, faith in the stars and planets as controllers of human destiny was unshakeable. Those born during the ascendancy of a particular planet were thought to be particularly susceptible to its powers. Mercury was the swift and sprightly messenger god, known for his volatile temperament. Anyone born during his planet's dominance in the skies was said to be 'mercurial': highly changeable or fickle. Thanks to its mobility, alchemists also gave the name Mercury to the liquid metal quicksilver. In the nineteenth century, the long-term use of the metal as an additive in the hat-making trade caused a spectrum of effects ranging from tremors and slurred speech to hallucinations, viewed as a form of insanity. It is from these sorry beginnings that the expression 'mad as a hatter' is said to have evolved.

mercy: compassion; clemency.

'The quality of mercy is not strained ... It is twice blest;/It blesseth him that gives, and him that takes': Portia's famous speech in *The Merchant of Venice*, in which she tries to persuade Shylock not to demand 'a pound of man's flesh' in exchange for an unpaid debt, positions mercy as a key attribute of a Christian God. This is very much how Shakespeare's audience would have perceived the word. In the Latin of the early Christian Church, *merces* stood for the rewards of Heaven. As 'mercy' in English, the same word described clemency towards those with no right or claim to kindness or forgiveness, as well as the forbearance shown by God to sinful humanity. After the Norman Conquest, such intensity had weakened a little, and 'I cry you mercy' became a standard equivalent to 'I beg your pardon'. But 'mercy' has never really lost its power, and to be at someone's mercy even today is arguably as perilous as it ever was.

merry-go-sorry: the circle of pleasure and sadness.

'A lifetime of happiness! No man alive could bear it: it would be hell on earth.' A curious sentiment on the face of it, but with those words George Bernard Shaw was simply voicing the familiar truth that life will always shift between light and dark, pleasure and sorrow. It will, to use a sixteenth-century expression, always be a 'merry-go-sorry'.

The poet Nicholas Breton, writing in the early seventeenth century, offers a useful example: 'Thou hast told me of such a

Merry goe sory, as I have not often heard of: I am sory for thy ill fortune, but am glad to see thee alive.' A sentiment that seems just as applicable to recent years.

metanoia: a transformative change of heart.

'Metanoia' describes a journey in which a person's mind, heart, or entire way of life undergoes a conversion. It comes directly from the Greek for 'second thoughts' or 'repentance'. More loosely, it has come to mean a turning point or change of heart. (Should you think of it more as a change of 'mind', you can always opt for the Latin 'mentimutation'.)

mischievous: waggish and playfully annoying.

'Mischievous' is living up to its name, for today's younger generations are opting for the pronunciation 'mischievious', adding an 'i' into the mix to follow the pattern of 'devious' and 'previous'. However you wish to pronounce it, 'mischievous' remains the perfect articulation of mild misbehaviour, especially on the part of children or pets. It wasn't always this way, however, for in its earliest days, 'mischief' was much more about misfortune and severe distress. It came to English from the Old French *meschever*, to 'come to an unfortunate end'.

misdelight: delight in something wrong.

There are **guilty pleasures**, and there are 'misdelights'. A misdelight might inspire a little more condemnation, however, for it describes a pleasure that you *really* shouldn't be indulging in. Modern misdelights might include the pleasure of seeing someone glued to their phone screen walk into a lamp post, or the quiver of gratification when your IT boss can't get Zoom to work. Not quite as strong as **Schadenfreude**, the word has just one mention in the *Oxford English Dictionary*, taken from a sixteenth-century sermon that implies that misdelights are the work of the Devil or a 'wyked sprete' [wicked spirit]. Perhaps guilty pleasures are the better option after all.

misery: wretchedness; extreme unhappiness.

> 'I am the most miserable person who ever lived,' he said . . .
>   'You are young, and in love,' said Primus. 'Every young man in your position is the most miserable young man who ever lived.'

Many of us would relate to these words from Neil Gaiman's *Stardust*. But if youth is a guarantee of occasional misery, the emotion's linguistic source is less certain. We do know it came from the Latin *miser*, which entered English untouched to describe someone both downcast and stingy with it, but its route to that point remains a mystery. The word may be a relative of 'misericord', 'compassion', implying that any miserable person is deserving of pity. But even if its ultimate history is a little patchy, the state of abject wretchedness that misery describes is never in doubt. Franz Kafka put it like this in his *Diaries*: 'People label themselves with all sorts of adjectives. I can only pronounce myself as "nauseatingly miserable beyond repair".'

mislove: to love the wrong person.

For all its popularity at the office party, the act of improper smooching has been charted in language since at least the fifteenth century, when it was known as 'miskissing'. A touch more seriously, however, the *Oxford English Dictionary* also includes the now-lost 'misloving', which it defines as 'loving in a sinful manner'. English needs a word for loving the wrong person, and the 500-year-old 'misloving', simple as it is, will do nicely.

moi tout seul [French: mwah-too-serl]: utterly alone.

Moi tout seul is the French articulation of absolute aloneness, said to have originated among the Huguenots, who were persecuted by the French Catholic government in the sixteenth and seventeenth centuries and who fled to many countries, including Germany. They embraced *moi tout seul* to convey their sadness at their exile and dislocation from home. It (and its German equivalent *Mutterseeelenallein*) are probably best reserved for those moments when isolation is so extreme that it induces acute longing and despair.

mono-no-aware [Japanese: mono-no-a-wahr-eh]: an empathy towards things.

Mono-no-aware is of great importance in Japanese culture and aesthetics. The term is made up of *mono*, meaning 'things', and *aware*, a 'pathos' or 'sentiment', while the *no* in the middle indicates something an object possesses. *Mono-no-aware* thus describes the powerful emotions that objects can instil in us.

The phrase is perhaps best known as a wistful description of cherry blossom, a richly symbolic emblem of Japan that is celebrated annually and steeped in ritual. This act of observing spring's blooming foliage even has its own name in Japanese – *hanami*. Translated as 'flower viewing', the custom, observed since at least the eighth century, sees families and friends gathering to picnic under the trees and to appreciate the cherry blossom, whose evanescence is associated with both mortality and new life.

Japanese art and literature are equally full of images and metaphors of impermanence. *Mono-no-aware* combines the sad anticipation of loss with an intense enjoyment of beauty in the moment.

mood: a state of mind.

'Mood' has always been a versatile word. These days, it's enough to say someone is 'in a mood', or that we are 'getting in the mood', without having to specify which one. This generalized sense of a temporary state of mind has been constant since the thirteenth century, when it emerged from the Old English *mod*, meaning a 'frame of mind', 'spirit', or 'courage'. It was a much more expressive, robust word then however, and was also used widely with other words to specify which emotion was prevailing. *Orgelmode*, for example, was 'pride', and *modecare* 'sorrow' or 'grief', while to be *modleste* was to be 'cowardly' indeed.

morbid: unusually preoccupied with disturbing and unpleasant subjects.

Often used to describe black-clad teenagers and their taste for true crime, as well as horror films and heavy metal, 'morbid' was originally all about disease, thanks to the Latin *morbus*, a 'sickness' or 'ailment'. When used as an adjunct in the name of an illness, it intensified it to a life-threatening degree – 'morbus Gallicus', for example, the 'French disease', was once another term for syphilis. Fittingly, then, 'morbid' may come from the same stable as *mori*, 'to die', implying that anyone suffering from a morbid condition 'looks like death'. Whatever its source, morbidness is characterized by excessive gloom or unwholesomeness, and a 'morbid fascination' is a particularly unusual or unhealthy one.

morose: sullen; gloomy; sour-tempered.

'Cheer up, it might never happen.' Anyone who has ever had this said to them will probably have felt their moroseness grind up a gear. For the Romans, to be *morosus* was to be hard to please and extremely pernickety. With pernickitiness often comes sullenness and sour temper, as well as pessimism and gloom – which is more or less exactly where 'morose' glumly sits today.

mortified: deeply humiliated; embarrassed.

Like the 'mortgages' we take out on our homes, 'mortification' is rooted in death. In the case of the first, a 'mortgage' is a 'death pledge', not because it kills us to pay it off, but because at the end of it, the debt is 'dead'. The first meaning of 'mortification', meanwhile, in the fourteenth century, was the action of 'mortifying' or deadening the appetites of the body in the cause of religious devotion, often via the self-infliction of bodily discomfort. More literally, and in medicine, 'mortification' means the death or necrosis of tissue, such as in one's fingers and toes in extreme cold.

It might seem curious that the act of numbing or deadening was then transferred to an acute and heightened sensation of embarrassment and humiliation, but the connection lies in the killing off of pleasure and the resulting destruction of vitality and energy.

mouton enragé: a normally calm person who becomes suddenly enraged.

Little more needs to be said about this epithet, borrowed into English in the nineteenth century to describe a usually calm person who suddenly becomes enraged, other than that it is French for 'mad sheep'.

mubble fubbles: a fit of despondency.

Most of us are familiar with the sense of impending doom that besets us on a Sunday evening. In the sixteenth century, a low mood such as this was known as a bout of the 'mubble fubbles', a term whose bounciness might take the sting out of even the gloomiest of prospects.

The expression may be a riff on the expression **mulligrubs**, which once described a similar fit of despondency. Such feelings might even lead to a **humdudgeon**, an eighteenth-century term for an imaginary illness for which there is no known cure other than retreating beneath the covers.

As for the 'mubble fubbles', we should perhaps respond to them in the manner set out in a novel called *The Christmas Prince*, from around 1610, aimed at one who is similarly downcast:

> And when your brayne, feeles any paine,
> with cares of state & troubles
> We'el come in kindnesse, to put your highnesse
> out of ye mubble fubbles.

mudita [Pali: moo-deeta]: joy, especially in the well-being of others.

From the Sanskrit and Pali for 'joy', *mudita* is a key tenet of Buddhism, where it is one of the *brahmaviharas*, the four highest qualities of the heart (alongside loving, compassion, and equanimity). Here it applies specifically to joy that is unadulterated and selfless, experienced upon witnessing happiness beyond ourselves. As most of us will recognize, this is not always easy. Summoning pleasure at your colleagues' promotion, or your friend's child's exam success, can be a challenge. But in Buddhism happiness is contagious, and shared joy is twice the joy, which is a compelling motivation in itself.

mulish: stubborn and dogged.

The mule has had a particularly bad rap when it comes to language, and for no good reason. On the face of it, this industrious animal has everything going for it – it combines the strength of a horse with the sure-footedness of an ass. And yet for almost three centuries it has worn the metaphorical saddle of stubbornness and obstinacy. To be 'mulish' is to be considered cranky, sulky, and generally intractable.

mulligrubs: a fit of pique or depression.

An episode of despondency, in the 1500s, was known by the puzzling term 'mulligrubs', as well as the **mubble fubbles**. The *Oxford English Dictionary* even allows us to be a 'mulligrub' ourselves if we are sullen or ill-tempered. No one quite knows the origin of the term, and what insect larvae might have to do with it, but its heavy, **Eeyorish** sound seems just right for a wearisome attack of the **blues**.

mumpish: depressed in spirits; sullen.

Cranky, withdrawn, and glum, 'mumpish' individuals tend to carry their gloom around with them, infecting all those in their wake. The adjective is recorded in Nathan Bailey's *Universal Etymological English Dictionary* of 1721, where it is defined pithily as 'angry, and silent withal'. To do something 'mumpishly', meanwhile, is to do it with plodding weariness.

mumpsimus: an individual who is obstinately reactionary.

The sixteenth-century 'mumpsimus' is a term that has inexplicably fallen out of use, for its application might be even more relevant today, in the age of social media. It describes an individual who insists they are right, despite clear evidence they are not.

The term originated in a much-told story about a less than literate Catholic priest who consistently trips up while reciting the post-Communion prayer. Whenever he gets to the line *Quod ore sumpsimus, Domine* ('What we have received in the mouth, Lord'), the priest substitutes the non-existent word *mumpsimus* for *sumpsimus*. Every time someone tries to correct him, he gives the stubborn response that he will not change his old *mumpsimus* for his critic's new *sumpsimus*.

mustard: full of fire and enthusiasm.

'Obtain Keen's genuine mustard and full approval is guaranteed!' promised an advertisement in the London newspaper *Field* in 1864. Could this be the origin of the expression 'as keen as mustard'? Certainly by that time the manufacturers Keen had been producing hot mustard for over a century. To be as 'keen as mustard', however, is recorded much earlier – as far back as 1672, when it is mentioned in a Latin–English dictionary by the English schoolmaster William Walker.

The simile is a straightforward one, of course, implying that someone passionate about a cause has a fire in their belly as hot as our favourite pungent condiment. 'Mustard' even stood on its own in the 1900s as a byword for being sharp and accomplished. To 'cut the mustard' – which draws on the slang sense of 'cutting it', i.e. achieving something – has meant (to use another eye-watering metaphor) 'fully up to snuff' since the late 1800s.

naches [Yiddish: NACH-uhs]: pride or gratification.

Naches is the burst of joy that accompanies pride in another person's achievements. You might *shep naches* when witnessing your child walk for the first time, for example, or you might wish them *naches* on their wedding day. For such a timeless emotion, the word came to us surprisingly late: it is an early-twentieth-century borrowing from the Hebrew *naḥat*, 'contentment', and *nach*, meaning to 'rest'. It is a largely private emotion, as opposed to **kvelling**, which likes a public audience. *Naches* really belongs not to some fleeting accomplishment but, as the *Jewish Chronicle* puts it, to 'the achievement of bringing up a mensch'.

narrow-minded: rigid and conservative.

The earliest reference in the *Oxford English Dictionary* to 'narrow-minded', from 1611, offers it as a translation of 'pusillanimous' – 'faint-hearted' or 'timid'. Just a few decades later, however, it was starting to flex its muscles and to settle in as a byword for rigid illiberalism and a lack of receptiveness to new ideas. In this, of course, it is the antithesis of 'broad-minded'. All quite straightforward, and some might be tempted by one of the lesser-used synonyms from the same century, such as 'tub-brained' and 'cat-witted'. More recently, an obstinate or blinkered person might be described as 'nippit', 'unenlarged', and 'chinchy'. Perhaps we're just too narrow-minded to use them?

naughty: disobedient or misbehaving.

Naughtiness has quite a story to tell. While it wears its heart on its sleeve, its meaning has changed so much we no longer see it. To be 'naughty' in the fifteenth century was to be 'poor', 'humble', and 'needy' – to have or be worth 'naught'. The temptation to associate those on the lowest rung of the ladder with poor morals was clearly irresistible, and before long the word had swerved to mean 'wicked' or 'improper'. Today, its wickedness may have faded, but the 'improper' aspect has not. To be naughty is to misbehave, and by the twentieth century this included indulging in sexual shenanigans, an aspect fully enjoyed in the 1970s ad slogan for cream cakes, 'Naughty but Nice', said to have been the choice of the copywriter and future novelist Salman Rushdie.

nausea: a feeling of sickness with an inclination to vomit; loathing and disgust.

Anyone who has experienced intense seasickness will appreci-ate the fact that it was sailors who first experienced 'nausea'. The word is founded upon the Greek *naus*, 'ship', making it a sibling of both 'nautical' and 'naval'.

More surprisingly, 'nausea' also gave us 'noise', based on a shift in the sense of the former from 'seasickness' to 'malaise' and on to a 'disturbance' – one that we might possibly find 'nauseating', a word now with a firm metaphorical sense of being 'disgusting' and 'loathsome'. When we talk about something 'ad nauseam' it is to a sickening degree.

nefandous: too odious to speak of.

Some words are only to be used *in extremis*, reserved for those situations that push us to the limit. 'Nefandous' is one of these. Made up of the Latin *ne* 'not', and *fandus* 'to be spoken', and a sibling of 'nefarious', 'nefandous' describes something so shocking or abominable that it simply should not be mentioned. Judging by the evidence of the dictionary, the sources of nefandousness have encompassed blasphemy, Acts of Parliament, and the selling-on of cadavers in 'that nefandous Burke and Hare business'.

nepenthe [ni-pen-thee]: a substance that brings forgetfulness or relief.

A 'nepenthes' is a drug or potion that induces a welcome forgetfulness in all who take it. The idea has a magical history, even if we now seek its refuge in more prosaic forms. It appears in Homer's *Odyssey*, as the drug that Paris gives to Helen after he abducts her in order to make her forget her old home. Built upon the Greek *ne*, 'not', and *penthos*, 'grief', it moved into English in the 1500s to describe a potent substance that liberates the mind and soul. In the eighteenth century, the name was given to a potent sherry-based tincture of opium and morphine, designed to dull any pain. In both senses the idea was of an emotional anaesthetic that drives away melancholy.

nervous: easily agitated or alarmed.

In Roman times, anyone earning the description *nervosus* would have been rippling with energy thanks to a physique that was sinewy, tough, and 'full of nerves'. In English, as 'nervous', it was essentially the fifteenth-century equivalent of 'buff'. Indeed, 'nerve' and 'sinew' were synonymous as terms for the cord-like structures of the body for centuries. 'Nervous' wasn't just reserved for the human body – a 'nervous leaf' had conspicuous veins running through it, while 'nervous insects' had flecked, multi-coloured wings. A 'nervous crossbow', meanwhile, would have been strung with an animal's guts. So how did the word shift from meaning 'tough' to 'trembling at the knees'? The answer lies in the dual meaning of 'nerve' itself, which can encompass both boldness – 'You've got a nerve' – and a state of stress – 'I'm a bag of nerves'. Each looks back to the physical nerves of the body that connect our brain with our sensory receptors.

Like **hysteria**, 'nerves' were for a time viewed as an exclusively female complaint, a belief mercilessly satirized by Jane Austen in *Pride and Prejudice* in the figure of Mrs Bennet:

> 'Mr Bennet, how can you abuse your own children in such a way? You take delight in vexing me. You have no compassion on my poor nerves.'
>
> 'You mistake me, my dear. I have a high respect for your nerves. They are my old friends. I have heard you mention them with consideration these twenty years at least.'

nesh: feeble; highly sensitive to the cold.

Among the first things to be 'nesh' was fruit, for in Old English, the adjective meant 'soft', 'mushy', or 'juicy', yielding easily to pressure. When used of a person, however, 'nesh' has lived a double life, conveying negative qualities such as cowardice, laziness, and temptability, as well as positive ones such as empathy or pity. It is the negative side of things that triumphed in the most recent leg of its journey: in modern English dialect, to be 'nesh' is to be 'weak', 'feeble', and – above all – 'highly susceptible to the cold'. *See also* **gwenders**.

neurotic: abnormally sensitive or anxious.

Like **nervous**, 'neurotic' first meant 'acting on the nerves'. The term was commonly used by apothecaries and herbalists for remedies that soothed disorders of the nervous system. By the nineteenth century, it had escaped its strictly medical moorings and was applied to people who were excessively anxious, tense, or obsessive. The term was significantly redefined by psychoanalysts such as Sigmund Freud, who viewed neurosis as a coping strategy, caused by the resurfacing of repressed emotions attached to past experience; such unconscious conflict is then expressed through physical and mental disturbances. For Carl Jung, neuroses were simply exaggerations of the normal self: for his part, he believed that over-emphasis on the past removes the desire for change.

The adjective 'neurotic' has largely broken free of these complex beginnings, and is frequently used of people displaying any degree of emotional instability.

nice: pleasant or attractive.

'Nice' people were to be avoided in medieval England. They were likely to behave like fools, or at the very least to not understand very much. The adjective is a descendant of the Latin *nescius*, meaning 'ignorant' or 'not knowing'. With ignorance go assumptions of stupidity and unsophistication, and 'nice' went on to develop a panoply of largely negative senses, from 'wanton', 'showy', and 'cowardly', to 'fragile', 'strange', and 'coy'. It wasn't until the sixteenth century that the word began to be used positively, first in the sense 'fine or subtle' and, later still, 'pleasant' and 'kind'. Jane Austen had a lot of fun with it in *Northanger Abbey*:

> 'I am sure,' cried Catherine, 'I did not mean to say anything wrong; but it is a nice book, and why should not I call it so?'

'Very true,' said Henry, 'and this is a very nice day, and we are taking a very nice walk, and you are two very nice young ladies. Oh! it is a very nice word indeed! – It does for everything.'

There are not many words that have made the journey from bad to good, rather than the other way round, but there may yet be a postscript to its story. When you are asked to judge someone's new haircut, and declare it to be simply 'nice', the reaction may well bring things back full circle.

nidificate: to make a nest.

The impulse to 'nidificate' has never been stronger than in the last few years – for humans, at least. The word really belongs to the birds, however, for 'nidificating' is the act of building a cosy nest and staying there for some time.

nightmare: a frighteningly unpleasant dream or situation.

No one welcomes a nightmare, an experience Bryan Adams described as being 'caught in the crossfire of a silent scream'. When the word first emerged in English in the fourteenth century, a 'nightmare' was even more scream-worthy, for it denoted a female spirit or monster that was said to settle upon the chests of sleeping victims and suffocate them. In some cases, the 'nightmare' was an incubus or succubus, seeking to satiate their sexual desire. Rather than being a female horse, this 'mare' is a relative of the early Irish *morrigain*, queen of the elves, and the Russian *kikimora*, a female house spirit.

The interpretation of dreams and nightmares has long rested upon the psychoanalytical theory that dreams are a door to the unconscious, betraying either hidden desires (Freud) or symbolic representations of our reality (Jung). Neurocognitive theories suggest that dreams are a way of making sense of stored memory. For many of us, the unpleasantness of nightmares is suffocating enough, even without a monster crushing our chest.

nikhedonia: the pleasure of anticipated success.

The build-up of emotion as your home team looks certain to clinch victory; the discovery that your exam paper contains all the questions you've revised, or the smug assessment that your Scrabble word is utterly unbeatable – all these involve 'nikhedonia', the excitement of guaranteed success. The term is a new coinage, based on the Greek *nikē*, 'victory', and *hēdonē*, 'pleasure'.

nod-crafty: able to seem fully involved in a conversation when you're not really listening.

Even in the days before Zoom meetings and the endless parade of boxed human faces on our screens, many of us had already perfected the art of nodding vigorously as though in complete understanding of what's going on, when we'd actually tuned out hours before. Clearly this is not a new phenomenon, for in the eighteenth century someone came up with 'nod-crafty'. This highly useful adjective describes one who is 'given to nodding their head with an air of great wisdom'. The key word here is 'air', for 'nod-craftiness' is all about the affectation of understanding without putting in any effort whatsoever.

noggle: to achieve something only with difficulty.

According to the *English Dialect Dictionary*, 'noggle' has a geographical reach as far north as Yorkshire and as far south as Cornwall. The verb is defined as to 'manage anything with difficulty', especially walking as a result of weakness or carrying something heavy. For most of us, it is a useful way of marking a stuttering start to a day or activity, as in 'I could barely rouse myself to get out of bed this morning, but I noggled it somehow.'

nonchalant: calm, relaxed, and not concerned at all.

Can you be 'chalant' without the 'non'? Not exactly, but you can come close by using the now obsolete adjective 'calent', meaning 'warm' or 'hot'. Its source is the Latin *calere*, to 'be hot', which also gave us 'calorie' and 'chafe'. To be 'calent' is to be full of energy and zeal; to be 'non-calent' or, as we and the French now put it, 'nonchalant', is to be entirely lacking in either.

nonplussed: discombobulated.

For those who view the Americanization of English as a new infestation that is robbing British English of its sovereignty, any blurring of the distinctions between the two tongues can be a prime source of vexation and resentment. For the rest of us, however, there is pleasure to be had in these differences, and in the very pondering of how apparently straightforward words and expressions can lead such separate lives according to their geography.

Not all differences pertain to English. Words like 'gotten', 'trash', 'Fall', and 'sidewalk' aside (all of which happily existed in British English long before the *Mayflower* set sail), some borrowings from European languages have also gone separate ways. A New Yorker, for example, would probably quite enjoy looking 'nonplussed', for there it means 'coolly unruffled' and nonchalant. Call someone 'nonplussed' in Manchester, however, and the answer will be very different. If, indeed, there is any answer forthcoming at all, because to be 'nonplussed' in Britain is to be so surprised and confused that you are unsure how to react.

The British usage is, etymologically, the correct one, for 'nonplussed' is rooted in the French *non plus*, 'no more', conveying a frozen indecision as to which way to turn. The North American meaning is a new usage based on the assumption that *non-* is the normal negative prefix tacked on to an imaginary adjective 'plussed', and so to be 'non-' or 'un-plussed' is to be not very bothered at all.

nostalgia: a sentimental longing for the past.

Nostalgia, as they say, ain't what it used to be. The word has been with us since Georgian times as a combination of the Greek words *nostos*, a 'return home', and *algos*, 'pain'. Its first meaning was acute homesickness.

Nostos is a key theme in Greek mythology and literature, much of which involves an epic hero making their way home, facing trials and obstacles along the way. Homer's *Odyssey* sees Odysseus battling to return from the Trojan War, fending off the seduction of the Sirens and the Lotus-Eaters to do so. He achieves full *nostos*. Not all heroes manage it, however: Achilles notably realizes he will never make it home, and that his *kleos* ('renown') can only be reached through death in battle. 'My *nostos* has perished, but my *kleos* will be unwilting.'

'Nostalgia' itself was coined in 1688 by the Swiss physician Johannes Hofer, who introduced *nostalgia* or *mal du pays* as alternative names for the condition known as *mal du Suisse*, 'Swiss illness'. This was a sickness observed amongst Swiss mercenaries who, while fighting in the lowlands of Europe, yearned for their native mountains. Symptoms were not just psychological: this particular brand of homesickness was believed to include fevers, abdominal pain, fainting, vomiting, and even death. Military physicians attributed the mercenaries' singular malady to damage that had been done to their brains since childhood by the continuous clanging of Swiss cowbells. Consequently, they were forbidden from indulging in *Kuhreihen*, the melodies accompanied by an alpine horn that were sung by herdsmen as they ushered their cattle to pasture.

Inevitably, this nostalgia was not confined to Switzerland for long. In the journal he kept during the first voyage of Captain Cook in 1770, the naturalist Sir Joseph Banks noted with alarm that the crew 'were now pretty far gone with the longing for home which the Physicians have gone so far as to esteem a disease under the name of Nostalgia'. Later, the same malady was diagnosed among soldiers during the American Civil War and those who fought in the First and Second World Wars.

Today's sense of 'nostalgia', of a sentimental and affectionate longing assuaged by listening to old albums or TV eighties nights, is far removed from ancient Troy and the Alps of Switzerland, where nostalgic longing was once so intensely focused.

numb: deprived of sensation.

In the opening years of the fifteenth century, the word *nome* emerged to mean 'deprived of motion or feeling, powerless to feel or act'. It is an offshoot of the Old English *niman*, meaning to 'take', 'seize', or 'grasp', and so to be 'numb' was the result of sensation being 'taken' away from a limb or faculty. The word's silent 'b' appeared in the seventeenth century as an apparent riff on similar words such as 'thumb' and 'limb', whose own story began at a time when consonants were becoming simplified. 'Lamb' lost its 'b' sound, retained in spelling but not in pronunciation, as did 'plumb', 'womb', and 'climb'. The result was that people began to use the letter 'b' after an 'm' more liberally, either out of fashion or uncertainty. It was this hypercorrection that also informed 'numb'.

oblectament: a source of delight.

Oblectare, for the Romans, meant to 'entice' or 'delight'. It is the root of the seventeenth-century 'oblectament', a source of delight, which doesn't seem quite mellifluous enough for such a happifying circumstance. But English lacks a pithy word for something that inspires extreme pleasure, and 'oblectament' fills that gap.

oblivious: unaware of what is happening around you.

Fittingly, no one seems to remember quite how 'oblivious' began before it emerged in the Latin *oblivisci*, to 'forget'. The word has always been about things forgotten, and is part of the story of Lethe, 'Oblivion', the name of the Underworld river in Greek mythology that was said to create a state of forgetfulness in all who drank from it (*see* **lethargy**). By extension, 'oblivion' came to mean 'freedom from care or worry', as well as serving as a political byword for 'overlooking' or pardoning crimes of the past. 'Oblivion' can also describe the state of being forgotten or overlooked: it is defined wincingly by Ambrose Bierce in his *Devil's Dictionary* as 'fame's eternal dumping ground'.

obsequious: servile and fawning.

Catchfart, 'parasite', **toady**: English has shown no mercy to fawning flatterers. Yet 'obsequiousness', in its early days, was a form of obedience. Much like 'buxom', which first meant 'compliant' before moving on to 'jolly' and 'well-endowed', 'obsequious' meant 'willing to please and follow directions'. Its source is the Latin *sequi*, to 'follow'. Embrace submissiveness long enough, however, and you might turn into a **sycophant**.

obsess: to be excessively preoccupied with something.

Obsession has never been a comfortable word. In the fifteenth century, when it came into English from the Latin *obsidere*, it described the haunting and tormenting effect of an evil spirit upon its victim. This was an external force, as opposed to that of 'possession', used for the control of a person from within. A parallel meaning of 'obsess' at this time was to 'besiege', whether of an army or of a person's mind. Such preoccupying forces eventually informed our modern use of 'obsession' for a compulsive interest, be it good or bad. Whatever the context, it's worth remembering that the literal meaning of *obsidere* was to 'sit opposite', as of an influence or individual that is, stalker-like, omnipresent.

odd: unusual or different.

There is nothing particularly strange about 'odd' numbers, and yet they have borne that description since counting in English began. The original meaning of 'odd', taken from the Old Norse *oddi*, 'angle', was indeed mathematical: 'having one left over when divided by two' or 'in addition to a pair'. This led to the sense of something single or solitary, and from there 'odd' embraced the idea of being outside the norm. The metaphor informing all of these, clearly present in its Scandinavian origins, is the third point of a triangle, and so the unpaired member of any group.

oeillade: an amorous glance.

There is an 'ogle', and there is an '*oeillade*'. The first is lustful, and usually unwelcome, while an '*oeillade*' describes a secret look of affection or benevolence. At least that is how its story began in the sixteenth century, before – probably inevitably – a bit of heavier-handed flirtation crept in. It is based, of course, on the French *oeil*, 'eye'.

oleaginous: oily and ingratiating.

Sanctimony, diplomats, and comedians – such are the recipients of the unfavourable word 'oleaginous' in the earliest records. An extension of its literal meaning of 'oily' and 'greasy', and based on the Latin *olea*, 'olive tree', to be 'oleaginous' is to be unctuous in the extreme.

olfrygt [Danish: ohl-frigt]: the fear of running out of beer.

Translated literally, the Danish *olfrygt* means 'ale fright'. A modern coinage, it can be applied to the fear of running out of beer at home, or the disappointment of finding that your destination on a night out is entirely devoid of bars.

omertà: a code of silence.

For over a century, the operations of the Mafia were a closed book to the authorities. That all changed in 1963, when Joseph

237

Valachi, once a loyal soldier for the mob boss Vito Genovese, agreed to testify before the US Senate. In doing so, he was breaking a brutal code of honour known as *omertà*.

Omertà is an emotion to live or die for, a blood oath of allegiance and a fundamental ethic for its disciples. It dictates that no Mafia member should ever betray information about any crime to the authorities, whether committed by a brother or an enemy. The penalty for doing so, without exception, is death.

The beginnings of *omertà* are suitably murky. Some believe it began as a more general code among outlaws in the nineteenth century, when the Kingdom of the Two Sicilies was collapsing and Italian mercenaries began to form private armies. It was from these organized clans that the Mafia emerged. Its *uomini d'onore*, or 'men of honour', obeyed the principle that any crossing of the line between police and its members was the ultimate betrayal. As new Mafia clans established themselves in the US, capitalizing on the disaffection of Italian immigrants who had been poorly absorbed into city neighbourhoods, they ensured that these communities also adopted *omertà*, a code of silence rooted in respect as well as fear. The term may derive from the Spanish *hombredad*, 'manliness', itself based on the Sicilian *omu*, 'man'. The decision to be a *cascittuni* or 'informant' is therefore the gravest of all acts against manhood.

In November 1991, Salvatore Gravano (aka 'Sammy the Bull'), the right-hand man of John 'the Teflon Don' Gotti, agreed to turn state's evidence, delivering a mortal blow to the Mafia's celebrity image and, some might say, to the code of *omertà* that fuelled it.

omnisciturient: craving knowledge of everything.

Omni-, Latin for 'all', has been a useful component of English. From 'omnibus' to 'omnivore', it neatly conveys something all-encompassing or meant for all. Some of its partners trip more easily off the tongue than others. 'Omnishambles' has proved to be more than a match for situations (often political) that can only otherwise be described as 'clusterfucks'. But there are rarer finds in the recesses of the *Oxford English Dictionary*, such as 'omniswallowing' (useful for toddlers) and 'omniloquent': 'able to speak about anything' (sofa pundits). 'Omnisciturient' is more of a mouthful, but its description is no less useful. It describes someone who 'wants to know everything', and as such will fit comfortably both with a child who endlessly wants to know 'why?' as well as the keenest of polymaths.

onion-eyed: lachrymose; prone to weep.

We have Shakespeare's *Antony and Cleopatra* to thank for being 'onion-eyed': full of tears, as if from the effect of raw onions. 'Look, they weep / And I, an ass, am onion-eyed.' In *The Taming of the Shrew*, a nobleman who wishes his pageboy to weep as part of an elaborate deception comments that if the boy does not have 'a woman's gift' of being able to 'rain a shower of commanded tears', then an onion in a handkerchief will do just as well to 'enforce a watery eye'. But why do onions make us cry? The answer lies in a wholly unfriendly-sounding chemical known as syn-propanethial-S-oxide, which causes a distinct burning sensation when it floats up from the chopping board and hits your eyeballs. The brain quickly triggers a tear response to rinse the irritant away. 'Onion-eyed' may not be the most poetic of metaphors, but like the edible bulb itself, it certainly hits its target.

onomatomania: failing to find the right word.

It seems oddly cruel that the term for the failure to find the right word is itself so hard to remember. 'Onomatomania' leads a bit of a double life, describing both the vexation of being unable to find the correct word and an extreme love of names.

It is probably in the first category that most of us need the term. Assuming we can ever summon it.

oomph: excitement; energy; sexiness.

What do 'it', 'oomph', and 'X' have in common? All have at one time represented the indefinable quality that can make or break a movie star. 'It girls' have wowed audiences since the 1920s, while 'oomph girl', whose sound is surely deliberately redolent of lip-smacking wonder, also described a woman full of sex appeal and magnetism: 'Hollywood's gay, laughing, modern oomph girl' was one newspaper's description of the actor Ann Sheridan. By the 1990s, 'oomph' was evoking all manner of zest and 'pep', and there it has largely stayed.

optimism: hopefulness and confidence about the future.

In his *Mémoires de Trévoux* in 1737, the scholar Gottfried Leibniz spoke both of 'l'Optimum' and 'l'Optimiste', both derived from the Latin *optimus*, the 'best'. 'Optimism' appeared a couple of decades later in Voltaire's satirical story *Candide*, which popularized its use far beyond the confines of philosophy. Voltaire himself defined the emotion as 'the madness of insisting that all is well when we are miserable'. Brian May, the guitarist and co-songwriter of the band Queen, saw the upside: calling it 'the biggest emotion in creation'. While the world is mostly split into the two glass-half-full and glass-half-empty brigades, those of us in between are probably just realists.

orgasm: the climax of sexual excitement.

Sex has always been a contentious subject. In Ovid's *Metamorphoses*, Jupiter and Juno, the married king and queen of the gods, discuss orgasm. Jupiter puts his view that 'The sense of pleasure in the male is far / More dull and dead, than what you females share.' When Juno primly disagrees, they ask Tiresias, who had been both a man and a woman, to adjudicate. When Tiresias agrees with Jupiter, Juno is so furious that she strikes him blind on the spot. (Jupiter promptly lessens the blow by giving Tiresias the gift of foresight as well as a long life.)

The first 'orgasms' were not necessarily sexual, and the word is unrelated to 'orgy'. It was originally used to describe any sudden movement, spasm, or convulsion. A seventeenth-century guide for physicians notes that 'When there appears an Orgasm ... of the humours, we rather fly to bleeding as more safe.' A hundred years on, the term had shifted to refer to a surge of sexual excitement (the 'rut' as the *Oxford English Dictionary*, somewhat uncharmingly, puts it), and eventually to that excitement's highest point. Its linguistic sources are the Greek *organ*, to 'swell'. But that in turn is from *orgē*, which as well as excitement conveys temper and rage. In French, an orgasm is famously known as *le petit mort*, an idea that writers have enjoyed playing with over the centuries. 'I will live in thy heart, die in thy lap, and be buried in thy eyes,' Benedick promises Beatrice in *Much Ado About Nothing*. Death, rage, and bliss: that's quite some package.

ornery: scratchy; bad-tempered.

Mediocre, average, ordinary – not descriptions anyone would wish for these days, yet none of these words came from a negative place. It all depends on your outlook. 'Mediocre', for example, comes from the Latin for 'halfway up a rugged mountain', while 'average' was concerned with equal distribution. 'Ordinary' itself meant 'regular' or 'usual' – belonging to the expected order of things. And yet they have each ended up occupying a sphere that is distinctly commonplace. Take this gloomy note a beat further and you get 'ornery', a nineteenth-century respelling of 'ordinary' that took on even more associations of unpleasantness and inferiority. To be 'ornery', in North American English, is to be cranky and cantankerous – deliberately running contrary to the usual state of affairs.

outrage: shock; horror; indignation.

'Outrage' is an excellent example of how we bend foreign words to suit both our understanding and our tongues. The term has nothing to do with either 'out' or 'rage', but is based instead upon the Latin *ultra*, meaning 'beyond'. The French used this to produce *ultrage*, a term for extreme indignation and being 'beyond' self-control: it is the state of being 'ultra', in which *-age* is a standard suffix (in the manner of 'footage', 'shortage', or 'breakage'). When English adopted it in the four-teenth century, it did so on the assumption that the word's two components were 'out' and 'rage', because the idea of hitting out in anger fitted so neatly.

overmused: exhausted from thinking.

'Have you not over-mus'd, or over-thought your selfe?' asks a character in a play from 1653. And with that the dramatist Richard Brome introduced a word that neatly sums up our **dumfungled** state after hours of working and 'doomscrolling'. When we are 'overmused', we are simply exhausted from too much thinking.

oy vey [Yiddish]: an expression of dismay over a misfortune.

'Oh woe' is the closest, less heartfelt, equivalent to the Yiddish *oy vey*. Extend the latter a little to *oy vey iz mir* – 'oh woe is me' – and you'll get what the Yiddish glossary *Meshuggenary* describes perfectly as a 'cosmic ouch'.

pain: care; trouble; physical distress.

In Old French, *peine* was a weighty word, coming from the Latin *poena*, 'punishment' or 'retribution', and describing not just woes and suffering, but Hell's torments too. By 1300 *peine* was being used for the agony suffered by Christ. It is from here that 'pain' developed its broad spectrum of meanings for both emotional and physical distress. It retains a vestige of punishment in the phrase 'on pain of death'.

Keats saw pain as a prerequisite for feeling anything: 'Do you not see how necessary a world of pains and troubles is to school an intelligence and make it a soul?' A trained doctor and chronic sufferer from the TB that was to kill him, the poet was an expert in physical pain.

True to a word that can describe myriad physical sensations and mental anguishes, 'pain' has one of the longest definitions in the *Oxford English Dictionary*, finishing with an 'etc.' that invites a thousand possibilities: 'a continuous, strongly unpleasant or agonizing sensation in the body (usually in a particular part) such as arises from illness, injury, harmful physical contact, etc.' For all its ubiquity, 'pain's' synonyms are few: among them 'wrake' (a sibling of 'wrack'), 'bale', and 'dolour'.

pallesthesia: the perception of vibration.

It might be your mobile phone ringing in your pocket, or the feel of a train's engine as it reverberates through your seat: the awareness of a vibration that is transmitted through the body is known as 'pallesthesia', from the Greek *pallein*, to 'feel'. *See* **fauxcellarm**.

pandemonium: uproar and confusion.

In John Milton's epic seventeenth-century poem *Paradise Lost*, Pandemonium is the capital of Hell where Satan presides over his council of malevolent spirits. Milton chose the term, from the Greek *pan*, meaning 'all', and *daimōn*, 'spirit' or 'devil', for the gathering place of all demons. A century later, his dramatic coinage had become a synonym for any centre of vice, before moving on to a state of utter chaos and confusion.

Panglossian: unreasonably optimistic.

'Optimism. The doctrine, or belief, that everything is beautiful, including what is ugly': so reads another typically mischievous definition from Ambrose Bierce's *Devil's Dictionary*. And yet, optimism does assume the predominance of good over evil, and of happiness over sorrow. In its original form, it described a distinct philosophy, one embodied in the character of Dr Pangloss, a glibly passive character in Voltaire's eighteenth-century satire *Candide*, whose constant refrain is that '*tout est pour le mieux dans le meilleur des mondes possibles*' – 'everything happens for the best in the best of all possible worlds'. Pangloss is almost hanged, nearly dissected, imprisoned, and ravaged by syphilis, yet still he subscribes to the conviction that everything happens for a reason. To be 'Panglossian', therefore, is to be steadfastly and unrealistically optimistic.

panic: sudden, uncontrollable fear and anxiety.

Pan, inventor of pan pipes and pursuer of revelry and romance, was believed to be both a maker of mischief and a figure inclined to great rages – either way, his reputation is said to have instilled fear in anyone who encountered him.

According to Greek mythology, Pan possessed a stentorian voice that helped the gods vanquish a horde of giants. He liked to exercise his vocals in lonely forests and on remote mountain-tops, and so any loud or eerie noises emanating from the dark were, in the frightened imagination of travellers, immediately attributed to him. Such was the hold of the myth that the terms 'Panic frights' and 'Panic fear' moved into English idiom in the sixteenth century.

As knowledge of its story faded over time, 'panic' took on a broader embrace of extreme, unreasoning anxiety. Of course, one person's 'panic fright' is another person's mild inconvenience: in 1876, *Punch* magazine informed its readers that 'the Milliners and Modistes are in a state of panic, because while this cold weather lasts, they cannot sell their summer costumes.'

pantophobia: generalized fear or anxiety.

LUCY: Or maybe you have pantophobia. Do you think you have pantophobia?
CHARLIE BROWN: What's pantophobia?
LUCY: The fear of everything!
CHARLIE BROWN: THAT'S IT!

panurgic: ready for anything.

Mornings can be binary experiences. We can either jump out of bed ready to confront the world head on, or emerge blearily to the sound of the 'expergefactor' (a thing or person that wakes you up), unable to function without a drip feed of strong caffeine and a good few hours **quiddling** ineffectively on our phones.

'Panurgic' is for the former. Based on the name of a mirthful rogue in a series of novels by Rabelais, it can mean both 'ready for anything' and 'knavish'. The inspiration was the Greek *pan*, meaning 'everything', and *ergon*, work. Then again, the same *ergon* is also at the heart of the word 'orgy', which gives 'panurgic' an added layer of energetic potential should you need it.

parabore: protection against bores.

Should you be faced with a 'blatteroon', a relentlessly tedious conversationalist at a party or other gathering, you might enjoy a word for which the *Oxford English Dictionary* has just one record. A 'parabore', it informs us rather enigmatically, is a 'defence from bores'. You can see the appeal.

paranoia: unjustified suspicion and mistrust of other people.

For William S. Burroughs, 'Sometimes paranoia's just having all the facts.' For the Greeks, however, 'paranoia' was sheer madness. The word is based on *para*, 'beside', and *noos*, 'mind'. Its sufferer is therefore 'beside themselves'. Clinically, the term expresses a condition characterized by delusions of persecution, unwarranted jealousy, or exaggerated self-importance. In its loosest, vernacular sense, however, it can signify the simple mistrust of other people, and the usually unjustified suspicion that everyone is out to get you.

pareidolia: seeing images or hearing sounds in random stimuli.

In late July 1976, the spacecraft *Viking 1* captured the infamous 'face on Mars' photo, featuring a huge rock formation resembling a human head. Immediately, dozens of theories emerged as to how this 'human' face could have been etched upon the surface of another planet. Further investigation revealed it to be a landform known as a 'mesa'. To interpret its particular features as a face involved a phenomenon known as 'pareidolia': the human brain's instinct to find familiar concepts in random objects. These might involve shapes in clouds, hidden messages in audio tracks, and a surprising number of sightings of Jesus on a piece of burnt toast. 'Pareidolia' is made up of the Greek *para*, 'beside', and *eidōlon*, 'shape' or 'form'.

paroxysm: a sudden outburst of a particular emotion.

'Paroxysm' – whether one of tears, or of laughter – came to us from a Greek word meaning 'exasperation'. Its early senses in English included both 'violent sorrow' and a 'savage impulse'. The word is a sibling of 'oxymoron' (literally 'sharp/dull', and itself an oxymoron), and is made up of *para*, 'beside' or 'beyond', and *oxys*, 'sharp'. A 'paroxysm' is therefore something that cuts you to the quick.

passion: intense, barely controllable emotion.

'Passion' is built upon the Latin *pati*, to 'suffer'. The word's original use in English referred specifically to the Passion of Christ through the last days of his life and his suffering on the Cross. When European missionaries travelled to South America in the seventeenth century, they used the structure of the native 'passion flower', or *Passiflora edulis*, to illustrate the crucifixion. The flower's five petals and five sepals represented the ten faithful apostles, and its corona represented the crown of thorns, while the three stigmas symbolized the three nails, and the five anthers Christ's five wounds. Finally, the plant's tendrils represented the whips used in the flagellation of Christ.

By the thirteenth century, 'passion' was used to convey any extreme hardship or suffering, be it mental or physical. It was frequently prefaced by an indication of which part of the body was distressed – medical journals spoke of 'cardiac passion' and 'hysteric passion', while one seventeenth-century manual states that 'Thirst is a Passion of the Mouth of the Stomach'. Passion also became a frequent component of medieval oaths. 'Passion of my soul!' and 'Christ's passion!' were popular right up until the eighteenth century, joining an arsenal of euphemisms when Christ's name was invoked.

By the end of the Middle Ages, 'passion' could encompass any overpowering feeling or emotion, whether rage or attraction, madness or longing. The philosopher Descartes perceived such strong feelings as 'passions of the soul', which corresponded roughly to the sentiments we now know as 'the emotions'.

But it was physical desire that soon became 'passion's' chief focus, and during the nineteenth century such terms as 'passion-monger', 'passion-stung', 'passion-pale', and 'passion-tossed' emerged as tropes of Victorian potboilers and melodramas. The trajectory continued in the twentieth century, producing such military coinages as 'passion-killers' (standard-issue underwear) and 'passion-wagons' (trucks used to take troops to the nearest town for 'recreational' purposes).

Today, 'passion' still holds its own, without the need for the hyperbole required for such words as 'tragic' and 'hero'. True passion is just that, and, as most of us have discovered, the experience continues to reflect the word's journey through madness and pain – which are only ever as far away from desire as the other side of the coin.

passive: inactive; unresistant; yielding.

It's a strange move that takes us from **passion** to 'passivity', but the two words are inextricably linked. Both come from the Latin *pati*, to 'suffer'. To be 'passive' is to be acted upon by an external agent, and thereby exposed to the risk of suffering.

pathetic: arousing pity; miserably inadequate.

'To be honest, I think bananas are a pathetic fruit.' The tennis champion Andy Murray is presumably not moved to tears by the sight of every tournament's standard accompaniment to barley water, yet that was the earliest meaning of 'pathetic', in the sixteenth century. Its journey into English, where it first described something so moving or stirring that it intensely affected the emotions, began with the Greek *pathētikos*, meaning 'sensitive' or 'capable of feeling'.

Its ultimate root is, of course, *pathos*, 'suffering', reflected still in uses such as 'they cut a pathetic figure' – one deserving of our pity or compassion. The colloquial, Andy Murray sense of 'so inadequate as to be ridiculous' emerged in the 1930s.

pathetic fallacy: the attribution of human feelings to inanimate objects or nature.

'All violent feelings . . . produce . . . a falseness in . . . impressions of external things,' noted the art critic John Ruskin in 1856. 'This', he continued, 'I would generally characterize as the "pathetic fallacy".' For him, the tendency of poets to project feelings externally was a form of distortion or falsehood, and he used as an example some lines from Oliver Wendell Holmes's 'Astraea':

> The spendthrift crocus, bursting through the mould
> Naked and shivering, with his cup of gold.

These lines, Ruskin maintained, demonstrate 'the fallacy of wilful fancy'. Nonetheless, he also recognized that such externalization isn't all bad, for it can be highly revealing of a poet's state of mind. In this, he believed, poetry offers a powerful counterpoint to science, which looks at hard facts; 'pathetic fallacy', by contrast, offers a window onto the truth of experience.

peccable: fallible and open to sin.

'Peccable' is a rare example of a lost negative. It joins 'maculate', 'wistless', and 'defatigable' in the remote recesses of the historical dictionary.

Both 'impeccable' and 'peccable' are rooted in the Latin *peccare*, to 'sin', and so the original distinction was between being incapable of sin, and only too capable of it. If we are 'peccable', we, or our efforts, are fallible, imperfect, and flawed. The word's outings are often in deliberate contrast to its more illustrious sibling, as illustrated in one example from the *New York Times*: 'Its credentials are about as impeccable as you can find in the peccable atmosphere of Hollywood.'

peevish: querulous and ill-tempered.

From the start 'peevish' has meant 'querulous' or 'irritable', a state that was once seen as the likely result of fasting or another form of religious asceticism. Perhaps **hangriness** was what prompted its earliest outings, but today peevishness is all about being bad-tempered in a petty kind of way. Its origin seems to be the Latin *perversus*, 'contrary'. There is a small handful of decidedly odd-sounding alternatives if you are too bad-tempered to stick with simple peevishness, including 'teethy', 'frampold', 'frappish', and 'froppish'.

penchant: a liking or tendency.

'Penchant', which must be pronounced with a French accent, means a 'leaning'. Its inspiration was the French *pencher*, to 'slope' or 'incline', itself from the Latin *pendere*, to 'hang'. To have a 'penchant' for something, be it jazz or cheesecake, is to have a distinct inclination for it.

perception: the awareness of something through the senses.

On Sunday, 3 May 1953, under the careful supervision of a friendly psychiatrist and his wife Maria, Aldous Huxley took mescaline – a psychedelic compound of the peyote cactus, used in shamanic rituals for centuries. At the time, mescaline was still regarded as a research chemical rather than a drug; the US Navy's Project Chatter had been examining its potential as a truth-revealing agent since the end of the Second World War, and it was not illegal. The experience of his first trip was everything Huxley had hoped for – even the flowers in his garden were 'so passionately alive that they seemed to be standing on the very brink of utterance.' The book he wrote about his mind-expanding experiences, *The Doors of Perception*, became a counter-culture classic, inspiring everyone from Timothy Leary to Jim Morrison, who even named his band the Doors after it.

To 'perceive' something is to capture it with the mind through our senses. Its root is the same as 'capture' – the Latin *capere*, to 'seize'. 'Perception' was used chiefly in philosophical contexts to mean 'awareness' and 'consciousness'. By the eighteenth century, it had come to describe 'an intuitive insight' or 'understanding'. 'There are things known and there are things unknown,' runs a famous adage, 'and in between are the doors of perception.'

perky: cheery and lively.

The first thing to be 'perky', at least in the dictionary, was 'wheat'. A farmer's manual of 1732 declares that 'Pirky Wheat is the most convenient for our chiltern lands.' This was a crop that was early or precocious in its growth, and so was considered to be full of vim and vigour. The earlier verb 'perk', of mysterious origin, meant to 'behave proudly' or 'impudently', or to have a 'jaunty' or 'conceited manner'. It is from here that we get the idea of feeling 'perky' − that is, lively, jaunty, and perhaps a tiny bit cocky to boot.

pertolerate: to endure and withstand.

'Grit and determination', 'strength and stamina' − we often resort to tautology in order to convey the teeth-clenching ability to endure. And yet it turns out we might only need a single word to pack the punch we need. 'Pertolerate', from the seventeenth century, has all those meanings and more. Defined as to 'endure steadfastly to the end', its strength lies in the Latin prefix *per-*, which here conveys the meaning of 'thoroughly', or 'to completion'. If you are able to 'pertolerate' a situation, you will most definitely see it through.

pervicacious: headstrong and wilful.

'A bully; a blustering, turbulent, pervicacious, noisy fellow.' Such was Dr Johnson's definition of a 'hector'. 'Pervicacious' itself he defines even more pithily: 'Spitefully obstinate; peevishly contumacious'. The word rests upon the Latin *pervicax*, 'stubborn, headstrong', from *pervincere*, to 'thoroughly win a point'.

pessimum: the least favourable environment for survival.

When we hit rock bottom, our standard emotional vocabulary can seem almost as lacking as the situation itself. For the very worst of times, however, we might borrow from the lexicon of science and declare that we have reached the 'pessimum', a Latin word for 'the worst thing' that articulates the least favourable environment in which an organism can survive. Such an environment can also be described as 'pessimal'. 'Pessimum' is of course linked to 'pessimism', the tendency to assume the worst.

philocalist: a lover of beautiful things.

> What is this life if, full of care,
> We have no time to stand and stare.

The famous admonishment from William Henry Davies encourages us all to appreciate the small things in life. Most of us are 'philocalists', if only we knew it. The word defines a 'lover of beauty', wherever we may find it.

philodoxical: to be in love with one's own opinions.

Any group of people united in a cause or passion is made up of 'homodoxians', a term based on the Greek for 'same opinion'. Those with a different opinion, on the other hand, are 'heterodoxes' (*hetero-* meaning 'other; the opposite').

As we know, however, the world is also full of those for whom the only opinion that matters is their own. These are the 'philodoxes', from *philo-*, 'loving', and *doxa*, 'opinion', because they are entirely in love with their own views. Worse, if they are philodoxical 'stiffrumps' or **mumpsimuses** (those who obstinately refuse to change their mind), they are to be avoided at all costs.

phlegmatic: calm and stoical.

An abundance of phlegm is not exactly an attractive thought. And according to the ancient physiological doctrine of the four cardinal humours, an excess of the viscous, clammy substance was the cause of constitutional indolence or apathy. Both 'phlegm' and 'phlegmatic' are built upon the Greek *phlegma*, meaning 'inflammation'.

The sense of apathy associated with phlegm eventually shifted to an absence of excitability or a stolid calmness in the face of adverse events. Such suggestions of even-temperedness and self-possession are the ones that prevail today, although the *Oxford English Dictionary* does make one exception with 'phlegm-cutter': a strong alcoholic beverage, typically taken in the morning, and the potential cause of an excitability that a phlegmatic individual might abhor.

phobia: an extreme or irrational fear.

Everybody fears something, and helpfully English will usually provide a word for it. From a fear of ants ('myrmecophobia'), long words ('hippopotomonstrosesquipedaliophobia'), and baldness ('phalacrophobia'), to being alone ('autophobia'), blushing ('erythrophobia'), and body odour ('bromidrosiphobia'), someone somewhere has borrowed a word from ancient Greek and paired it with 'phobia' to name an irrational aversion. Sometimes a bit of inventiveness is required – the Greeks had no word for 'clown' in our modern sense, and so 'coulrophobia', today's term for a terror of them, literally means 'stilt-walker fear'. 'Phobia' itself is rooted in the Greek *phobos* meaning 'fear' or 'flight'.

piblokto [Inuit: pib-lokto]: hysteria prompting wild and dangerous acts.

There is no exact word in English for the jitters and malaise
that accompany **crapulence** after a night of indulgence.
Piblokto might in this instance be useful, even if it is an invoca-
tion of something far more sinister than a warm glass of wine
at 1 a.m.

   Also known as 'Arctic hysteria', *piblokto* is a highly specific
and culture-bound term for a condition affecting Inuit peoples
in winter, characterized by episodes of wild excitement and
irrational behaviour followed by a period of stupor. News of it
began to emerge from the accounts of explorers in the late
nineteenth century, which means that it has invariably been
viewed through a Western lens. The condition is said to provoke
taciturnity and sullenness in its victim, before inspiring acts
such as eating excrement or running out into frigid temperatures. Stretched to its limits, it could be a highly useful description of the aftermath of the office party.

pigritious: extreme laziness.

Being 'pigritious' has nothing to do with pigs, sadly, for all their
(unfair) reputation for laziness. It comes instead from the Latin
piger, 'slothful', which could also describe the animal that is a
sloth itself: 'The beast in Brasil,' notes the writer Thomas Fuller
in 1642, 'which the Spaniards call *Pigritia*, goes no farther in a
fortnight than a man will cast a stone.' If you prefer to look
for other sources to express extreme donothingness, look no
further than 'limaceous', 'slug-like'.

pigsney: darling; sweetheart.

The history of endearments is packed with terms that to
modern ears sound either offputting or positively ridiculous –

words such as 'pigsney' (pig's eye), 'bagpudding', 'nutting', 'cabbage', 'prawn', 'creep-mouse', and 'ding-ding' have all been sweet nothings in the last 600 years or more.

Elsewhere, taste is a pretty dominant theme in our linguistic loving-up. Beyond 'cabbage' and 'prawn', you'll find 'honey-bun', 'cinnamon', 'crumpet', 'lamb-chop', 'munchkin', and 'tart'. Most of these were reserved for women, who also attracted such flowery endearments as 'rosebud', 'honeysuckle', and 'primrose'. Animals are high on the list too: 'duckling', 'dove', 'ladybird', 'pussy', and 'chuck' have been sealed with a kiss for centuries.

Amongst the storehouse of male-friend-to-male-friend monikers were 'bollock' (once used by one man to another in the same way as they might choose 'mate'), 'prick', 'bawcock', and 'pillicock'. Pet names for children, meanwhile, included 'sparrow' and 'snookums', 'pumpkin' and 'poopsie'.

pique: indignant irritation.

Anyone who has ever sought a remedy in a French chemist for a wasp or mosquito bite might recognize the word *piqure*, 'sting'. It is this that informs an English fit of 'pique': an outburst of sulky resentment and indignation at the very idea that anything unpleasant or 'stinging' should happen to *you*.

pissuprest: the retention of urine.

The seventeenth-century 'pissuprest' is the word you need when stuck in a traffic jam or any other tight spot and desperate for a pee. Put simply, as a shortening of 'piss-suppressed', it means 'the holding in of urine'.

pity: sorrow and compassion.

For the Romans, *pietas* encompassed not only 'piety', but a whole raft of moral values, including loyalty, compassion, and the fulfilment of family duties. The word passed into English through French in two forms, 'pity' and 'piety', which remained interchangeable in meaning until well into the seventeenth century. They each replaced the Old English *mildheortness*, 'mild-heartness', which itself was a translation of the Latin *misericordia*. (The daily allowance of food handed out by monks to paupers, meanwhile, was a further offshoot, and became known as a 'pittance'.) 'Pity' alone eventually came to embrace the profound human reaction of grief or distress at the misfortunes of others, although the religious sense of devotion lingered for some time.

The word has moved on, however, and the distinctions between 'empathy', 'compassion', and 'pity' have become much clearer. While most of us appreciate others' compassion, very few of us want to be pitied. Friedrich Nietzsche believed that 'suffering itself becomes contagious through pity', and that although those offering pity believe they are doing so through altruism, the emotion's 'seductive allure' can easily turn a fellow-feeling into contempt or condescension. As such, 'pity' and 'sympathy' are very distinct. As the novelist Karen Marie Moning puts it in *Bloodfever*: 'Sympathy says, I know how it feels, doesn't it just suck? Pity means they think you're defeated.'

As for 'misericord', this is also the name given to the wooden ledges in choir stalls – 'pity seats' for choristers who need to remain standing for hours on end.

pleasure: a feeling of happy satisfaction and enjoyment.

'Pleasure' was a relative latecomer to English, arriving in the late fourteenth century as a borrowing from the Normans' *plaiser*. Then, as now, it meant 'enjoyment' or 'delight', the antithesis of pain. The sensual gratification side of things didn't appear for another century or more, when its more hedonistic applications took the driving seat. The full-on sexual sense of 'pleasure' – particularly of 'pleasuring' someone – followed soon after. For the most part, however, pleasure is the quieter sister of happiness, and is possibly the most enduring of the two emotions: as the nineteenth-century US writer Christian Nestell Bovee remarked, 'Tranquil pleasures last the longest; we are not fitted to bear long the burden of great joys.'

plobaireacht [Irish: plob-uh-rucht]: babbling or blubbering.

English lacks a word for convulsive, sob-drenched conversation and the feeling of helplessness that accompanies it. The Irish *plobaireacht* helps us out: it means to 'talk whilst crying': a tearful mixture of babbling and blubbering.

ploiter: to feel aimless and ineffectual.

The first meaning of dialect's 'ploiter', or 'plouter', was to dabble about in water or mud. By the 1820s it had come to mean dabbling of any sort, especially when applied to an aimless or ineffectual attempt to work. As one character put it rather damningly in a novel from the same century: 'Your mither has dune naething but plowter aboot the hoose.' Both senses, though, neatly convey the idea of wading through something sticky and getting precisely nowhere.

pluviophile: a lover of rainy days.

Some of us relish a heavy shower or 'thunderplump', while others just get wet. For the former, there is the word 'pluvio-phile', a rain-lover – as simple in its meaning as the pleasure enjoyed by those who thrive beneath the clouds.

poignant: evoking sadness and regret.

When it comes to tears, 'pungent' and 'poignant' are brothers in arms. They are both descendants of the Latin *pungere*, to 'prick'. In the Middle Ages, daggers or swords were 'poignant' because of their sharpness, while any particularly strong scent or sauce might also be described that way. 'Pungent', conversely, originally meant 'painful' or 'distressing', as well as something 'telling' or 'to the point'. As time went on, 'poignant' took on the emotional aspects of sharpness, while 'pungent' embraced strong tastes and smells. 'Compunction', meanwhile, is another relative, and is etymologically all about the hard stings, or 'pricks', of guilt.

polite: respectful and courteous.

'Politeness is one half good nature and the other half good lying,' concluded the US author Mary Wilson Little, implying that courtesy is as skin-deep as beauty. Her words fit neatly with the etymology of 'polite', which originally went hand in hand with 'polish'. Both descend from the Latin *politus*, a descriptor of something burnished or shiny. 'Polite' behaviour is therefore the smooth and polished kind. It may be nothing but veneering, Mary Wilson Little continued, 'but a veneered slab has the advantage of being without splinters'.

polrumptious: obstreperous; overconfident.

Its origins may be hazy, but 'polrumptious' does an admirable job of conveying a disputatious kind of arrogance. Its first part may be related to the 'poll' that was once a 'head' (there in 'tadpole' too, a 'toad-head'), while the second has the kick of the word 'rumpus'. In the end, the thumping sound of 'polrumptious' is really all you need.

poppycock: stuff and nonsense.

When it comes to bywords for 'rubbish' or 'nonsense', English has often looked to culinary metaphors. 'Balderdash' was once an unappetizing mixture of wine and ale, with the occasional addition of pigeon's dung and quicklime. One half of 'codswallop' is thought to be based on the dialect 'wallop', meaning cheap beer ('cod' seems to be a nod to Hiram Codd, who introduced stoppered bottles for fizzy drinks considered inferior to the stronger stuff). 'Baloney', meanwhile, is said to be a corruption of 'bologna' sausage. 'Poppycock' bucks this trend, although its story is equally unflavoursome. It comes from Dutch, where *poppekak* means simply 'doll's shit'.

praise: to express admiration.

The medieval word *pris*, borrowed from the conquering Normans, was clearly a very useful one. It produced not only 'praise', but also 'prize' and 'price'. The thread common to all of them is the idea of value, and of holding something in high esteem. The curious expression 'praise the pigs' is a probable mangling of the 'pyx', the vessel in which the host or consecrated bread of the sacrament is stored, making the phrase the equivalent of 'praise God' or 'God willing'.

pregret: to regret in advance.

'Pregret' is a recent blend that perfectly articulates modern impetuosity. It might sum up the act of sending an instant, ill-thought-out reply to a text or email, for example, or the making of a crazy online purchase at midnight – each comes with the momentary realization that you will regret what you are about to do, with the sure knowledge that you're going to do it anyway.

prejudice: a preconceived or unreasonable opinion or bias.

'Prejudice, a dirty word, and faith, a clean one, have something in common: they both begin where reason ends.' Harper Lee's 'dirty word' is all about prejudgement, and that is precisely its etymology, for the Latin *praejudicium* described a judgment reached before a trial – in other words, a preconceived opinion based not on facts but on presupposition and, more often than not, intolerance.

pride: satisfaction or pleasure in one's own achievements.

When *Pride and Prejudice*'s Mr Darcy makes his first appearance, 'haughty, reserved ... continually giving offence', the reader assumes, like Elizabeth Bennet, that he is the villain of the piece. Sure of his position, and brutally frank about the inferiority of Elizabeth's family and friends, Darcy is astonished to have his marriage proposal turned down flat. He is the embodiment of the 'pride' of Austen's story, at odds with the more modern sense of the term, which tends to express a positive sense of delight in someone or something.

Austen's reading of the word is in keeping with its earliest outings, which appeared in surnames of the twelfth and thirteenth centuries. Tofig Pruda, Orgar le Prude, Richard Prude, and Walterus le Prude were each 'proud' rather than 'prudish', despite their names' appearance, for 'prude' didn't arrive in English until the seventeenth century. The Prudes would not have been particularly popular, however, for this was a time when surnames were frequently selected to reflect an individual's personality, and the suggestions here would have been ones of haughtiness and arrogance rather than a sense of self-worth. Indeed 'pride' was the first of the seven deadly sins, for which the symbol was a lion – the collective noun 'a pride of lions' dates back to the depiction of the creature as the embodiment of the sin of pride in medieval bestiaries.

The ultimate source of 'proud' and 'pride' is the Latin

prodesse, meaning to 'be of value' – in this case, the value is all about oneself. Such value can be entirely positive, of course, as when we take pride in our own achievements or in those of our 'pride and joy', a stand-in for a cherished person or thing since the 1900s (and for the penis a couple of decades after that).

profanity: irreligious or irreverent behaviour or language.

Few football matches pass without profanity, and the latter is a word that fittingly belongs in the same family as 'fan' and **fanatical**. It is made up of Latin *pro*, 'before', and *fanum*, 'temple' – in other words, something 'profane' was beyond the boundaries of what was considered sacred.

The act of uttering profanities has long had a mixed press: for some, it is the linguistic crutch of the inarticulate, while Mark Twain spoke for many of us when he declared, 'Let us swear while we may, for in heaven it will not be allowed.'

pronoia: the belief that the world is conspiring to do good.

The converse of 'paranoia' is 'pronoia', the belief in the good-will of others, as well as in the power and pervasiveness of serendipity. All of which might sound idyllic, but 'pronoia', like its unwelcome sibling, is also classed as delusional, on the basis that this too is a form of conspiracy theory, albeit one expecting positive results.

'Pronoia' has had many advocates in literature, even before the term was coined in the 1980s. In J. D. Salinger's *Raise High the Roof Beam, Carpenters*, the protagonist Seymour Glass confides to his diary, 'Oh, God, if I'm anything by a clinical name, I'm a kind of paranoiac in reverse. I suspect people of plotting to make me happy.'

More loosely, 'pronoia' has been extended to encompass the narcissism of those who believe that the world revolves around them – as expounded by the actor John Cleese when speaking about one of recent history's most divisive characters, Donald Trump: 'A pronoid person is someone who thinks, without any basis in reality, that everybody likes them.'

psyched: excited and full of excitement.

Psyche was the beautiful mortal princess loved by Cupid, son of the goddess of love. Her name has become shorthand for the 'self' or 'soul': the literal meaning of 'psychology' is 'the story of the self'. In ancient myth, Psyche was represented as a butterfly, and it's possible that Sigmund Freud chose 'psychoanalysis' as a term for his field on the basis that 'analysis' comes from the Greek for 'loosen' or 'release' – the idea, then, would be of the liberation of the butterfly as a metaphor for the soul.

To 'psych' someone or something, back in the 1920s, was to analyse them psychologically, or alternatively to try to manipulate their minds. By the 1960s, we had begun to 'psych' people 'up' by giving them a pep talk (or psychedelics), leading to feelings of intense excitement known as being 'psyched' ('psyching' someone 'out', conversely, is tantamount to intimidating them.) It wasn't until the early 2000s that the word really found its feet in the slang of US teens, where it sat excitedly alongside 'stoked' and 'pumped' as a term of high approval.

purblind: short-sighted and foolish.

The 'pur' of 'purblind' is a stand-in for 'pure'. In its literal senses – of being, variously, 'blind in one eye', 'short-sighted', or 'completely blind' – and its figurative ones – of 'foolish' and 'undiscerning' – the idea is of thoroughly impaired vision.

quake-buttock: a coward.

A *Dictionarie in English and Latine for Children*, published in 1608, defines the rather clinical Latin *excors* with a far more expressive translation: 'a faint-hearted fellow, a quake-breech, without boldnes, spirit, wit; a sot'. A century later, 'quake-breech' was joined by a similar expression of cowardice: the 'quake-buttock', for which no further explanation is necessary.

quarrelsome: argumentative.

'Rixosous', 'brangling', 'stickling', 'barratous', 'wranglesome' – those who love a good argument are well served in the histor-ical thesaurus. 'Quarrelsome' is probably the most transparent of all of them, recorded from the sixteenth century and of course based on 'quarrel', from the Latin *queri*, to 'complain', which also gave us 'querulous', meaning 'fault-finding' or peevish. The sense of one-sided disgruntlement was echoed in the early twentieth century by the Dean of St Paul's, William Inge: 'It takes in reality only one to make a quarrel. It is useless for the sheep to pass resolutions in favour of vegetarianism, while the wolf remains of a different opinion.'

queem: satisfied and in harmony.

If you were 'well-queem' in the thirteenth century, you were highly satisfied with life. Something 'queem' was fitting, convenient, and therefore pleasing. This strange-looking word has relatives in both Germanic and Scandinavian languages: in each it carries the entirely positive attribute of something or someone that fits with ease, ensuring perfect harmony. 'Queem' had an extra edge, however: used as a verb in Old English, it meant to please and gratify a superior by slotting in with their desires. To queem the queen, therefore, would have been a high priority for any courtier.

quiddle: to waste time on unimportant things.

'Quiddling', from eighteenth-century New England, is more than just futzing about. While it involves the same time-wasting and pottering, it has the important extra dimension of attending to trivial tasks as a means of avoiding the important ones.

quidnunc: a gossip.

'The famine continues in the world of news, and quidnuncs are at their wits' end for want of something to feed them with.' This headline in the *Inverness Courier* from September 1845 suggests that the newspapers' silly season has been around for a while. The 'quidnunc' here is an older version of a 'stickybeak' – an overly inquisitive individual who sticks their nose into everything. Coined from the Latin for 'what now?', the term is ideal for anyone who eagerly chases down the latest gossip.

rage: violent, uncontrollable anger.

For those living in the Middle Ages, someone afflicted with 'rage' was probably 'raving' mad. At its heart is the Latin *rabere*, meaning to 'rave' through delirium or insanity and the source of 'rabid', now inextricable from the disease rabies, but originally attached to violence as a result of a disturbed mind. The same sense of frenzy continues to pervade 'rage', whether it's of the berserk, road, air, or trolley variety.

ranço [Brazilian Portuguese: ruhn-so]: an irrational dislike.

We surely all recognize the experience of taking an instinctive dislike towards someone without being able to explain why. We can't quite pinpoint it, and may even try to overcome it, but the aversion somehow persists. In the slang of Brazilian Portuguese, this is *pegar ranço*, to 'feel repugnance'. *Ranço* consequently fits nicely for all those occasions when you just don't hit it off.

rapport: a connection; an understanding.

A 'rapport' is at the heart of what we look for in human relationships. It is a mutual understanding, a harmonious accord. A relative of 'report', it arrived via the French *rapporter*, meaning to 'bring' or 'carry' back – in this case, the bringing back is of a mutual and sympathetic connection.

rapture: intense joy.

There is a thin line between 'rapture' and 'capture', for behind both is the idea of seizing something. Both words are descended from Latin words meaning to 'take' or 'carry off' – *rapere* and *capere* respectively. In the case of 'rapture', the seizing is entirely one of joy and delight – a transporting to a place of elation. 'The Rapture' is also a theological position held by some Christians which professes that at the end of time all Christian believers will be 'snatched away' or 'seized' into the clouds to meet the Lord.

rational: clear-thinking and logical.

A *ratio*, in Latin, was a 'reckoning' – a calculation based on mathematical reasoning. A rational person is just as measured. While 'rational' kept its affinity to *ratio* in its spelling, the words 'reason' and 'reasonable', which are very much part of the same family, came to us with a French twist.

Human rationality has long attracted varying schools of thought. Some see us as a fundamentally rational species, albeit with the capacity to err and exercise bad judgement. Others interpret all human decisions as being informed by instinct and impulse rather than reasoning, with any rationalization happening after the event – on Shakespeare's stage, reason is regularly trumped by emotion.

The eighteenth-century philosopher David Hume reacted against the prevailing view that passions should be moderated by reason: 'Reason is, and ought only to be, the slave of the passions, and can never pretend to any other office than to serve and obey them.' This tension has been explored by many others: Friedrich Nietzsche put it in unusually simple terms when he stated, 'One ought to hold on to one's heart; for if one lets it go, one soon loses control of the head too.'

rebellious: resistant to authority or convention.

At the heart of 'rebellion' is war – in this case the Latin *bellum*. To be or feel 'rebellious' is to resist authority or control by rising up against it, but rebellion is considered less respectable than either war or revolution. Less respectable again is a 'revolt', which comes from the Latin *revolvere*, to 'roll back'. The 1381 Rebellion of Wat Tyler and his peasant armies forced Richard II to issue edicts abolishing serfdom, and came very close to overturning the oppressive aristocratic order 500 years before the storming of the Bastille. Had they won, we might now be reading about Wat Tyler's Revolution. When they lost, their rebellion was rapidly downgraded to the title of 'Peasants' Revolt'. It's no coincidence that 'revolting' has since come to mean 'disgusting and repulsive'. History is, after all, written by the victors.

reckful: full of consideration.

'Reck' is so close to 'wreck' that it's hard to imagine it has any positive associations at all. No wonder 'reckless' – 'unheeding of consequences' – is its only survivor in modern English. Yet 'reck' is part of a large Germanic family united by the theme of care and heed. To 'reck' was to be full of concern and diligence; yet even in its earliest uses in English it was more often than not accompanied by 'nought', 'not', 'little', or 'not much'. Which probably explains why 'reckful' – 'full of care and consideration' – never really stood a chance.

recognition: the feeling that someone or something has been encountered before.

'Recognizing' is all about 'knowing again', thanks to the Latin *recognoscere*. But for the Romans this meant not just being familiar with something already felt or seen; it was also to examine or acknowledge it. It was in a legal context that 'recognize' first entered English in the fourteenth century, where it was all about accepting the validity of a claim or title. We retain that early sense when we 'give recognition' to someone as a way of honouring them formally, and when we 'recognize' a fact by acknowledging it. 'It's a helluva start', mused the comedy pioneer Lucille Ball, 'being able to recognize what makes you happy.'

redamancy: the act of loving back.

'Redamancy' is a rarity in the lexicon of love in that it has reciprocity at its heart. It is from the Latin *redamare*, in which is hidden *amare*, to 'love'. The word featured in one of the earliest English dictionaries, Thomas Blount's *Glossographia* (1656), where it is described as 'a loving of him, or her, that loves us; a loving again, a mutual loving' – in other words, the very best kind.

redeless: ill-advised.

The tenth-century king Æthelred was notoriously indecisive. His reign saw repeated attacks by Danish invaders, leading him to offer lavish payments in the form of Danegeld in an attempt to buy them off. Such a move may have been expedient, but it also mocked the heroic tradition of the Anglo-Saxons, and later historians would saddle the king with the epithet 'The Unready'.

But 'unready' here does not mean 'ill-prepared'; rather it draws on the Old English *rede*, meaning 'counsel' – Æthelred was viewed as ill-advised (if advised at all) and foolish. As such, the moniker is an oxymoron, for Æthelred's first name, typical of other compound names in the royal House of Wessex such as Æthelwulf ('noble-wolf'), Ælfred ('elf-counsel'), and Eadweard ('rich-protector'), means 'noble counsel'. Æthelred the Unready therefore translates as 'noble counsel the no counsel'.

For the rest of the Anglo-Saxon population, 'redeless' was a choice insult meaning 'heedless; foolish; perplexed' and generally clueless. The Redes were even considered to be a class of people impoverished by their ignorance, in need of both 'rede-craft', logic or reasoning, and a 'rede-purse', a set of good ideas.

regret: sorrow over something you can't repair.

'Regrets, I've had a few,' in the immortal words of Frank Sinatra. Haven't we all? *Regreter*, in Old French, was to 'bewail the dead'. Weeping in lament connects it with similar words in different languages – the Old English *gnætan*, to 'weep', for example, which is matched in Old Norse, the language of the Vikings, by *grata*, to 'groan'. Such physical grieving soon gave way to the mental kind, a remorse or repentance that comes from reflection upon past events and actions, when we did it our way.

rejection: a dismissal or spurning.

Anyone who has suffered rejection – which means all of us – will appreciate the etymology of the word. It comes from the Latin *rejectus*, meaning 'thrown back'. As the disgraced cyclist Lance Armstrong said, 'a boo is a lot louder than a cheer.'

relish: to anticipate with pleasure.

'What one relishes, nourishes,' mused Benjamin Franklin. For the French-speakers of the Middle Ages, a *reles* was an aftertaste. It is this that eventually morphed into the English 'relish'. From an aftertaste it moved to the smack of something good, which we can in turn relish or savour. The 'relish' that is the condiment arrived in the late eighteenth century; its name suggesting all the scrumptious enjoyment it intends to deliver.

remorse: deep regret or guilt.

Like 'sarcasm', which rests on the image of something caustic 'eating away' at the victim, 'remorse' is a grisly word. At its heart is the Latin *mordere*, to 'bite' or 'sting'. The scientific term 'premorse' describes something that has been truncated, as though it has had a piece of itself bitten off. 'Remorse' – a profound regret or guilt – is in turn something that 'bites back' or gnaws away at you. The emotion tends to be attached to something morally wrong, although its use has extended to encompass regret over less 'sinful' actions, such as buying an expensive car and experiencing 'buyer's remorse' straight after. Nonetheless, the words accompanying 'remorse' over the last 500 years underscore its weightiness, from 'remorse-stricken' and 'remorse-stung' to, in an etymological double whammy, 'remorse-bitten'.

requited: returned; repaid.

We know 'requited' largely through its lonely partner. 'Unrequited' love has been the heartbeat of songs and poetry for centuries; perhaps it's time to bring back its lost positive, one that meant simply 'returned'. Then again, author of *Peter Pan* J. M. Barrie decided that 'even love unreturned has its rainbow.'

resentment: indignation at having been treated unfairly.

'Resentment', wrote Carrie Fisher, 'is like drinking a poison and then waiting for the other person to die.' The term is relatively new to the English lexicon, crossing over from the older 'resent' in the seventeenth century. The root of both is the French *ressentiment*, 'memory of an injury'. Alcoholics Anonymous cites resentment as one of the greatest threats to an alcoholic. Several of their Twelve Steps involve identifying and dealing with the emotion as part of the path towards recovery, including acknowledging one's own role in resentment and praying for it to be taken away.

The seventeenth-century lexicographer John Florio defined the word in his magnum opus, *Queen Anna's New World of Words*, as 'a remembrance or effect of some wrong received, or revenge for it'. Revenge was in fact central to resentment, and the term articulated far more anger than it does in modern times, placing it among the most widely used terms in the lexicon of furious feelings. Friedrich Nietzsche believed that 'nothing on earth consumes a man more quickly than the passion of resentment.' Today, poison aside, the emphasis is more on silent begrudgement than the desire for retribution or oblivion.

resigned: accepting of something unwanted.

If you are 'resigned' to a situation, you have essentially given up fighting it. The Latin *resignare* meant to 'annul', 'cancel', or 'give back' – all based on the metaphor of reversing a signature or breaking a seal, thereby taking back an approval once given. Put differently, when you resign from something, you renounce control and let go.

resilient: able to spring back into shape.

'Resilience' is about bouncing back, a fact neatly reflected in its etymology, the Latin *salire*, meaning to 'leap'. This makes it part of an unlikely family, all involving jumping of some kind. 'Desultory', for example, meaning 'lacking a plan or purpose', was built upon *desultor*, 'one who leaps down', used of a Roman acrobat and entertainer who would amaze spectators by leaping from one galloping horse to another. To be 'desultory', by extension, is to be rather unmethodical. 'Salacious' is another relative, first referring to male animals 'jumping up' to mate. Finally, 'salient' was originally used in English to describe jumping animals in heraldry; such 'jumping' was later applied to the beating pulse of an embryo as a symbol of the essence of life – the 'salient point' of any argument today lies at its very heart.

resipiscence: a return to a better frame of mind.

The sound of the three letters at the heart of 'resipiscence', a rare word from the seventeenth century, might suggest that its inspiration is invariably alcohol. And yet the term's range was originally both broader and loftier, embracing both 'coming to one's senses' and 'returning to a more acceptable opinion'. Its journey began with 'repentance', which was the meaning of the Latin *resipiscentia* (itself from *re-*, 'again', and *sapere*, to 'be wise'), and the earliest outings of 'resipiscence' focused on a recognition of one's past misdeeds or errors. Today's potential applications are vast, however, suggesting long baths and sossing on the sofa at the end of a hard week – not forgetting the arrival of 'quafftide' and a restorative glass or two.

resistentialism: the malice of inanimate objects.

'Resistentialism' is the belief that inanimate objects are out to get you – the mean mischief that prompts our toast to land butter-side down, sharp edges of furniture to cut into us, and car keys to bury themselves in soft furnishings the moment we're about to exit the house.

This highly useful term, a pun on 'existentialism' in which *res* means 'thing', was coined in the 1940s by the humorist Paul Jennings with the slogan *Les choses sont contre nous*, 'Things are against us.' Rather than *deus ex machina* ('god from the machine': the person or thing that arrives in the nick of time to solve a difficulty, a nod to the ancient Greek theatrical device in which actors playing gods swoop down onto the stage, suspended by a crane), this is *malitia ex machina*, 'malice out of the machine', and most of us have the bruises or buttery floor to prove it.

respair: a recovery from despair.

'Respair' is a word that feels so entirely necessary to modern times that its disappearance is quite perplexing. The word is, of course, the antithesis of 'despair', in which *spair* is a descendant, via French, of the Latin *sperare*, to 'hope'. The *Oxford English Dictionary*'s definition is beautiful in its simplicity: 'fresh hope, or a recovery from despair'. Gratifyingly, 'respair' is also a verb, when we long for better days.

respect: deep admiration; due regard.

There are few emotional anthems more memorable than that delivered by the Queen of Soul, Aretha Franklin, whose 'R-E-S-P-E-C-T' of 1967 became a groundbreaking signature song for female empowerment. Franklin had taken the lyrics of Otis Redding's original and flipped its narrative, so that this time it was a woman demanding respect from a man.

Having 'respect' for someone was originally all about turning your gaze upon them. For *specere*, in Latin, was to 'look', the mother of 'spectacle', 'spectator', and 'expect' (to 'look out for'). In the case of 'respect', the idea is of 'looking back', of taking note and giving something or someone due regard. It can be a tall order sometimes, as a character in J. D. Salinger's *Franny and Zooey* observes: 'I'm sick of just liking people. I wish to God I could meet somebody I could respect.'

retrouvailles [French: RUH-troov-ayee]: the joy of reuniting with someone after a long time apart.

The happiness of a reunion after an extended period of absence is something many of us have felt acutely in recent times. English offers just a handful of bland synonyms for the instance of meeting someone dear after a separation – 'ralliance', 'rejoining' among them– but from French there is the glorious *retrouvailles*: literally, 'refindings'.

revenge: retribution for wrongdoing; returning a harm.

'Revenge' is, most famously and according to a saying from the nineteenth century, 'a dish best served cold'. Whichever temperature you choose, the source of the word is simple enough: the Latin *vindicare*, to 'claim' or 'avenge', which had quite a journey before arriving in English, passing first through Portuguese, Spanish, Italian, and French.

'Revenge' is usually defined as a harmful response to a grievance. The ancient passions that are generally translated as 'anger' in modern English, such as the Greek *orgē* and the Latin *ira*, were extreme states in which the desire for vengeance featured prominently. Francis Bacon saw the emotion as a form of 'wild justice' that was legally and morally indefensible. And yet the thirst for revenge and the actions it precipitates were once enshrined in law. In Old English, the word 'murder' denoted *secret* murder, which alone was regarded as a crime; an open homicide was a private wrong that called either for payment of a compensatory *wer-gild*, 'man price', or for blood revenge. The twin concerns of family and vengeance remained pillars of law and justice for centuries. In the Elizabethan and Jacobean periods, dramas in which vengeance was a dominating motivation for their characters, were known as 'revenge tragedies', reaching a climax in Shakespeare's *Hamlet* and its conclusive line, 'And so he goes to heaven / And so am I revenged.'

reverence: deep respect.

The Latin *revereri* meant to 'stand in awe of'. Emerging in English in the early fourteenth century, 'reverence' was as much about veneration for the sacred as it was about deference to status or position. Used to address a member of the clergy, 'reverend' means 'person to be revered'.

revulsion: repugnance or abhorrence.

'Revulsion' is really all about being 'pulled back' – usually by recoiling from something repulsive. It is built upon the Latin *revulsio*, a 'plucking away'. In sixteenth-century medicine, revulsion was the process of withdrawing **humours** – black or yellow bile, phlegm, or blood – in the attempt to cure or correct disease. This idea of drawing away was gradually extended to flinching in the face of something abhorrent.

ridicule: mockery or scorn.

'"Don't be ridiculous, please." The most insulting words in the world!' It's hard to disagree with the musings of L. M. Montgomery's Anne of Green Gables. But 'ridiculous' is one thing, and 'ridicule' another entirely. Subject someone to ridicule and you are openly mocking them. The Latin *ridere*, to 'laugh', gave us 'risible', 'ridicule', and 'ridiculous', all suggesting an object of derision or amusement at another's expense (otherwise known through the centuries as a **scoffing stock**, a 'japing-stick', and a 'make-mirth'). The state of being 'ridiculous' has softened a touch, however. It is now a throwaway dismissal of anything foolish or unreasonable – or, as Anne Shirley herself might have put it, decidedly 'cockamamie'.

rire dans sa barbe [French: re-uh don sa barbe]: to chuckle to oneself.

'Checkling', 'shuckling', 'keckling' – English has a fair few words for the suppressed laughter generally known as 'chuckling'. It doesn't, however, have a word for a *secret* chuckle, one you keep entirely to yourself. French can help us out with *rire dans sa barbe*, literally to 'laugh into one's beard', especially at a memory of something funny. Rather than being snide, it is an entirely private moment of enjoyment.

rivalry: competitiveness.

Muhammad Ali and Joe Frazier, Ernest Hemingway and William Faulkner, Marvel and DC, Al Capone and Bugs Moran – history is peppered with beefs and epic rivalries. The description of such feuds – friendly or otherwise – hides a surprisingly literal story. Water has always been a precious commodity, a truth reflected in the word 'rival', for it shares the same source as 'river'. A 'rival' was originally someone with whom you shared your water supply and competed to 'derive' as much of this essential asset as possible. Recorded in English from the late sixteenth century, 'rival' goes back to Latin *rivalis*, which originally meant 'a person living on the opposite bank, using the same stream'.

road rage: violent anger induced in one driver by another.

In 1987, a year before 'road rage' was first recorded in a splash headline in Florida's *Orlando Sentinel* about a fatal highway shooting, a warning about 'roid rage' was attracting attention in a book about drug abuse in sport. The *Oxford English Dictionary* suggests that the name for the sudden anger we display while driving may have been a riff on the heightened aggression that comes from the overuse of anabolic steroids by bodybuilders. Whatever its beginnings, the meaning of 'road rage' is crystal clear, and most of us have experienced it, because the person going faster than us will always be a 'maniac', and the one driving more slowly, an 'idiot'. This is an emotion felt just as strongly by cyclists towards drivers, and vice versa. Take this joke: a strip of tarmac goes into the pub and orders a pint. After serving him, the barman asks if he wants to join the other strip of tarmac in the corner. The strip of tarmac shakes his head violently. 'I'm not going near him,' it says. 'He's a cyclepath!'

romantic: characterized by feelings of love.

The story of 'romance' began in the fifth century, when the Roman Empire was falling and the Gauls – inhabiting a region encompassing modern-day France as well as parts of Italy, Germany, and Belgium – spoke a language derived from Latin that they knew as *Romanicus*, 'of the Romans'. Although the Gauls were eventually conquered, *Romanicus*, and the French derivative *Romanz*, remained very much alive. But the language this described was not formal Latin itself, but rather the spoken dialects of Old French and Old Occitan descended from it. Poems and stories written in these 'Romance languages' were known as *romans* (still the French term for 'novels'), and their focus was popularly upon tales of gallant knights and the chivalrous pursuit of their lady loves. It is from this winding journey that 'romantic' appeared as a description of anything concerning heroic adventures of love. As for 'romance', it was the Victorians who gave us our modern senses of idealized, sentimental affection, as well as a love affair itself. To this day, the French are still said to be the most romantic of all – according to Stephen King, 'French is the language that turns dirt into romance.'

rose-tinted spectacles: an idealistic view of things.

The first thing to be described as 'rose-tinted' was Modesty (with a capital 'M'), while it was 'thoughts' that were the first to be 'rose-coloured'. Both are recorded from the 1780s, and both describe a cheerful optimism or tendency to see things in the best possible light. The Queen of Pink and author of some 723 romances, Dame Barbara Cartland, summed up the filter of rose-tinted spectacles best when she insisted: 'Who on earth wants to read about the cockroaches in the kitchen? People want romance and happy endings; it brings them comfort.' (Cartland bracingly insisted that a rosy pink was the most flattering colour for all women to wear, as well as to see life through. Beige or brown, she mused, simply made them 'look like a baked potato'.) Cartland was also the step-grandmother of Princess Diana, an enthusiastic teenage reader of her books. According to Tina Brown's biography of the Princess, Cartland once remarked, 'The only books Diana ever read were mine, and they weren't awfully good for her.'

rudesby: one who is consistently ill-mannered and badly behaved.

The suffix *-by* is simple enough, for it is found in many Scandinavian place names, where it means a place of habitation. But it is its use in surnames that seems to have gifted the greatest punning potential, and in the middle of the sixteenth century several jokey formulations emerged with the implication that those who bore such names amply fulfilled the characteristics they described – a medieval medley of what linguists know as nominative determinism. Shakespeare introduced us to the notion of a 'Rudesby' for someone unruly and argumentative, while the *Oxford English Dictionary* also records 'Idlesby', 'Lewdsby', 'Sneaksby', and 'Sureby' (who was presumably very smug). The potential, of course, is endless.

ruthful: to be full of compassion.

'Ruthful' is the long-lost cousin not only of 'ruthless', but also of 'rue' – to regret something and wish it undone. Each came from the Viking word-hoard for 'pity' and 'sorrow'. If you have 'ruth', however, you are unlikely to 'rue', for it means 'compassion'. The name 'Ruth' comes from Hebrew and means 'compassionate friend', a quality amply borne out in the Book of Ruth, written in Hebrew in the sixth–fourth centuries BC. Here Ruth commits to Jahweh, the God of the Israelites, and tells Naomi, her Israelite mother-in-law:

> Where you go I will go, and where you stay I will stay. Your people will be my people and your God my God. Where you die I will die, and there I will be buried. May the Lord deal with me, be it ever so severely, if even death separates you and me.

sad: unhappy or sorrowful; uncool.

To be sad is to be sated with life – at least for a while. It is fitting, then, that 'sad', 'sated', and 'satiated' are all relatives of the Latin *satis*, meaning 'enough'. When *sæd* came into Old English it meant both 'weary' and 'sorrowful', as well as being a marker of no appetite – a combination found in our looser expression 'fed up', which suggests the image of being stuffed, heavy, and over-full. For a while, 'sad' could also describe someone steadfast and firm, but by the fourteenth century its use for feelings of mournfulness, sorrow, or heavy-heartedness had properly bedded in. It eventually displaced the Old English word *unrot*, meaning 'distressed' or 'displeased'.

Modern usage has added some new meanings, however: 'sad' can be a slur against someone considered pathetic or desperately uncool, who then becomes a 'saddo'. Slang, meanwhile, has performed a traditional flip and made something 'sad' suddenly very good indeed.

sanguine: optimistic and hopeful.

> A sanguine temper, though for ever expecting more good than occurs, does not always pay for its hopes by any proportionate depression. It soon flies over the present failure, and begins to hope again.

Jane Austen's description of 'sanguinity' in her novel *Emma* is as good a definition as you'll find. This emotional state is one of positivity and optimism, and of 'hoping again', especially in the face of adversity.

Originally, 'sanguinity', from the Latin *sanguineus*, was all about blood. In the medical theory of humorism, it belonged to one of the four 'complexions' (a word which literally means 'entwined together'), and was believed to be characterized by the predominance of blood over the other three humours. The physical sign of a sanguine person was a ruddy countenance, in this case not the result of an alcoholically induced 'grogblossom' or two, but rather a reflection of courage, hope, or even amorousness.

The effects of a large quantity of blood were not always judged to be positive. For some it was the source of irresponsible mirth, or of optimism that was both superficial and blind to reality. For most of us today, however, Austen's definition still holds firm – a sanguine person will always look to **respair**, and their mind does indeed fly over any present setback to look for hope again.

sapiophile: one who is attracted to intelligent people.

A recent coinage based on the Latin *sapiens*, 'wise', and Greek *philos*, 'loving', 'sapiophile' neatly fits the bill for those whose romantic attachment to others is based largely on intelligence. It reflects the modern embrace of the geek after centuries of rejecting those considered too nerdy to be attractive. And if you wanted to make things a little more physical, 'sapiosexual' is the word you need.

sarcasm: contemptuous irony.

'Sarcasm' is a word that openly bares its teeth. It comes from the Greek *sarkazein*, to 'tear flesh', referring to the caustic nature of a sarcastic remark that might 'sear' the skin of its recipient. The word is a sibling of 'sarcophagus', the stone coffins believed to be 'flesh-eating' thanks to the properties of the limestone once used, which would rapidly decompose the bodies lying within.

sardonic: grimly mocking or cynical.

It was Homer, the Greek epic poet, who first used the word *sardanios* to describe bitter, scornful laughter. Later Greeks and Romans decided the word must have been a miswriting of *sardonios*, 'Sardinian', and accordingly the myth arose that sardonic behaviour was caused by 'the Sardinian plant', or *herba Sardonia*. If ingested, the plant was believed to cause extreme facial convulsions that resembled hideous laughter, invariably followed by death. The ghosts of those deadly convulsions remain in the lip-curling sneer of the sardonic smile. In medical terms, a *risus sardonicus* is the fixed, uncontrollable grin of those afflicted by tetanus.

satisfied: content and fulfilled.

To be 'satisfied', from the Latin *satis*, 'enough', is to have your desires met and wishes fulfilled. Perhaps not all of them, though, for 'satisfactory', in today's hyperbolic world, is often a begrudging judgement that something is 'good enough'.

saturnine: gloomy in outlook.

Saturday, the happiest day of the week, belongs to the Roman god Saturn. But for the ancients, the planet named after him was associated not with joy but with heaviness and specifically with lead, thanks to its cold temperatures and slow orbit around the Sun. The first metal to be extracted from ores some 9,000 years ago, and the 'basest' of the traditional seven metals, lead has been put to a wide range of uses, from coffins to bullets, and from car batteries to the pewter goblets routinely quaffed from in medieval taverns. The metal's toxicity, however, has also left its mark, and 'saturnism' was one of the first industrial diseases to be formally recognized. It owes its name to symptoms of depression and sluggishness associated with 'saturnine' humour, a characteristic of those born under the influence of Saturn. Anyone described as 'saturnine' today is deemed to have a thoroughly gloomy take on life.

saudade [Galician-Portuguese: sow-dah-dji]: a bitter-sweet yearning.

To experience *saudade* is to feel longing for a past that may never have existed, or for an alternative present that may never materialize. In his study of Portugal at a complex period in the country's history – between the 1910 revolution and the coup d'état in 1926 – Aubrey Bell described *saudade* as an 'indolent dreaming wistfulness'.

The emotion's roots may lie in the Latin *solitas*, 'loneliness' or 'solitude', for it can express a deep nostalgia for what is lost, combined with the knowledge that it may never be had again. It is both sadness and desire. *Saudade* can even express a longing for longing itself, and is often captured in *fado*, a Portuguese genre of music infused with melancholy and a sense of loss.

The myriad interpretations of *saudade*, and the slipperiness of its definition, are perhaps highly suited to a word conveying a longing that is as hazy as it is powerful. *See also* **Sehnsucht**.

scapegoat: one blamed for the mistakes of others.

Anyone bearing a 'hangdog' expression may not realize that the term was born at a time when courts would regularly try and execute animals blamed for 'criminal' behaviour – perhaps the theft of some food, or the biting of a passer-by. They were not the first: the Normans would burn cockerels they accused of witchcraft, while St Bernard even excommunicated a swarm of flies that provoked him. These are but a handful of scapegoats in history, creatures to whom others have assigned guilt for wrongdoings they haven't committed.

The idea of the 'scapegoat' was, of course, inspired by a different animal altogether, as told in the biblical Book of Leviticus, in which God instructs Moses to ask the Jewish people to take two goats and cast lots to determine their fate. The sins of the people were laid upon one before it was pushed out into the wilderness, while the other goat was sacrificed. The animal that was banished was thus the 'escapegoat' – allowed to survive but bearing the full weight of sin on its back.

scaramouch: a boastful but cowardly person.

The introduction to the 'scaramouch' came for many of us via the airwaves, thanks to Queen and their 'Bohemian Rhapsody', in which we hear Scaramouch being invited to 'do the fandango'. Scaramuccia, a stock figure in the Italian *commedia dell'arte* whose name means 'skirmish', was a cowardly and foolish servant who was forever getting into tricky situations from which he would triumphantly extricate himself, always at other people's expense. As for Queen's Scaramouch, some believe that the fandango in question – a lively Spanish dance – is more precisely the 'hemp fandango', a grisly euphemism for hanging.

sceptical: inclined to doubt accepted opinions.

For the Greeks, *skepsis* meant both 'doubt' and 'investigation', while to be *skeptikos* was to be thoughtful. The ancient Sceptics subscribed to a school of philosophy that denied the possibility of total knowledge. Its followers described themselves as investigators, and as *ephektikoi*, 'those who suspend'. But the Sceptics didn't just suspend disbelief while investigating; for them doubt was omnipresent, denying the possibility of total knowledge of a particular sphere. In this they were vigorously opposed to stoicism, which taught that virtue, the highest good, is based upon total knowledge. By contrast, a Sceptic's life was devoted to inquiry – it was, in other words, a life without belief.

At the forefront of the Sceptic movement was Pyrrho, a poor painter and one of a group of philosophers said to have accompanied Alexander the Great to India. In the course of the expedition Pyrrho encountered some *Gymnosophistai*, or 'naked wise men', a meeting that was later to help him cement his philosophy and attract many followers. Most of Pyrrho's beliefs have been reconstructed from the accounts of others, for he wrote nothing himself. There are many anecdotes too, referring for example to the fact that he always kept the same demeanour no matter what, and that if anyone left him in the middle of a discourse he would carry on regardless. Another describes how he once underwent torturous surgery without flinching. Far from doing any of these for attention, Pyrrho was apparently unmotivated by the desire for approval, or by the fear of disapproval. He was greatly revered by his disciples as well as, it seems, by the state, who even suspended taxation for anyone calling themselves a Sceptic.

Today's sceptics, with a small 's' and a British 'c', still question the validity of something that is purported to be fact, without the broad sweep that existed in ancient times. Nonetheless, they continue to challenge life's **ipsedixits**.

Schadenfreude [German: sha-duhn-froy-duh]: pleasure in another's pain.

If you ask someone for the German word with which they are most familiar, they are likely to say *Schadenfreude*. Its usefulness is largely built on the fact that English has no real equivalent.

Schadenfreude entered English in the late nineteenth century. A compound of *Schaden*, 'harm', and *Freude*, 'joy', it is defined in the *Oxford English Dictionary* as 'the malicious enjoyment of the misfortunes of others' – strong stuff, more reminiscent of sadism than today's looser applications, such as witnessing the comeuppance of an obsequious colleague or the injury record of a rival football team. Nonetheless, the feeling it describes is clearly a universal and ancient one: the Greeks knew it as *epichairekakia*, 'rejoicing over disgrace', and the Romans as *malevolentia*, the root of our 'malevolence'. The French know all about the *joie maligne*, and the Russians about *zloradstvo*.

It is not an emotion to be proud of, and yet it is strangely enjoyable for all that. As a Japanese saying has it: *tanin no fukou wa mitsu no aji* – 'the misfortune of others is sweet like honey.'

schmaltzy: excessively sentimental.

Schmaltz is a basic tenet of Jewish culture. A staple of kosher food, you might use it instead of butter in the form of chicken or goose fat – a use that dates back to the eighteenth century. To describe something or someone as 'schmaltzy', therefore, is to imply that they exhibit so much sentimentality that they are positively oozing with it. And a 'schmaltzfest' is an event so full of unrestrained emotion that you're either all in, or definitely out.

scoffing stock: an object of laughter.

No one wants to be scoffed at, particularly while locked in the stocks and exposed to the public's ridicule and tomato-throwing. This is the metaphor for a 'scoffing stock', the more expressive relative of a 'laughing stock', which has described an object of derision since the 1500s.

scorn: mockery or derision.

> I know I have the body of a weak and feeble woman; but I have the heart and stomach of a king, and of a king of England too; and think foul scorn that Parma or Spain, or any prince of Europe, should dare to invade the borders of my realm.

Elizabeth I's speech to her troops on 9 August 1588 demonstrates one of the most popular companions to scorn at the time: 'foul'. To 'think foul scorn' upon someone was to revile them utterly. Elizabeth's rallying cry contributed to the defeat of the Armada and a victory for her nation's self-confidence.

The source of 'scorn' is a Germanic word meaning 'mockery' or 'sport', suggesting that humiliation was always at its heart. It may also have been influenced by the Old French *ecorner*, meaning to 'deprive of horns', which brings the emphasis round to one of dishonouring the recipient.

The English writer William Congreve, in his play *The Mourning Bride*, gave the emotion a whole new level in the seventeenth century with the words, 'Heaven has no rage, like love to hatred turned,/Nor hell a fury, like a woman scorned.' The observation became enshrined in proverbial law as 'Hell hath no fury like a woman scorned.'

scrouge: to crowd out or sit too close.

There is 'manspreading', and there is 'scrouging'. While the former is clearly gender-specific, sitting alongside 'mansplaining' and 'hepeating' (when a man repeats what a woman has said and takes all the credit), 'scrouging' is multi-purpose. A possible blend of 'screw', 'bruise', and 'gouge', it is the eighteenth-century version of encroaching upon someone's personal space by sitting or standing too close.

scrupulous: careful, thorough, and attentive to detail.

If you have ever stepped barefoot onto a pebble beach and walked gingerly across it, you will appreciate the metaphor behind 'scrupulous', which comes from the Latin for a 'small sharp stone' and which as a result became a byword for anxiety. To be 'scrupulous' is to be as 'careful and painstaking', as if you are walking with a sharp pebble in your shoe. To be 'unscrupulous', meanwhile, is to ride roughshod over everything with no care or attention at all.

seemly: conforming to good taste.

'Of a pleasing or goodly appearance, fair, well-formed, handsome, "proper"': thus the description in the *Oxford English Dictionary* of all that is required to be 'seemly'. Of course, it survives mainly in its opposite form, 'unseemly', depriving us of opportunities to praise someone because they are just right, as in this description in the *Pall Mall Magazine* of 1900: 'He was a man of seemly outward parts.' Perhaps his inner parts were not quite so proper.

seen: 'clocked'.

For centuries, the word 'seen' was a long way from registering an emotion. It meant simply 'perceived with the eyes' or 'viewed', senses which it has kept to this day. In the past decade, however, the word has taken on a new mantle, so that being 'seen' is tantamount to being stripped back so far that people know what's *really* going on. It might be as flimsy as a GIF of a yawning cat that reflects your own soporific state, but when you're seen, you immediately recognize that someone is feeling exactly the same way as you.

Sehnsucht [German: zehn-zoocht]: a wistful longing.

To experience *Sehnsucht* is to feel a longing for something intangible. Some psychologists use the word to represent thoughts and feelings that are unfinished or imperfect, paired with a yearning for ideal alternative experiences. Above all, *Sehnsucht* is 'wisftfulness' – the desire for something that you can't quite contain in your hands or head, but that draws you nonetheless. *See also* **saudade**.

seijaku [Japanese: say-ya-ku]: tranquillity amidst chaos.

The concept of *seijaku* is surely one to aspire to. It is a state found most frequently in nature, inspiring a calm equanimity amidst the cacophony of modern life, and offering the opportunity for serenity in the midst of chaos.

selcouth: strange; wondrous.

Something 'selcouth' is 'strange and marvellous', and is probably being viewed for the first time. Based on the Old English *sel*, 'seldom', and *cup*, 'familiar', it is an ideal word for the awe and wonder we might feel when we witness something truly new. Anyone uttering 'me thinks selcouth' in the thirteenth century, meanwhile, would simply be saying 'I wonder'. The field of physics has taken the word one step further, however: here, 'selcouth' sits right at the theoretical horizon, describing a hypothetical form of matter.

sense: meaning, intelligibility; the faculties of feeling.

The word 'sense' has, fittingly, dozens of senses listed in the dictionary. Some of them seem directly opposed to each other: in a lexical definition, for example, a word's 'senses' are its meanings or usages – things to be grasped by the intellect. Yet the bodily 'senses' are the faculties of sight, hearing, smell, taste, and touch – those that are 'felt' rather than 'thought'. The psychiatrist Fritz Perls demonstrated the difference more pithily when he wrote, 'Lose the mind, and come to your senses.' The link between these apparently contradictory uses is that of natural understanding and consciousness: they come together in our notion of 'common sense', an instinctive intelligence innate to all.

The story of 'sense' began with an ancient word meaning variously to 'go', 'have in mind', or 'perceive'. It is echoed in the French *sentir*, which manages to deliver the whole sensory and emotional package in combining the senses of smell, touch, thinking, and feeling.

sensibility: the quality of sensitivity.

In 1771, Henry Mackenzie's novel *The Man of Feeling* delivered what the historian of emotions Thomas Dixon describes as 'the most famously tear-soaked text ... in all of English literature'. That is quite a claim for a period in which sentimental novels dominated the literary scene, from Fanny Burney's *Harcourt* to Samuel Richardson's *Clarissa*. The simultaneous act of weeping and reading was encouraged – in fact, lachrymal responses were sought in every area of creativity during this period, including paintings, which often depicted characters in high states of emotion in order to inspire the same in their beholders. Participating in the 'cult of sensibility' became a near-requirement of cultured ladies and gentlemen, who sought to experience the world as much through the senses as through intellect.

By the time Jane Austen wrote *Sense and Sensibility*, the competing impulses of reason and emotions were hotly vying for attention. 'Sensibility' was not, in her time, the quality of being 'sensible' or rational, but rather the power of sensation.

As for Mackenzie's *The Man of Feeling*, the story is said to have moved the poet Robert Burns so much that he carried a copy everywhere until it fell to pieces. Such an emotional reception was not to last – Thomas Dixon notes that a Victorian edition of the novel included a satirical 'Index to Tears (Chokings, etc., not counted)', inviting readers to laugh rather than cry. Sensibility had been trumped by sense, even if the journeys of both were far from complete.

sensual: gratification of the senses, especially through sexual pleasure.

'Sensual' and 'sensuous' are not quite brothers in arms. Though both are often used to mean 'gratifying the senses', it was traditionally only 'sensual' that carried that idea. 'Sensuous' was thought to have been the creation of John Milton as a deliberate sidestep from the sexual connotations of 'sensual'. Their interchangeability today at least reflects their common origin: the Latin *sensus*, the 'faculty of feeling', itself from *sentire*, to 'feel'.

sentimental: prompted by feelings of tenderness or nostalgia; overindulgent or mawkish.

'I am proud of my heart alone, it is the sole source of everything, all our strength, happiness and misery': Johann Wolfgang von Goethe's *The Sorrows of Young Werther*, which deals in the agony of unrequited love, is a defining work of the German *Sturm und Drang* ('Storm and Stress') movement, which championed feelings and individualism over the rationalism of the Enlightenment. Such sentimental novels demanded strong emotions from its readers as much as their characters.

'Sentiment', as well as 'sensibility', 'sensitivity', and the less appealing 'sentimentality', all originated in the Latin *sentire*, to 'feel'. To be 'sentimental' was to be 'determined by feeling rather than by reason' – a neutral description that was frequently used to describe literary compositions that involved and appealed to the sentiments. The tide began to turn in the early nineteenth century, when the 'sentimental classes' were, according to the poet Robert Southey, 'persons of ardent or morbid sensibility, who believe themselves to be composed of finer elements than the gross multitude'. Not long after, the novelist Mary Elizabeth Braddon confirmed 'sentimental's' slide to the dark side: 'You have no sentimental nonsense, no silly infatuation . . . to fear from me.'

sequacious: prone to slavishly following a person or belief.

'Sequacious' was coined in the seventeenth century as a description of one who, as defined in the *Oxford English Dictionary*, is given to 'the slavish or unreasoning following of another in matters of thought or opinion'. The word is based on the Latin *sequi*, to 'follow'.

'Sequacious' quickly gathered momentum to describe other contexts of unthinking and unwavering adherence, including monotonic musical notes and individuals who are easily bent to another's will. As a feeling, 'sequaciousness' and 'sequacity' convey the compulsion to follow others without question, showing a total lack of independent thinking. Social media, consequently, might be described as hotbeds of both.

serendipity: the making of happy and unexpected discoveries by chance.

Serendip was an Old Persian name for Sri Lanka (and in earlier times Ceylon). It is said to come from the Sanskrit *Siṃhaladvīpa*, 'Dwelling-Place-of-Lions Island'. In 1754, the writer and politician Horace Walpole created the word 'serendipity', basing it upon the title of his 'ridiculous' fairy tale, *The Three Princes of Serendip*. Its heroes, he wrote, 'were always making discoveries, by accidents and sagacity, of things they were not in quest of'.

The three princes, in the course of their travels, follow the tracks of a camel. Through analysing such clues as the patches of grass at which the camel has grazed and the imprints it has left in the ground, they conclude that the animal is lame, blind in one eye, missing a tooth, bearing a pregnant woman, and carrying honey on one side and butter on the other. When later they meet the merchant who has lost the camel, and repeat these observations to him, he accuses them of theft and denounces them to the king. Escaping execution thanks to yet more detective work, the princes go on to have many more adventures that end happily, powered by coincidence and the fortunate alignment of circumstances.

serene: smooth and tranquil.

Serene weather is the calm, cloudless kind, while serene stars and planets shine with a clear, tranquil light. Such were the earliest meanings of 'serene', which came to English from the Latin *serenus*, 'fair' and 'calm'. A serene individual is therefore untroubled, unruffled, and unperturbed – outwardly, at least, for a swan might appear serene as it glides along a river, while paddling frantically below the surface, much like the rest of us.

serious: considered; earnest; grave.

'Unfeastly', 'unlaughter-mild', 'solemned', 'moy', and 'dreich': such have been the heavy and sober synonyms of 'serious' over the centuries. The root is the Latin *serius*, used of something weighty and important. Fittingly, it has not really wobbled an inch since then.

seventh heaven: extreme happiness.

> To feel oneself the object of general attention is for the Englishman misery, but for the Frenchman and the Italian it is to be in seventh heaven.

Such was the conclusion of the *London Evening Standard*'s Rome correspondent in April 1872 when comparing national characteristics. Used rather loosely these days, 'seventh heaven' occupies an exalted place in Jewish and Islamic theology. In the Talmud, it is there that God is believed to dwell with the angels, alongside the souls of the unborn and the righteous. The expression moved on to embrace any place of supreme bliss, even for an Englishman.

shame: humiliation or regret arising from the knowledge of wrong behaviour.

For the Vikings, it was *kinnroði*, 'cheek-redness', while the Romans knew it as *pudor*, 'ignominy'. For Carl Jung, it was a 'soul-eating emotion'. 'Shame' has always packed a punch, eroding equanimity since ancient times. While the Greeks distinguished bad shame (*aischynē*) from the shame of modesty (*aidōs*), which they saw as a form of humility, the shadow of the first was long. Public shaming was decided via the casting of an *ostrakon*, a pottery shard, which carried the name of an individual deemed unfit for society and thus condemned to exile; *ostrakon* eventually gave English the word 'ostracize'.

Such acts of humiliation continued throughout the centuries, whether by bodily stigmatization, stocks, tar and feathers, a scold's bridle, cucking stool, bride's muzzle, dunce's cap, the pillory, or even 'baffling' (a word that originally entailed hanging a disgraced knight by his heels from a tree). The punishment of 'shame' was high entertainment for many, and frequently fatal for the victims. And when illegitimacy was regarded as a moral sin, 'child of shame' became a synonym for 'bastard'.

'Shame derives its power from being unspeakable,' according to the research professor Brené Brown. Her view is supported by the word's etymology, which lies in an ancient root meaning to 'cover' or 'hide'. Perhaps this lack of exposure explains why we have sought no other word for 'shame' since its entry into English in the eighth century. The word has lost little of its bite since, other than in the curious yet liberally used expression 'that's a shame', uttered at even the slightest disappointment.

shamefaced: abashed.

The word 'abashed', thanks to its similarity to 'bashful', has come to mean a gentle embarrassment over something unfortunate. Its etymological beginnings were much stronger, however, for to be 'abashed' was to be stunned or open-mouthed as a result of some humiliation. Its roots lie in the Old French *es*, 'utterly', and *bair*, 'astound'. The alternative expression 'shamefaced' shares some of its sting, although that too began as something rather different, in that one's 'face' has nothing to do with it. The original expression was 'shamefast', suggesting a state of being rooted to the spot in mortification. Clearly the idea of bearing such humiliation on suitably reddened cheeks was a more vivid image, and 'faced' eventually took over.

shibui [Japanese: si-boo-ee]: improvement with age.

The aesthetic of *shibui* is a counterpoint to the modern ideal of youthfulness and a lesson to us all, for it describes a subtle beauty that increases with age. It can be applied to anything from a wrinkled face to a time-honed piece of wood.

shirty: testy or irritable.

'"I am exceedingly obliged," grunted Tomkins, in rather a shirty tone, and continued reading.' So runs the *Oxford English Dictionary*'s first record, from *The Swell's Night Guide* of 1845, of 'shirty', meaning 'cantankerous' and 'annoyed'. It is an extension of the phrase 'keep your shirt on', a reference to the practice among fist-fighters of symbolically shedding their shirts before entering the fray.

shivviness: the scratchy feeling of new underwear.

Some words die away even when their usefulness clearly hasn't. 'Shivviness' arguably isn't one of them, but we can at least revel in the fact that a word once existed for the uncomfortableness of new underwear. Its base is the dialect 'shiv', meaning either a husk of oat or a small piece of foreign substance in woollen materials, suggesting that eighteenth-century undies were very scratchy indeed.

shock: surprise or deep upset.

'Shockvertising' was a buzzword of the 1990s, when brands began to realize the value of a previously under-utilized emotion. When the sanitary pad-makers Bodyform replaced the blue liquid traditionally used to show a pad's absorbency with real blood, they confronted taboos which had held firm for centuries. While some recoiled, others argued that the power of shock was as valuable here as when governments produce highly graphic drink-and-drive adverts. Not only can shock sell, it educates too.

The word 'shock' dropped into English in the mid sixteenth century as a borrowing of the French *choc*. Its earliest uses were military ones: to 'shock' enemy troops or opposing jousters was to throw them into disarray by charging at them. From here it developed the notion of a 'sudden violent blow or impact', of the kind delivered by shockvertisers today. The use of 'shocking' to mean 'very bad', meanwhile, is first found at the end of the eighteenth century, in a collection of letters called *The Paget Papers*: 'Shocking Weather since you left.'

shock horror: unsurprised or unshocked at something.

The essence of 'shock horror' is that it is, in fact, anything but. The phrase is used entirely ironically in response to something entirely predictable – meaning there is little horror, and certainly no shock.

shy: timid and nervous in company.

The Old English word *scéoh* was originally applied exclusively to horses that were easily frightened or that 'shied away'. It wasn't until the seventeenth century that it was used of people who were timid in company or who avoided others altogether by 'eschewing' them – a word that shares the same ancestor.

silly: lacking in good judgement; foolish or absurd.

Silliness was once a badge of honour. To label someone 'silly' in the Middle Ages was to consider them 'fortunate' or 'happy'. That's because the earliest form of the adjective was 'seely', a Germanic borrowing that is a sibling of the modern German *Seligkeit*, 'bliss'. 'Seely' could also mean 'pious' or 'lucky', but shifted to embrace defenceless souls who were deserving of pity. By the time 'silly' took over, a note of cynicism was beginning to bed in, thanks to the ageless equation between innocence, naivety, and foolishness. Both good and bad co-existed for a while, however, and the jury is out as to whether the medieval citizens John Silly and Will Sillyman were holy, pitiable, or just plain numpties. Since the late sixteenth century 'silliness' has settled firmly upon foolishness, albeit with a lighter and more affectionate touch.

simchah [sim-chuh]: gladness and joy.

At the heart of *simchah* is the Hebrew *samech-mem-chet*, which means 'to rejoice'. It can refer both to the celebration of a particular occasion, such as a wedding or barmitzvah, and to an entire ethos – an empowering approach to life that rests upon clutching joy wherever we can, even amid everyday irritations and sorrows.

simper-de-cocket: an affected, flirty manner.

To 'simper it', in the sixteenth century, was to smile in an affectedly coy and bashful way. To 'simper like a frumenty kettle' upped the flirting ante considerably. Any individual guilty as charged might be described as 'simper-de-cocket', a term generally applied to a woman that apparently suggested trembling lips, fluttering eyelashes, a heaving bosom, and all-round counterfeit emotion.

sincere: free from deceit; genuine.

Folk etymology will tell you that 'sincere' has a hidden connection with Roman art. It is said to be a nod to sculptors who used wax to patch over any costly mistakes when working with marble or other precious stone. A statue without any such blemishes was said to be *sine cera*, 'without wax', and therefore unadulterated. An alternative scenario takes us to Roman markets, where sellers of honey would shout '*Sine cera!*' to the throngs to assure them that their products were pure and clear of any additives.

There is, sadly, little truth in either colourful suggestion. The answer is rather more prosaic, although Latin is still involved. In this case it is *sincerus*, which seems to be related to *simplus*, in which *sim* means 'one'. In other words, to be sincere is to have only one story to tell – the truth.

sisu [Finnish: see-su]: determination in the face of adversity.

If you ask a Finn to explain their national character, you may hear just one word in response: *sisu*. Derived from *sisus*, meaning 'entrails' or 'guts', it represents tenacity and resilience in the face of adversity, and in particular courage against the odds. *Sisu* is stoicism and grit, equanimity and gutsiness. Above all, it is persevering when the odds are stacked against you. The popularity of the word coincided with the independence of Finland from Russia in 1917. In an eloquent article about the true nature of *sisu*, the writer Olga Smirnova describes it as the 'social glue' that helped define a nation.

English has no word that encompasses the spirit of *sisu*, besides, perhaps, the **stiff upper lip** in which the British take such pride. The Japanese have *ganbaru* to describe a dogged industriousness and a focus on seeing a task through to the end. But neither comes close to the perception of *sisu* as a near-mythical energy that transcends the expected limits of endurance.

skittish: nervous or excitable.

The rare word 'skit', a likely borrowing from the Vikings, meant 'to move rapidly' or to 'dart'. It is from here that we got the name of a short and snappy comedy sketch or piece of writing, as well as the idea of being 'skittish', meaning 'playfully frivolous' or 'nervous and excitable'.

sloth: indolence; a reluctance to move.

'Sloth', the deadly sin that took over from **acedia**, is very much how it sounds — slow. Its first incarnation was the Old English *slæwþ*, describing the sluggish movements that come with indolence.

Arguably, 'sloth' involves less of the self-preoccupation that lies at the heart of acedia. Nevertheless, both have been heavily condemned for their rejection of the seven gifts of grace conferred by the Holy Ghost, resulting in a slow spiritual progress or even a reversal of it. They are very much sins of omission rather than of action. In Dante's *Inferno*, one of the few ways of purging the vice of sloth was continuous running. Although there is a fine line between the results of 'laziness' and 'sloth', our perceptions of them — the one a throwaway indulgence, the other a disease of the soul — position them a million miles apart.

Today, sloth's intrinsic aversion to any effort is often viewed as an adjunct to depression. The lack of a desire to make any practical or moral decisions results in an apathy that in turn negates the desire to do anything, and so the cycle continues.

For all its concomitant risks and sinfulness, sloth will always have its advocates. The American journalist John Chancellor spoke for many when talking about his city's personality: 'The avenues in my neighborhood are Pride, Covetousness, and Lust; the cross streets are Anger, Gluttony, Envy, and Sloth. I live over on Sloth.'

As for the 'sloth' that is a slow-moving mammal, it seems positively cuddly by comparison. Though here too there is danger, for sloths famously defecate just once a week, risking peril from predators by having to reach ground to do so, and losing a third of their body weight by the end of it.

smell-feast: a parasite when it comes to food.

It might be the friend who always pops round when you're about to dish up, or the colleague who **groaks** at your plate of chips when you're out to lunch. When there's food to be had, a 'smell-feast' will usually be there, inspiring an all-too-familiar frustration. Defined in the *Oxford English Dictionary* as 'one who comes uninvited to share in a feast; a greedy sponger', they were once also known as 'lick-dishes' – or, more formally, as 'parasites', a word that shares the same etymological inspiration of one who sits alongside (the Greek *para*) and steals your food (*sitos*). We've all met one.

smellfungus: a constant critic.

Quite why 'smellfungus' fell out of use is a mystery, for it is as relevant now as it was in the eighteenth century, when Laurence Sterne coined the term as a name for an omni-critical character in *A Sentimental Journey*. Smellfungus travels from Boulogne to Paris with 'spleen and jaundice', and 'every object he pass'd by was discoloured or distorted'. A 'smellfungus', by extension, is one so querimonious and discontented that they find fault with everything.

smile: a pleased or amused expression.

Thank goodness for the word 'smile'. While the pleasure it reflects is often simple, the dictionary definition is anything but: 'a facial expression in which the eyes brighten and the corners of the mouth curve slightly upward and which expresses especially amusement, pleasure, approval, or sometimes scorn'. Where 'smile' came from no one quite knows – it seems to be Scandinavian and a cousin of the word 'smirk' – but we should always be grateful for it.

smug: pleased with oneself.

There is nothing good to say about someone who is 'smug' these days, but when it first set out it was a happy word meaning 'trim', 'neat', and 'spruce'. In nineteenth-century university slang, a 'smug' was even a quiet and hard-working student – not perhaps the coolest member of the team, and so almost imperceptibly the word shifted to describe someone with a self-consciously respectable and satisfied air.

smultronställe [Swedish: smull-tron-steh-luh]: somewhere that has sentimental value.

From the Swedish for a 'place of wild strawberries', a *smultron-ställe* is a special location that is treasured in the memory, and that may be returned to whenever solace and recombobulation are required.

snoodging: nestling snugly.

Language loves a snuggle. Search the *English Dialect Dictionary* and you will find a host of synonyms for lying comfortably and still. Here you will come across 'croozling', 'croodling', 'cummudging', 'neezling', 'nuddling', 'nuzzling', 'snoozling', and 'snuggening'. One of the best is surely 'snoodging', from Yorkshire, Warwickshire, and Shropshire, which is defined as to 'nestle or lie closely together'.

sober: serious; sensible; not drunk.

'Sober' has always had one elbow on the bar. For the Romans, *sobrius* was the opposite of *ebrius*, 'drunk'. When 'sober' passed into English in the early 1300s, therefore, it meant 'moderate' or 'temperate', both in the intake of food and drink, and in life in general. To embrace 'sobriety' was to resist all indulgences of appetite and excess. In the fifteenth century, *The Game and Playe of the Chesse*, the second book ever to be published in English, included the warning 'That the dronken men shold be punysshyd / And the sobre men be preysed'.

solace: comfort; consolation at times of distress.

To find 'solace' is to be 'consoled'. Both words stem from the Latin *solari*, to 'comfort'. 'Solace' is relief, the assuagement of sorrow, and what in the sixteenth century was simply called 'recomfortation' – a consolation that puts the heart and spirit back in play.

solastalgia: wistfulness at a fading landscape.

At the heart of 'nostalgia' is the sense of retreating memories. Combine that with the idea of staying at home while seeing your environment disappear around you, and you have 'solastalgia'. The word is the creation of Glenn Albrecht, a philosopher at the University of Newcastle in Australia. He devised it as a blend of 'solace' and 'nostalgia' to describe the feeling of distress associated with environmental change on your very doorstep.

solipsist: one who is selfish and self-centred.

The Latin *solus* meant 'alone', while *ipse* meant 'self'. Put those two together and you have one who only thinks of themselves. The word 'solipsist' was first used by German philosophers as a label for one who believes that their own self or consciousness is all that exists. In reality, such metaphysical 'solipsism' has rarely been subscribed to by any philosopher – rather it was used as a devil's advocate in philosophical debate. Any reference to a 'solipsist' today is likely to be an accusation of excessive self-regard, usually to the exclusion of all else.

solitude: the state of being alone.

Hamlet, hermits, anglers, poets, Carmelite nuns and Trappist monks – all seekers of the benefits of solitude. This fundamentally positive emotion is very different from the loneliness felt by those upon whom solitude is thrust. As the critic Terry Eagleton points out, 'solitude has rarely killed anyone, whereas loneliness can drive you to the grave.'

The motivations for seeking solitude are various. For some it is an escape from the vexations of daily life. St Simeon the Stylite, a monk in ancient Syria whose extreme devotion inspired hundreds of disciples and supplicants, resorted to climbing onto a sixty-foot-tall column, just six feet in diameter, to gain some peace. He found the results so refreshing he remained there for the next thirty years, albeit with the unintended consequence of attracting vast crowds who disturbed the precious solitude he had so fervently sought.

For the Romantics of the nineteenth century, the self-communion that comes from physical isolation was a catalyst for great art, allowing for a revelation of the self that is denied by constant company. Solo walking became a recreation for many – William Wordsworth apparently covered some 180,000 miles in the course of his lifetime. He both 'wandered lonely as a cloud', and 'alone / Amid the heart of many thousand mists' in order to benefit from the solitude. For the poet and his peers, the emotion was a wellspring of necessary introspection, one that had equally been sought by their eighteenth-century predecessors Thomas Gray, William Cowper, and others who became known as the 'Graveyard Poets' on account of their gloomy and solitary meditations on mortality.

Virginia Woolf, who taught us the rewards of a room of one's own, found solitude a prerequisite for any work of the imagination. She was also able to describe its profound effects on how we feel:

> How much better is silence; the coffee cup, the table. How
> much better to sit by myself like the solitary sea-bird that

opens its wings on the stake. Let me sit here for ever with bare things, this coffee cup, this knife, this fork, things in themselves, myself being myself.

sonder: the realization that other lives progress around you without your ever being aware of them.

John Koenig's glorious *Dictionary of Obscure Sorrows*, conceived in 2006, is the result of the writer's observation that English lacks hundreds of words to articulate particular emotions. Some of the terms he has gone on to create have received such a wide audience that they have moved into the mainstream and become largely untethered from their 'deliberate' beginnings.

Of all Koenig's creations, 'sonder' is perhaps the term most will recognize. It describes the realization that everyone else has a life as vivid and complex as your own, which continues irrespective of whether we witness it or not.

Many more of Koenig's creations may resonate too: 'vellichor', for example, is the smell of old bookshops, while 'dorgone' is wondering whether you can slip away from an event or conversation without anyone noticing your absence.

sorrow: mental distress caused by suffering or by loss.

> Sorrow is knowledge: they who know the most
> Must mourn the deepest o'er the fatal truth,
> The Tree of Knowledge is not that of Life.

Lord Byron's equation between sorrow and creativity was a hallmark of Romanticism, when suffering was the result of the gap between ideals and reality. Johann Wolfgang von Goethe articulated a similar sentiment: 'Only by joy and sorrow does a person know anything about themselves and their destiny. They learn what to do and what to avoid.'

Linguistically, the history of 'sorrow' is closely connected with the word 'sorry', although the two are etymologically distinct. While 'sorrow' has relatives in many other languages – from the German *Sorge*, 'care', to the Swedish *sorg*, 'distress' – 'sorry' shares a root with the word 'sore'. Nonetheless, thanks to their similarity in appearance, the two have followed parallel paths for centuries.

sour grapes: a negative attitude born of resentment.

In one of Aesop's celebrated fables, a fox stares longingly at a mouth-watering bunch of grapes. Tantalizingly, the branch bearing them is simply too high, and try as he might, the fox can't reach them. Eventually he gives up, sitting down in disgust and declaring himself a fool: 'Here I am wearing myself out to get a bunch of sour grapes that are not worth gaping for.' 'Sour grapes', subsequently, are ones you tell yourself you never really wanted anyway.

spite: malice; a grudge.

When Andrew Carnegie and Henry Clay Frick teamed up to become an indomitable force in America's steel industry, it seemed as though nothing could go wrong. But the pair's relationship eventually fell apart, and Carnegie engineered Frick out of the business. For the rest of his life, it is said, Frick plotted ways to get back at his former partner, from building bigger mansions to firing off telegrams informing Carnegie that his 'management of the Company has already become the subject of jest'. Even when Carnegie invited Frick to a reconciliatory meeting towards the end of their lives, Frick resisted – 'Tell him I'll see him in Hell, where we're both going' – thus providing one of history's most noteworthy examples of spite.

'Spite', 'despise', and 'despicable' are joined at the hip, each descending from the Latin *despicere*, to 'look down upon'. The difference in the appearance of 'spite' is down to the fact that we borrowed it from the French *despit* rather than directly from the Latin. Running through the whole family is the sense of contempt, hatred, and the desire to hurt – a complex mix, as Charles Dickens observed:

> Spite is a little word; but it represents as strange a jumble of feelings, and compound of discords, as any polysyllable in the language.

spleen: the seat of intense emotion.

Venting your spleen was once a physical imperative, at least in the eyes of Hippocrates and his followers. According to the theory of the humours, the spleen was both the seat of melancholy and, conversely, of laughter and mirth. To confuse matters even further, in sixteenth-century Scottish English 'from the spleen' meant 'from the heart'. The connection between the various beliefs seems to be an intensity of feeling – the spleen is a filter for the blood, and therefore the metaphorical channel for emotions. If these were negative – be they depression or vexation – then venting the organ by airing one's grievances was believed to metaphorically detoxify it.

sprezzatura [Italian: sprets-a-tu-ra]: an artful nonchalance.

Sprezzatura describes the kind of studied **nonchalance** that gives the firm impression that not a hair on your head has been ruffled in the process of achieving something impressive, even if behind the scenes the effort has been gargantuan. The essence of *sprezzatura* is a confident toss of the head and a casual smile that radiates assurance.

The term emerged in English in the 1950s, but its history in Italian is far older, beginning in the Renaissance. The sixteenth-century writer Baldassare Castiglione extolled it in his etiquette manual *The Book of the Courtier*, which was intended to advise noble gentlemen on manners and comportment. Castiglione notes the desirability of a casual elegance that belies any suggestion of hard work: 'a certain nonchalance, so as to conceal all art and make whatever one does or says appear to be without effort and almost without any thought'.

In later centuries, *sprezzatura* became associated with slight but deliberate imperfections or deviations from the norm. In fashion terms, it is a form of aesthetic rebellion, whereby a wristband is worn over a shirt cuff, or a tie is tied slightly wonkily. The desired impression at all times is one of insouciance because other things are more important, even if all the while such eccentricities have been carefully constructed.

Perhaps in modern, looser, terms, *sprezzatura* covers the knack of receiving a compliment on an effortfully chosen outfit with the response, 'Oh, *this* old thing?'

stamina: the ability to sustain prolonged effort.

'Stamina' comes from the Latin *stamen*, a word now used for the threadlike part of a flower or plant. For the ancients, however, it was even more important, for the *stamen* denoted the thread spun by the Fates at a person's birth, the length of which determined the duration and course of one's life. When the plural 'stamina' entered English in the 1700s, it described the collective influences and characteristics that decide a person's life expectancy. Before long, it took on the metaphorical sense of the vital impulse that each of us possesses.

stiff upper lip: uncomplaining stoicism.

Charles Darwin's pioneering work *The Expression of the Emotions in Man and Animals* of 1872 presented a hierarchy of emotional expression according to race (and presumably gender). Darwin's view was that 'savages weep copiously from very slight causes', whereas 'Englishmen rarely cry, except under the pressure of the acutest grief'. What could be more quintessentially British, then, than our stiff upper lip, the ability to be resolute and unyielding in the face of distress or attack? Yet the very first records of the expression are from the US, dating back to the mid nineteenth century in works such as *Uncle Tom's Cabin*: 'Well, good-bye, Uncle Tom; keep a stiff upper lip.' Not until the century's closing decades was it readily adopted into British English. After several more had passed, its American moorings were long forgotten and a stiff upper lip was readily assumed to be a typical display of good old English reticence.

stoical: forbearing; enduring without complaint.

The story of the Stoics is widely believed to have begun with a shipwreck. It involves the story of a merchant from Cyprus called Zeno of Citium, who is sailing back from Phoenicia with a cargo of precious purple dye – used to stain the robes of kings and emperors – when a vicious storm hits. The ship goes down but Zeno is washed ashore, left to wander the streets of Athens without fortune or clothes, making his way eventually to the Oracle at Delphi, who instructs him to wear the colour of dead men.

On his way back, thoroughly bemused, Zeno stops at a bookstall and picks up a volume by a famous Athenian general called Xenophon, a disciple of Socrates. In this book Xenophon had set down Socrates' truth that good is within rather than outside us. Zeno understands then that the Oracle, by instructing him to wear the colour of dead men, is telling him to study the words of the greatest philosophers of the past.

Whatever his inspiration, real-life Zeno trained to become a prominent philosopher in his own right: through reason, he believed, we can harness the calm and order of the universe by learning to accept events with a tranquil mind, freeing it from the turbulence of high emotion and passion. He eventually established his own school in Athens called the *Stoa Poikilē*, or 'Painted Porch'.

Such was the importance attached to the seats of learning in this period that many schools took on the name of the buildings they used. The first Cynics, for example, who espoused the belief that wealth, luxury, and pleasure were contemptible ambitions that distracted an individual from the quest for self-knowledge, took their name from the *Kynosarges*, the gymnasium where one of their founders, Antisthenes, taught. The name translates as 'white dog', suggesting perhaps that the Cynics were considered dogged in their pursuit of asceticism. As for Zeno, his school produced the name 'Stoics' for his followers. Centuries on, 'stoical' is interpreted more broadly, to describe one who is calm and unflinching in the face of hardship.

stound: a momentary pang of emotion.

Many of us have come across an old photograph that unexpectedly stirs our memories. We may feel a stab of grief when we smell a remembered perfume, hear a certain musical refrain, or revisit a place of our youth. Such brief but powerful emotions are captured in 'stound', a word of many faces that has moved from a simple description of a moment in time to a fleeting flash of pain or, less frequently, of pleasure. Of Germanic ancestry, 'stound' was also once a verb, meaning to 'affect with a pang of pain'. It appears to have no clear relationship with 'astound', even if the searing effect on the mind and body can be just as shocking. And its journey continues still: in a nineteenth-century glossary of North Country words, 'stound' is defined as 'the sensation or first impression of sudden pain, arising from a knock or blow' – in other words, the instant response of the body before the brain catches up.

stress: mental and emotional strain.

When the physician Hans Selye wrote up his collective observations of hospital patients in the 1920s, he noticed that they all had one thing in common: they were suffering from physical 'stress'. Borrowing from physics, in which 'stress' is a physical force, Selye was one of the first to formalize the term for a non-specific strain on the body that resulted in the release of certain hormones. His subsequent research pioneered the efforts to understand stress in both its physical and psychological forms.

Selye identified three stages of stress, in what he called the General Adaptation Syndrome. The first is an alarm reaction: the immediate and fearful response to a stressor in which the human fight-or-flight instinct takes hold. The second is resistance: as the body accustoms itself to repeated stress, so it expends a lot of energy in trying to combat it. The third stage is the inevitable outcome of the first two: exhaustion.

Today, at any given time on YouGov's 'mood meter', Britons' stress levels hover around 40 to 50 per cent. Stress's spectrum now is broad, reflecting the many emotions that emerge when the body and mind are put under pressure. The term became in the twentieth century what 'trauma' is fast becoming in the twenty-first: a word for all manner of psychological and emotional suffering, so broad as to include almost everyone and every kind of negative experience.

The etymology of 'stress' fits closely with the sense of extreme pressure or anguish, for it is a shortening of 'distress', which comes from the Latin *distringere*, to 'stretch apart', an early version of being entirely 'strung out'. The word was also influenced by the Old French *estresse*, 'narrowness' or 'oppression', which in turn looks back to the Latin *strictus*, 'drawn tight'. Both emphasize the restricting forces of the emotion on our lives. 'It's not stress that kills us,' wrote Selye, 'it's our reaction to it.'

strikhedonia: the pleasure of saying 'to hell with it'.

'Strikhedonia' is one of those recent coinages adopted in corners of the Internet as a historical term for an emotion we've always wanted to express. Not that this makes the word any less 'legitimate' – like all words, it is usage that will decide on its success – but the process involves the *de facto* acceptance of an ancient past that on closer inspection isn't borne out. In this case, 'strik-' appears to be an obsolete form of the verb to 'strike', which originally meant to 'take a new direction' – a sense we still use when we 'strike out' to a new destination – while 'hedonia' is straight from the Greek *hēdonē*, meaning 'pleasure' (*see* **nikhedonia**). Put the two elements together and the meaning becomes 'pleasure in leaving for somewhere new'. More loosely, the translation becomes 'the pleasure of saying "to hell with it"' – a very recognizable sentiment, which probably explains the word's traction on the Web.

stroppy: grumpy and argumentative.

A traditional companion to 'teenager', 'stroppy' emerged in the 1950s to describe someone awkward and cantankerous. It seems to be a shortening of 'obstreperous', which in turn came from a Latin word for 'opposing noisily or troublesomely'.

struthious: inclined to bury one's head in the sand.

An adjective meaning 'ostrich-like', 'struthious' suits the individual who greets every crisis with 'Problem? What problem?'

sturmfrei [German: shtorm-fry]: free to do what one wants.

To be *sturmfrei*, or 'storm-free', is to be liberated from any supervision from parents, flatmates, or children. Put simply, it is the joy at the sudden realization that you can do whatever you want.

sublime: of great excellence or beauty.

Edmund Burke, whose *Philosophical Enquiry into the Origin of Our Ideas of the Sublime and Beautiful* was published in 1757, maintained that the human response to danger or pain is all-powerful, and that the terror it inspires 'is productive of the strongest emotion that the mind is capable of feeling'. That strongest of the emotions he called 'the sublime'.

For Burke, the sublime is not exclusively an unpleasant emotion: by overwhelming us and depriving us of rational thought it can also induce delight. He held it to be 'an irresistible force' that obscures all other emotions, much like darkness. And indeed darkness too was for him a source of the sublime – he notes how 'the druids performed all their ceremonies in the bosom of the darkest woods, and in the shade of the oldest and most spreading oaks'. Darkness creates a sense of vastness, which is also built into our perceptions of the sublime because we are unable to perceive any boundaries. The result, thanks to the uncertainty such a lack of control produces, is a 'delightful horror . . . the truest test of the sublime'.

If this all seems a far cry from our modern use of 'sublime' for something almost impossibly perfect, it pays to look to the word's etymology, which enshrines that same sense of vastness. It comes from the Latin *sublimis*, 'lofty'. As for its frequent companion, 'the ridiculous', that relationship began with the saying 'from the sublime to the ridiculous is only a step', a remark attributed to Napoleon Bonaparte following his retreat from Moscow in 1812. He was not the first to make the link, however. In 1795, the English political writer Thomas Paine had already mused:

> The sublime and the ridiculous are often so nearly related,
> that it is difficult to class them separately. One step above

the sublime, makes the ridiculous; and one step above the ridiculous, makes the sublime again.

subtrist: a little bit sad.

'Subtrist' is a nineteenth-century word from Scotland meaning 'somewhat sad'. 'Trist' itself, from the French for 'sadness', *tristesse*, has been used of melancholy since the fifteenth century. The addition of *sub-*, meaning 'below' or 'up to', suggests a low-level sadness that never quite takes over, but which is debilitating nonetheless.

suffering: undergoing something distressful or unpleasant; tolerating.

At the heart of 'suffer' is the Latin *sufferre*, made up of *sub*, 'from below, under', and *ferre*, to 'bear' (from an ancient root that could also mean to 'bear children'). In other words, to suffer is to *undergo* pain, death, judgement, punishment, or sorrow. The idea of submission runs through an additional sense of the word, meaning to 'tolerate': the Bible instructs that 'For ye suffer fools gladly, seeing ye yourselves are wise'.

supercilian: an individual who considers most people to be beneath them.

No one admires a 'supercilian'. Like its far more familiar relative 'supercilious', this seventeenth-century word comes from the Latin for 'eyebrow', implying such haughtiness and disdain that this individual looks down on others with an arrogantly arched eyebrow.

surly: churlishly bad-tempered or rude.

When you know that the adjective 'surly' was originally spelt 'sirly', all becomes clear. From the start, it was associated with an imperious, haughty arrogance that follows entitlement and privilege. A similar description is 'high-horsed', first used of those with pedigree horses who quite literally looked down upon everyone else.

surprise: the feeling caused by something unexpected or unusual.

'Surprise is the greatest gift which life can grant us,' wrote Boris Pasternak. Those living in the fifteenth century would have disagreed, for to witness a 'surprise' in their lifetime was to be subject to attack or to a forceful seizure of land and property, whether expected or not. Its source was the medieval Latin *superprehendere*, to 'seize'. It took some time for the suggestion of force to fade away, and for a sense of being seized by the unexpected to come to the fore instead.

suspire: to sigh.

Of all the members of the family descended from the Latin *spirare*, 'suspire' is surely the most evocative. Put simply, it means to 'breathe out with a sigh'. Whether that sigh is one of relief, exhaustion, melancholy, or resignation is entirely down to you.

swadder: to grow weary with drinking.

Depending where you are in Britain, to 'swadder' is either to 'dabble in water or mud', or to 'grow weary from drinking'. The first is Cumbrian, where ducks are regularly seen to be swaddering. The second application, born in south-east England, is arguably the more useful of the two. Here, 'swaddering' describes the gradual glazing-over of eyes and pallor of face that comes at the end of a drinking session, and which is usually relieved only by a late-night curry or a final succumbing to sleep. *See also* **zwodder**.

swasivious: persuasive; cajoling.

It has just one mention in the *Oxford English Dictionary*, yet you have to wonder why 'swasivious' ever went away. Its sound says it all: it is the manner of being soothingly, unctuously, or cajolingly convincing – or, as the *OED* puts it, 'agreeably persuasive'. It is the perfect adjective for winning someone round without them realizing a thing.

sweary: given to profanity.

The earliest sense of the verb to 'swear' was to 'profess allegiance to a person or cause'. Its story began with the Old English *swerian* (of which the past tense was *swor*, and the past participle *sworen*), meaning to 'make a solemn oath'. It is a close relation of 'answer', originally a sworn statement that rebutted a charge or accusation.

Collateral is always useful, and those making their oaths would often swear on their lives, their lord, or their honour. Eventually, they might swear to God, a highly serious utterance that carried the heaviest conviction of all, as well as the risk of divine retribution. Today's primary use of 'swearing' to mean profanity and 'bad language' descends from the belief in the Middle Ages that the unnecessary or extravagant use of God's name was wholly blasphemous.

sycophantic: fawning and obsequious.

'I couldn't give a fig' is not a sentence you'd expect from any flatterer, intent as they would be upon ingratiating themselves. But the exotic fruit is at the heart of the word 'sycophant', whose beginnings might lie in ancient Athens and its laws preventing the export of food. This ban encouraged a black market in which particularly desirable items were smuggled over the border, including the luscious fig. But if an enemy decided to denounce you to the authorities, they became a *sykophantes* or 'fig-shower'.

So runs one of the most entertaining stories from English etymology, and it may indeed be true. The more plausible suggestion is arguably even more colourful, involving the making of the obscene gesture of a 'fig' (in which the thumb is pushed between two fingers to represent the female vulva) to any informer. When 'sycophant' entered English it duly meant a 'tell-tale' or spreader of malicious rumours, before shifting from slander to ingratiating servility.

Either way, it's a long journey from figs to flattery. But English rarely takes the direct route home.

symbel-gal [Old English]: intent only upon feasting.

Symbel-gal is the Anglo-Saxon description of being distracted by food and drink. It translates literally as 'feast-lustful', and is the adjective you need for someone who is so eyes-down intent on imbibing or scoffing that they have no time for anything or anyone else.

sympathy: pity or sorrow at someone else's misfortune.

Sympathy has been a hot topic for centuries, but never more so than today, when it is an active area of research within experimental psychology, neuroscience, economics, and politics. Its history is inextricably bound up with that of empathy, yet these are two distinct emotions that are often blended into a single emotional mash-up.

To take the linguistic story first, 'sympathy' comes from the Greek *sympatheia*, 'fellow-feeling' or, more literally, the 'state of being affected together'. Whereas empathy is made up of the prefix *em*, 'in', plus *pathos*, implying the ability to get *inside* another's head and see things from their point of view, at the heart of 'sympathy' is *sym*, 'with' or 'together', reflecting its meaning of coming alongside someone and helping them in their suffering, whilst at the same time remaining a separate agent.

Sympathy played a central role in the philosophy of the Stoics, for whom *sympatheia* depended on the unity of all souls in the universe. The philosopher Plotinus believed that this unity accounted for the occult working of magic and prayer, a concept picked up again in the Middle Ages when sympathy became both a medical principle and a foundation of astrology, a key aspect of education at the time. As knowledge and its sources began to be re-evaluated, sympathy began to be discussed as a much wider concept, affecting social, political, and cultural life.

In his *Descent of Man*, Charles Darwin believed sympathy to be the crux of morality in human civilization. But his views were far from straightforward. Some Darwinists believed that those who would normally be considered deserving of sympathy were actually 'unfit' and therefore a danger to society and to evolution. The debate intensified over whether the emotion depends on individual or collective morality.

Today, discoveries about the so-called mirror neurons of the brain – which make us flinch when we hit someone in the face, or our hands sweat when watching a hazardous mountain climb on TV – have placed sympathy once more at the heart of discussions about social behaviour. While the emotion's definition has been decidedly slippery, it has played a key role in the reflection of what it means to be human.

synaesthesia: a perception by one sense that is different to the one being stimulated.

Those with synaesthesia perceive the world very differently. They might see music as colour, or discern a flavour in certain sights. The sensory crossovers it involves can inspire great creativity. Kanye West, David Hockney, Marilyn Monroe, Franz Liszt, Richard Wagner, and Billy Eilish are all said to be, or to have been, 'synaesthetes'. The name of the condition is founded upon the Greek *syn*, 'together', and *aisthēsis*, meaning 'perception' or 'sensibility' (its close relative 'anaesthesia' means to be without any sensibility at all).

tabanca: the pain and anger of unrequited love.

In matters of love, while we all hope for **redamancy**, 'being adored in return', some of us are also a little too familiar with the pain of unrequited love. This is 'tabanca', a word that has the added dimension of being driven by one-sided passion to irrational or destructive behaviour. It comes from Caribbean English, and may have begun with the Kikongo term *tabaka*, meaning to 'buy up or sell out completely', a fitting choice for the sense of overwhelming rejection and emptiness that follows a break-up. In short, this is lovesickness with an edge.

tantalized: teased or excited by something unobtainable.

'Tantalizing' these days is applied to anything from a TV cliff-hanger to a delicious aroma emanating from the kitchen. Originally, however, to be 'tantalized' was to be in a state of deep torment, as is clear from the story that inspired it. According to Greek myth, Tantalus, King of Lydia, killed his son Pelops and served him up at a feast for the gods. His punishment, decreed by Zeus, was to be forced to stand for eternity up to his chin in a pool of water, which receded whenever he tried to drink it. Above him hung branches of fruit that moved away when he tried to reach them.

The name of Tantalus whispers through other words in English beyond 'tantalize'. A 'tantalus' is a stand in which decanters of spirits are visible but locked up and out of reach. In the early nineteenth century, meanwhile, a newly discovered metal was given the name 'tantalum' on account of its inability to absorb acid, just as Tantalus was fated never to drink.

tantrum: an uncontrolled outburst.

The first mention of a 'tantrum' is in relation to a woman's 'vapours coming out'. The implication was that any outburst of petulance was the result of hysteria or similar 'woman's complaint'. This eighteenth-century conviction took a while to shift, and tantrums remained a predominantly female preserve for some time – 'Where did the wench get these tantarums into her head?' asks the physician John Shebbeare in *The Marriage Act* from 1754. The origin of the word is as mysterious as female anatomy clearly was back then, and its beginnings are not yet pinned down. Today's tantrums, at least, are generally witnessed in toddlers rather than hysterical women.

tarab [Arabic: ta-rab]: the emotions that flow from music.

Victor Hugo believed that 'music expresses that which cannot be put into words and that which cannot remain silent'. Arab culture has nonetheless given voice to the transformative power of music with a word that has no equivalent in Western languages. *Tarab* describes the enchantment and intense spiritual responses that flow through us when we listen to music. It is a transcendent emotional state that, particularly in a live performance, is shared by both audience and musician – a collective summoning of cultural and personal memories.

tartle: to hesitate in recognizing or introducing someone.

The *Dictionary of the Scots Language* includes the invaluable word 'tartle', defined as 'to hesitate, to be uncertain as in recognizing a person or object'. In other words, tartling involves the extended and embarrassed pause you make when introducing someone to a friend, because you have completely forgotten their name.

tease: to gently make fun of someone.

'Tease' today is a playful word, but it wasn't always so innocent. The original meaning in Old English was to 'comb wool in preparation for spinning'. When we 'tease out' knots or tangles in our hair we are harking back to the same idea. To 'tease' a person, meanwhile, was to give them a great deal of vexation by rubbing them up the wrong way. Only later did teasing develop an affectionate side. There is also a third member of the family: the process of teasing wool was often done using a dried and prickly flower head from a plant subsequently named a 'teasel'.

temper: an individual's disposition or state of mind; a tendency to anger.

Both 'temper' and 'temperament' are in the mix of words derived from the Latin *temperare*, to 'mingle'. In the Middle Ages, 'temper' referred to the correct balance of various elements or qualities. This sense is preserved in metalworking, where to 'temper' a substance is to ensure its consistency or resilience, while an oenophile might also refer to a 'well-tempered wine' when it is considered finely 'tuned'. In terms of human nature, 'temper' was particularly associated with the combination of the four bodily humours, believed to control our personality and our 'temperament', which comes from the Latin for 'correct mixture'.

temptation: the desire to do something that may be wrong or unwise.

'The Lord's Prayer is less than fifty words long, and six of those words are devoted to asking God not to lead us into temptation,' wrote Aldous Huxley. In Christian theology, temptation begins of course with Adam and Eve, where it brings about the Original Sin and ensures the Fall of Man. According to the thirteenth-century Dominican friar Thomas Aquinas, the three sources of temptation are 'the world, the flesh, and the Devil'. Linguistically, the source is far less complex, for 'temptation' comes from the Latin *temptare*, meaning to 'put to the test'.

tender: gentle; kind; affectionate.

'Tenderness' is all about delicacy. We demonstrate it by being gentle and kind, while to have a 'tender' arm after an injection is to be sore to the touch. Both senses look back to the Latin *tener*, 'delicate'. While 'TLC' became the go-to abbreviation for making a fuss of someone in the 1960s, it was Shakespeare who gave us the full version in *Henry VI, Part 2*: 'Go, Salisbury, and tell them all from me / I thank them for their tender loving care.'

teng [Chinese]: to love; to hurt.

For all that love and sorrow often go together, we lack a word to express the pain that comes from love. You might love someone so much it hurts, or you might feel the anxiety of losing someone you cherish with your whole heart. There is perhaps truth in the fact that the Chinese character 疼 (*téng* in pinyin) can mean both 'soreness' and 'love'. It is sometimes used in Chinese for the sorrow inherent in the bond between parent and child: the words 'I love you' spoken by a mother or father is framed instead as *wǒ hěn téng nǐ*: 'My heart hurts for you.'

testy: irritable and impatient.

While 'testy' seems sure to be connected with 'testicles', 'testosterone', and being ballsy, it is actually much more about the head. Its journey into English began with the Old French *testu* (later *têtu*), meaning 'headstrong' and 'obstinate'. When Chaucer used 'testy' in *Troilus and Criseyde* he implied an impetuous brand of courage. The word's ultimate origin is the Latin *testum*, a 'pot', used in Roman slang to mean 'head' in much the same way we might employ 'loaf' or 'nut' today.

thinkache: mental exhaustion.

If your brain is frazzled and you simply can't live inside your head for a second more, you are suffering from 'thinkache', a pithily vivid word from the 1800s which originally meant 'a painful thought', but which has proved far more useful for what is less poetically known as 'brain fag'.

thirsty: feeling the need to drink.

You might expect the need to drink to be one of the earliest physical emotions to be expressed in any language. Certainly our English word 'thirsty' is a straight borrowing from the Old High German *durstag*, and is documented in early Old English texts. We are, however, quite unusual in making an adjective out of 'thirst' — as is the case with 'hunger', 'thirst' in other languages is often treated as an unwelcome possession. In modern German, you would say 'I have thirst' (*Ich habe Durst*), and the same pattern can be found in French, Spanish, Portuguese, and Romanian. Russian is even more direct: *ya khochu pit'* means 'I want to drink'.

thrill: to induce pleasure and excitement.

'Thrilling' was once tantamount to murder, or at the very least GBH. It comes from the Old English *thirl*, a 'hole', and originally described the result of stabbing someone with a sharp weapon. By the fifteenth century, a 'thirl' was also written as 'thrill', when it could represent a metaphorical piercing, especially of the heart by intense emotion.

Those 'thirls', or holes, also gave us 'nose-thirls': the holes beneath our nose that enable us to breathe. 'Thirl' became 'tril', and the 'nostril' was born.

throbless: hard-hearted; devoid of emotion.

Any glossary of feelings requires a word for the state of not having them. The *Oxford English Dictionary* offers an abundance of terms for a lack of emotion, including both the familiar 'callous' and the more curious 'frog-hearted' from the nineteenth century. 'Throbless' is another, first mentioned in Samuel Richardson's *Clarissa* in 1748 and in need of no further explanation, wherever the lack of a throb may be.

tickled pink: highly pleased.

Given the choice of being tickled to death or tickled pink, most of us would choose the latter. But why 'pink'? The answer is probably as simple as the fact that we turn pink with laughter when we are tickled. That kind of heavy, laughter-inducing tickling is known as 'gargalesis', while the light, feathery kind, as from a crawling insect, is known as 'knismesis'. For those with 'gargalaphobia', the idea of being tickled either pink or to death will provoke a shudder, not a smile. But when it's good, it's good, as expressed by Chaucer's Wife of Bath: 'it tickleth me aboute myn herte roote'.

tidsoptimist [Swedish: tidz-op-ti-mist]: someone who is always tardy.

If you are a victim of **Eilkrankheit**, it is quite likely you also have the habit of arriving too late even while confident of making it on time. For the Swedes, you are a *tidsoptimist* – literally, a 'time-optimist'. An obvious word, perhaps, but one which has yet to find its English equivalent despite the clear need for it in modern life.

tired and emotional: worse for wear.

'Tired and emotional' is more than the sum of its parts. It has been a euphemism for drunkenness since the 1970s, thanks largely to the satirical magazine *Private Eye*, which introduced the phrase 'tired and overwrought' to describe the British Labour politician George Brown, known to have a fondness for drinking.

This was not the only *Private Eye* euphemism that caught on: an 'exotic cheroot', for example, is double-speak for a cannabis cigarette.

titillating: suggestively exciting.

Ask a Roman for their word for 'tickle', and it would have been *titillare*. This tickling would have been more of a sensual stimulation than a full on gargalesis-fest (*see* **tickled pink**), which is why when 'titillate' emerged in the seventeenth century it meant to 'excite agreeably'. Three hundred years later, the excitement was mostly of a sexual kind, implying suggestiveness and mild arousal.

toadying: obsequious and fawning.

Were we to transport ourselves to a noisy marketplace in sixteenth-century Britain, some of the loudest voices would be those of the quacks and mountebanks selling their potions and wares. 'Quack' is short for 'quacksalver' – a Dutch term that translates as 'ointment-rubber'. It was a popular nickname for the bogus doctors who promised miraculous cures for every common ailment. One of their most notorious stunts involved making an assistant swallow a supposedly poisonous toad, only to promptly 'save' them by giving them a 'cure-all' which was then touted to the captivated crowd. Thanks to such quackery, the charlatan's assistant became known as a 'toad-eater', a word that soon took on the metaphorical meaning of a fawning servant determined to please his master at any price. By the nineteenth century, 'toad-eater' had been shortened to 'toady'.

torch, carry a: to feel passion, devotion, or tenderness.

The idea of 'carrying a torch' emerged in the early 1900s, when it described a love that was typically unrequited. But the metaphor was probably lit much earlier, perhaps even in ancient Greek and Roman times, when a wedding torch would be set aflame in the bride's hearth on her wedding night as a tribute to the gods of marriage. 'Torch' itself came to us from *torqua*, which in Latin described something twisted: ancient torches consisted of material twisted or wound around a stick.

The link between a burning torch and love also inspired the 'torch song', a sad or sentimental song about romance, particularly the kind that still burns inside the singer long after it has been extinguished in the object of their love.

torment: acute physical or mental pain.

The Latin verb *torquere* was prolific when it came to English descendants, and none of them are happy. The simple idea of twisting gave us 'contort', 'distort', 'extort', 'torture', 'tortuous', and, more obliquely, 'torment'. For the Romans, a *tormentum* was an instrument of torture, a rack for twisting the body, as well as an engine for hurling missiles. It has lost little of its bite since. Today's 'torment' suggests the repeated infliction of suffering upon someone – a persecution with little respite.

torpor: lethargy and inactivity.

The etymology of 'torpor' is simple enough: the Latin *torpere*, to 'be numb'. In some birds and animals, torpor involves heavily reduced activity and a lowering of body temperature and metabolic rate. In humans, it implies a degree of insensibility that is more apathy or lethargy than total shutdown.

'Torpor' has an unlikely cousin in 'torpedo', which despite its connotations of speed is equally inspired by slowness and paralysis. The electric ray, a sluggish sea fish that lives in shallow water, produces an electric shock both to capture prey and to defend itself. Its Latin name was *torpedo*, and when, in the late eighteenth century, the inventor of an underwater explosive sought a name for his missile, he borrowed it from the fish, leaving all sense of stupor behind.

Torschlusspanik [German: tor-shluss-pah-neek]: the fear that life is passing you by.

'Gate-shut-panic', German style, is the anxiety caused by the knowledge that, as we get older, doors of opportunity will close at an alarming rate. Some say the expression began in medieval cities, when peasants would rush to return to the city's gates at nightfall lest they be shut out in the cold with the wolves and bandits. In fact, the earliest records of *Torschlusspanik* date back only as far as the late nineteenth century. Nonetheless, the story offers a useful metaphor for the distinct sensation of time running out, as well as a mid-life crisis.

toska [Russian]: longing with no specific cause.

There is a particular type of anguish that has no focus. You know that you are lacking something but are not sure what; rather you simply feel its absence. For the Russians, this is *toska*, a longing that can be as superficial as not knowing what to do with yourself, or as spiritual as feeling devoid of any plan in life. In the words of Vladimir Nabokov:

> No single word in English renders all the shades of *toska*. At its deepest and most painful, it is a sensation of great spiritual anguish, often without any specific cause. At less morbid levels it is a dull ache of the soul, a longing with nothing to long for.

touched: moved by emotion.

'Touch has a memory,' wrote Keats, in a poem whose narrator is desperate to forget how it feels to hold someone he loves. At times in the past few years, we have had to resign ourselves to expressing feelings without being allowed to feel, to being touched without the touching. The double life of these words seems oddly fitting.

'Touch' has a vast entry in the *Oxford English Dictionary*. A legacy of the French of the Norman Conquerors, replacing the Old English *rine*, it has variously meant making contact with something, having sex, influencing, testing for gold, masturbating, running aground, getting drunk, bribing, playing a musical instrument, eating, drinking, and hitting. From the seventeenth century onwards, touching could also be non-physical: the kind that stirs the heart and mind – but not too much, in case you become 'touched in the head'.

Such complexity is perhaps not surprising. Touch is the first of the senses to develop, and the last to leave. In *Touch: The Science of Hand, Heart, and Mind*, the neuroscientist David Linden marvels at the effects of multiple forms of contact, from the essential touch that newborns need to thrive, or the electric touch of romantic love, to the caring touch of a doctor. Touch can provoke delight and disgust. Each and every one of our touch sensations 'flow from the evolved nature of our skin, nerves, and brain'. In modern terms, touching gives us **all the feels**.

tragic: bringing extreme distress or sorrow.

'Tragic' is a word that has almost been destroyed by hyperbole. In a world where even a slightly brave person must be a 'hero', and anyone who does someone a favour a 'star', it was inevitable that something even mildly sad or regrettable would become entirely 'tragic'.

The early tragedies were entirely fictional: narrative poems dealing with sorrow and disaster. The verse dramas that followed charted equal amounts of downfall and death. By the sixteenth century, a tragedy was a real event involving suffering, destruction, and distress, a meaning that has co-existed with the dramatic incarnation of the same emotions ever since. But while stage tragedies have retained their power, those on our daily radars have been reduced to minor misfortunes.

Perhaps, then, it is fitting that the etymology of 'tragedy' has a touch of bathos about it. The term *tragōidia* literally means 'song of the goats' – no one quite knows what the link between deep sorrow and our caprine friends might be, but goats were regularly sacrificed during the dramatic performances of the ancient Greeks, as well as awarded as prizes. Then again, as some have pointed out, have you ever heard a goat sing?

tranquillity: freedom from agitation or disturbance.

'Serenitude', 'evenhead', 'equilibrium', 'quietation': whatever you prefer to call it, 'tranquillity' is surely one of the most longed-for emotions of all. It entered English in the fourteenth century, when Chaucer wrote of the 'tranquillitee' of the soul. At its heart is the Latin *tranquillus*, 'quiet'.

triggered: provoked into a response.

Slang is the fastest-moving area of language. Designed as a code to be understood by the few and to keep the uninitiated out, it moves on as soon as outsiders scale the wall. 'Triggered' has gone from being a discipline-specific term – an electronic device, for example, is 'triggered' when it changes state in response to a momentary signal – to a multi-purpose one within a year.

In psychology, to be 'triggered' is to have an intense physical or emotional reaction to a reminder of a past trauma. It has been used frequently of sufferers of PTSD and anxiety disorders. Within slang, however, 'triggered' has come to refer to being unpleasantly affected by anything from a TikTok song to the sight of someone wearing odd socks. Videos now often come with a 'trigger warning' if they show nudity or blood. More insidiously perhaps, it is also used as a mocking term alongside **woke** and 'snowflake', directed at those who have a distinct emotional response to an event or point of view.

tripudiate: to dance, skip, or leap for joy.

'Tripudiation' is an ugly-sounding word for a celebratory emotion. It comes from the Latin *tripudium*, a stamping of feet as a sign of appreciation or pleasure, or as part of a religious dance. Ultimately, its heart lies in the Greek for 'three feet', implying that a 'tripudiator' hits the ground so quickly that the eye can't quite keep up.

twithought: a thought that disappears almost the moment you focus on it.

A daily occurrence for some, a 'twithought' is an indistinct musing or observation which, for all that it might seem to promise something highly significant or relevant, disappears almost as soon as it comes into your head.

ug: to fear something or look at it with revulsion.

The first Viking raid on British shores came in AD 793, when, as *The Anglo-Saxon Chronicle* relates, 'on the Ides of June the harrying of the heathen destroyed God's church on Lindisfarne, bringing ruin and slaughter'. From the language of these Norsemen, English eventually gained a significant word-hoard, characterized by its directness. 'Ransack' and 'slaughter', 'freckle' and 'egg', 'window' and 'knife' are all Viking legacies.

Many more words fell by the wayside. Among them is 'ugsome', a term that might have proved useful for the Britons encountering the marauders whose arrival must have seemed like a fury from hell. In Old Norse, *ug* represented everything that was repulsive to the eye and the senses. As a verb in English, to 'ug' was to 'be filled with an unparalleled sense of fear and dread'. Something 'ugsome', it followed, was 'hideous', 'horrid', or 'loathsome'. Their roots survive, of course, in our word 'ugly' – once an adjective with a sting not unlike the one delivered by the Vikings themselves.

uhtcearu [Old English: ucht-chay-a-ru]: the period before dawn when you lie awake and worry.

There is a particular time of night, before sunrise, when worries and fears loom unmanageably large. They take on gigantic proportions that, in the cold light of day and with a return to rational thinking, quickly shrink again. These seemingly endless hours, when we are caught in a dark spiral of anxiety, were known in Old English as *uhtcearu*, the 'sorrow before dawn'.

uitwaaien [Dutch: out-veye-en]: to clear the mind in windy weather.

Uitwaaien, 'to blow out', is the Dutch practice of jogging or walking into the wind, especially in the winter, for the purpose of feeling invigorated and revitalized. It carries much of the same sense of 'blowing away the cobwebs', with the extra boost of an energy lift.

ultracrepidarian: a presumptuous critic.

Perhaps it's because it's too much of a mouthful that 'ultracrepidarian' slipped away. As far as its meaning goes, however, it is as relevant today as it was centuries ago, for this nineteenth-century term describes someone who loves to hold forth on subjects they know absolutely nothing about. All thanks to a classical story of a cobbler who dared to pass comment on matters far beyond his expertise.

The cobbler in question lived in ancient Greece, and is said to have been critical of a painting by the renowned artist Apelles, finding particular fault with the rendering of a sandal, which in his opinion had one loop too few. Standing before the artwork, he then proceeded to criticize the subject's leg, too. In response, Apelles, who had overheard the whole exchange, is said to have retorted that the cobbler should stick to commenting on the shoes because they were the sole extent of his knowledge. The story inspired the Latin tag *ne ultra crepidam*, meaning 'not beyond the sole or sandal', and in turn produced the 'ultra-crepidarians' we reluctantly put up with today.

umarell [Italian: ooma-rel]: a retired individual who stands and watches construction sites.

In Italy's Bologna, there is a long-observed phenomenon in which elderly men with time on their hands stand to watch activity on building sites or at roadworks, stereotypically with their hands clasped behind their back, and usually offering a running commentary to anyone who wishes (or not) to hear. These are the *umarells*, an Italian-English coinage by Danilo Masotti based on a Bolognese dialect term *umarèl*, 'little man'.

umpty: mildly indisposed.

If you find yourself a little under the weather, there are several words with which to express your malaise. **Wabbit** or 'peelie-wallie', for example, are both evocative terms from nineteenth-century Scotland. Or you might opt for 'umpty', a word that has had several meanings since its first outing in the early 1900s, when it was a fanciful representation of the dash in Morse code (a dot followed by a dash was known as an 'iddy-umpty'). Given that a dash can be used as a marker for almost anything, 'umpty' produced the word 'umpteen' for a large but unspecified number of things. And it survived on its own as an adjective for something vaguely unpleasant or 'iffy', including one's state of body and mind. Perkin, a character in the 1970s animated children's programme *The Flumps*, explains it for all of us when he tells his mother that he's feeling distinctly 'umpty'. 'What's "umpty"?' she asks. 'It's a too-much morning,' he explains, before going off 'to be umpty on my own'.

unasinous: united in stupidity.

The *Oxford English Dictionary* is awash with words for fools, from the 'saddle-goose' of the 1400s and the 'clumperton' of the 1500s to the 'niddicock' of the seventeenth century, right up to today's 'wally' and 'plonker'. Were all those fools to come together and act in combined idiocy, they would be 'unasinous', a word from the seventeenth century that is related to 'asinine' and built upon the Latin *unus*, 'one', and *asinus*, 'ass'.

uneasy: disquieted; perturbed.

'Uneasiness', like 'disease', wears its heart on its sleeve. It describes a 'lack of ease' and an absence of comfort. Originally this discomfort would have been of the entirely physical kind, but by the fifteenth century the disquietude was largely of the mind. 'Uneasy lies the head that wears a crown,' as Shakespeare had it.

upset: disappointed; unhappy; anxious.

'Set' is famously one of the longest entries in the *Oxford English Dictionary*, offering 154 main senses explained in 60,000 words. Among them is the phrasal verb 'set up', which is how 'upset' is first defined: an 'upset sail' in the 1300s was one that was 'set up' by being hoisted and flew high. By the nineteenth century, the word had fittingly been turned on its head and its meaning had become one of overturning or capsizing. An 'upset stomach' was, and still is, physically disordered and in all kinds of bother, while an upset mind is just as agitated and perturbed.

urle: to curl up or draw in.

To 'urle', in old Yorkshire dialect, is to 'draw ones self up on a heap', as one seventeenth-century glossary put it. Such drawing-in happens particularly when we're ill or in what was once known as 'hunch-weather': the kind that is bitterly cold.

uxorious: especially fond of one's wife.

The adjective 'uxorious' describes an individual who dotes excessively, perhaps obsessively, on their wife. The reverse, strangely, is less popular. The dictionary provides a single, isolated, instance from 1607: 'maritorious', meaning to be excessively fond of one's husband.

valentine: to greet with song, at mating time.

Strictly speaking, using 'valentine' as a verb is for the birds. For them it means to 'greet or woo' during the mating season. In the human world, nineteenth-century children would set off 'valentining' on Valentine's Day by going from house to house asking for small change. Both uses were inspired, of course, by St Valentine, patron of sweethearts who is commemorated on 14 February, a day known for centuries as 'pairing time'.

vanity: excessive pride in one's own appearance or achievements.

'We are so vain that we even care for the opinion of those we don't care for.' The Austrian writer Marie von Ebner-Eschenbach, born in the nineteenth century, might easily have been commenting on our modern chases for likes. But in its earliest uses in the fourteenth century, 'vanity' was less about conceit and much more about futility, a sense retained when we do something 'in vain'. The idea of inflated pride came soon after, an extension, perhaps, of the idea of someone quite worthless who tries to persuade others of the opposite. This is the quality condemned in 'vanity of vanities; all is vanity', from the Book of Ecclesiastes. 'Vainglory', meanwhile, is its most extreme incarnation, a term for inordinate pride as well as idle vaunting. The source of both words is the Latin *vanus*, 'empty, without substance'.

In John Bunyan's *Pilgrim's Progress* of 1678, Vanity Fair is held in the town of Vanity, a thoroughfare for pilgrims on their way to the Eternal City. The fair sells all kinds of 'vanity' or trumpery finery, worth very little. The name 'Vanity Fair' went on to represent the world as a place of frivolity and idle amusement – most notably for William Makepeace Thackeray in his novel of the same name, in which we learn that, ultimately, 'All is vanity, nothing is fair.'

vapid: offering nothing stimulating.

It was originally food that was 'vapid', specifically when it was lacking in flavour and extremely bland. The adjective slipped into human focus in the eighteenth century, to describe a person, or conversation, of an equally flavourless nature. It is likely to be a relative of 'vapour', thanks to the sense of something as flimsy and insubstantial as a puff of smoke.

vehement: forceful; intense.

In the fifteenth century, 'vehement pain' was particularly intense, and a 'vehement wind' (bodily or not) blew with great violence. Sounds, flavours, medicines, and smells duly followed as the objects of 'vehemence', until the word settled largely upon human emotions, especially wrath, passion, and excitement. The root of all these senses is the equally powerful *vehemens*, Latin for 'fierce', 'intense', and 'violent'.

velleity: the act of wanting something but not doing anything to achieve it.

'Velleity', from the seventeenth century, is a rather high-sounding word for being all mouth and no trousers. Rooted in the Latin *velle*, to 'wish', it describes the fact of desiring something without any accompanying effort to get it. As one eighteenth-century writer put it: 'Velleity can scarce be called a power, for a power which never operates is no power at all.'

venomous: poisonous.

For the ancients, 'venom', like 'poison', could be either a deadly substance or a love potion. It seems to have begun with an ancient term meaning to 'strive for' or 'desire' – in this case either love or death. By the thirteenth century it had firmly settled on the poisonous side, and when applied to human behaviour describes someone full of malice and with an uncompromising bite.

ventosity: pompous conceit.

If you think that 'ventosity' might be all about wind, you'd be right, for in fourteenth-century medical manuals it described a state of extreme flatulence otherwise known as *colica passio* – apparently a regular companion of constipation. Perhaps it was inevitable that things took a metaphorical turn, so that by the 1500s it described the puffed-up vanity and arch pomposity of an over-inflated individual.

vernalagnia: romantic feelings in springtime.

The beginning of spring, when buds are erumpent and torpor begins to shift, is a time of 'vernalagnia'. A recently invented word that combines the Latin *vernalis*, 'relating to spring', and the Greek *lagneia*, 'lust', 'vernalagnia' describes romantic urges brought on by the advent of spring.

vestry: the sleeping smiles of children.

From nineteenth-century Cornwall comes 'vestry', a word we should surely never be without. It is defined in the *English Dialect Dictionary* with beautiful simplicity: 'the smiling of infants in their sleep'.

vibe: a distinctive feeling or quality.

'"You give off bad vibes." That's what George said to her, and we both sat through it. And I didn't hit him, I don't know why.' John Lennon often spoke about the uneasiness of the other Beatles at the continual presence of Yoko Ono in the recording studio. His words from 1972 give us only the second record in the *Oxford English Dictionary* of 'vibes', a shortening of 'vibrations' – of the kind the Beach Boys knew all about. These are essentially intuitive signals about a person or thing that create a distinct atmosphere or feel.

vigilant: watchful.

Both 'vigilant' and 'vigil' descend from the Latin *vigilia*, 'wakefulness'. A 'vigil' was originally the night before a religious festival, when people would stay awake in prayer. By extension, to be 'vigilant' was to keep one's eyes open or, to use a similar phrase from the sixteenth century featuring a different part of the anatomy, to be 'prick-eared'.

villainous: wicked or criminal.

'Villain' is an example of an innocent word tainted by associations of class. In medieval England, *villein* denoted a feudal tenant who was entirely under the rule of the lord of the manor – or indeed of the *villa*, from which the word derives. Before long, the associations of rural workers with ill breeding and bad manners put paid to the neutrality of the term, and it shifted from meaning a 'peasant' to someone guilty of heinous crimes.

vim: vitality and enthusiasm.

These days, 'vim' scarcely steps out without 'vigour'. It wasn't always that way. This byword for energy and enthusiasm began to emerge in the mid nineteenth century, some 500 years after its vigorous companion. The story of 'vim' seems to have begun straightforwardly enough, with the Latin *vis*, 'energy', but it may also have been born purely for its sound, which has all the pep and revved-upness of similar formulations such as 'va-va-voom'. *See* **oomph**.

violent: involving physical force with the intention of harm.

Archaeological evidence of violence, such as blows to the head or the impact of projectiles and other weapons, has been found in human bones dating back to the Palaeolithic era. There is, however, little evidence from that time of collective violence, characteristic of concerted attack or warfare. The hunter-gatherers relied on mutual defence and cooperation, essential for survival and reproduction. Violence became far more common during the Neolithic period, whose wall paintings frequently depict armed encounters between archers. As migration increased, so violent power struggles began to emerge, and war weapons fashioned out of metal became ever more sophisticated.

The graph has only gone one way since. Both the Bible and Shakespeare's plays are full of violence, from the story of Cain and Abel to what Horatio in *Hamlet* describes as episodes of 'carnal, bloody, and unnatural acts', of 'casual slaughters' and 'deaths put on by cunning and forced cause'. This is to say nothing of the violent emotional impulses that drive so many of Shakespeare's characters.

The root of all is the Latin *violentus*, itself from *violare*, to 'violate' – for this is what violence does, it violates or destroys a physical body or state of mind by force. Although the word is a relative of the Latin *vis*, 'energy' and 'strength', this is strength turned outwards and inflicted either upon another person, or upon oneself.

visceral: based on deepest feelings as opposed to the intellect.

One of the most important modern theories of emotion in the nineteenth century was put forward by William James (the philosophical brother of the novelist Henry). In his 1884 article 'What is an emotion?', James was one of the first to propose that our mental state is inextricably bound up with changes to our body, and that the 'bodily disturbances' produced by such strong feelings as fear, anger, lust, greed, and surprise, are actually the raw material of the emotions themselves. Without these physical states, he believed, our feelings would be 'colourless in form'. It followed, therefore, that we are sorry because we cry, afraid because we tremble, and angry because we hit out, just as much as the reverse. Such reactions in this interplay of flesh and feeling are 'visceral', a term based on the Latin 'viscera', the soft contents of the cavities of the body including our entrails or bowels. When something strikes us 'viscerally', therefore, it hits us in the very **guts**.

volatile: liable to change rapidly and unpredictably.

'Volatile' people make a habit of flying off the handle. Etymologically, the metaphor is entirely appropriate, for 'volatile' comes from the Latin *volare*, to 'fly'.

voluptuate: to luxuriate.

Sunday morning lie-ins, croissants and papers in bed, a hot bath with a glass of wine – the focus of 'voluptuating' is pleasure. The Latin *voluptas* became 'volupty' in Middle English, meaning absolute 'delight', while 'voluptuous' described anything characterized by indulgence in sensual pleasures and sumptuous living. Such gratification of the senses became associated with 'fullness and beauty of form', which is how 'voluptuous' also came to mean 'curvaceous'. To 'voluptuate', meanwhile, is happily still all about the little luxuries of life.

voorpret [Dutch]: pre-fun.

Go out for 'pre-s' as a student and you'll be getting in the drinks before you even set foot out of the door. The same sense of pre-partying informs the Dutch *voorpret*, 'pre-fun'. In this case, however, the fun need not be alcoholically induced; rather, it is the thrill of anticipation and knowledge of enjoyment to come that hits you before the main event begins.

Vorführeffekt [German: faw-fuer-effekt]: the effect of things going wrong when there is an audience.

It's rare to find a word that fills not just one but two gaps in English. The German *Vorführeffekt* does just that.

On the one hand, it describes the highly identifiable phenomenon of demonstrating a skill or action that you have practised a thousand times, only to find it goes wrong the minute someone is watching. The same can be said of an inanimate object that works perfectly well until there is an audience (all users of PowerPoint will recognize this).

Secondly, *Vorführeffekt* covers those situations in which you wish to show that something *isn't* working, only to find it works perfectly at the crucial moment. Organizing a repair to your washing machine, for example, which then operates faultlessly when the technician finally turns up. Or taking your child to the doctor with a hacking cough and hearing it miraculously disappear as soon as you step into the surgery.

All in all, it's a pithy and highly useful word. Simply translated, *Vorführeffekt* means 'demonstration effect'.

vril: a mysterious source of energy.

When Napoleon III needed an effective means of feeding his soldiers during the Franco-Prussian War, he ordered a million cans of beef, but there wasn't enough to meet the demand. Spying an opportunity, an Edinburgh butcher called John Lawson Johnston created a derivative meat product to fill the gap. He originally gave it the name 'Johnston's Fluid Beef' but, after reading one of the most successful novels of the day, decided upon something better.

Edward Bulwer-Lytton's *The Coming Race* is a utopian piece of science fiction in which the narrator accompanies an engineer into a natural deep chasm in a mine and encounters a mystical subterranean people who exist entirely without poverty, envy, or any of the other evils of human society. These are the 'Vril-ya', for whom 'vril' is a mystical source of energy. The myth of Vril was later co-opted by many cults and movements, including, it was claimed, the Nazis.

As for John Lawson Johnston, he took the Latin word for 'ox', *bos*, and added some 'vril' of his own. Bovril, advertised with the slogan 'Bovril is the substance of the beef, not the shadow' not only met Napoleon III's demands, but also became an instant success in Britain.

wabbit: played out; without energy.

'Exhausted', 'tired out', 'knackered', 'feeble' – all of these physical and mental states are encompassed in the Scots 'wabbit', first recorded in the late nineteenth century. It might sound as though it stepped straight out of Looney Tunes, but it seems to be a riff on another Scots term, 'oobit', meaning 'withered' or 'faded'. 'Wabbit' is the gentler articulation of another Scots term, 'depooperit'.

wabi-sabi [Japanese]: the transience of things.

For the writer Andrew Juniper, there is a particular emotion that demonstrates three simple realities: 'nothing lasts, nothing is finished, and nothing is perfect'. This emotion is known in Japanese as *wabi-sabi*, which describes the acceptance of imperfection and impermanence.

Wabi-sabi was at first a melancholy concept. Its two words – *wabi*, 'remote', and *sabi*, 'lean' – suggest isolation and insufficiency. Over time it has, however, transformed into something of an ideal: an acceptance that nature is fundamentally flawed yet beautiful, and that while a vase may be asymmetrical and cracked, it can be all the more exquisite as a result.

Waldeinsamkeit [German: vult-ein-zam-kite]: the spiritual feeling of being alone in the forest.

The Japanese know it as *shinrin-yoku*, 'forest bathing'. The benefits of solitude beneath a canopy of trees have been borne out in research which shows it lowers cortisol levels and blood pressure rates, and increases the feel-good chemical that is serotonin. The Germans, too, have a word for the spiritual response to being alone in a forest, namely *Waldeinsamkeit*, or 'forest aloneness'. Once again, the idea is of a spiritual solitude in a space that restores perspective and serenity.

wanderlust: a lust for travel.

'For my part,' wrote Robert Louis Stevenson in *Travels with a Donkey*, 'I travel not to go anywhere, but to go. I travel for travel's sake. The great affair is to move.' Those with 'wanderlust', from the German for 'desire to wander', don't necessarily need to go anywhere in particular, they just don't care to stay in one spot. The first documented use of the term in English is from 1902, and refers to what was then seen as the German impulse to wander, one that characterized much of German Romanticism. In recent years, *Wanderlust* is less commonly used in German, having been largely supplanted in the sense of 'desire to travel' by the evocative *Fernweh* ('the longing for faraway places').

weird: strange; uncanny.

'Luck, like a Russian car, generally only works if you push it.' Had the novelist Tom Holt made the same observation to the Anglo-Saxons, he would have used *wyrd* or *weird* instead of 'luck', for that was the word that for them signified 'fate' or 'destiny'. 'The Weirds' were the Fates, the three Greek goddesses who presided over the life of humans. Our modern use of 'weird' to mean 'bizarre' looks back to a profound sense of the uncanny or supernatural.

well-woulder: a conditional well-wisher.

There are those who are 'good-willy' – benevolent and well disposed towards others – and those who are **ill-willy**. Then there are the 'well-wishers': those who desire the well-being and happiness of others. In amongst this regular slice of humanity we will probably also find the 'well-woulder', a seventeenth-century term for those who are entirely conditional in their offer of good wishes: they wish other people success, just as long as it's not more success than them.

Weltschmerz [German: velt-schmairz]: world-weariness or pain.

We often turn to German for expressions of yearning and anxiety. We adopted **angst**, for example, in the nineteenth century, using it to pinpoint an intense, non-specific, anxiety. *Weltschmerz* has become another staple in our lexicon of sorrow. With a literal meaning of 'world-pain', it is defined in the *Oxford English Dictionary* as 'a weary or pessimistic feeling about life', as well as 'an apathetic or vaguely yearning attitude'. In other words, *Weltschmerz* is a melancholy that, rather than being focused inwards, comes down to the condition of being human in a thoroughly imperfect world.

wet: feeble.

A metaphorically 'wet' person is considered to be both inept and ineffectual. They are quite frankly a 'drip'. The image may be of a person 'wetted' by too much alcohol, who is therefore clumsy and not up to much. A political wet, meanwhile, is traditionally one who holds liberal or middle-of-the-road views on contentious issues – a 'mugwump', in other words, who prefers to straddle the fence.

whelmed: totally submerged by a strong emotion.

Today, we encounter 'whelmed' only in the company of 'over' and 'under', but it originally managed to convey the idea of being overturned or capsized all by itself. To 'whelm' a vessel was to turn it upside down or submerge it. John Milton wrote of the 'whelming tide', while a seventeenth-century historian lamented 'the all-whelming deluge of Time'. It didn't take long before 'over' was added to emphasize the idea of a complete overturn or upset, while 'underwhelmed' appeared in the middle of the twentieth century. If we pare both words back to their essence, however, 'whelmed' could clearly still do the job on its own.

whiffling: indecisive.

When the wind 'whiffles', it blows in puffs or little gusts. When a ship 'whiffles', it is carried here and there by the swell of the ocean. It follows, then, that when the 'whiffler' is an individual, they are vacillating, hesitant, and generally ineffectual. The root of all this is the word 'whiff', used mostly these days in the sense of a bad smell carried in the air.

The indecisive 'whiffler', unable to decide on matters as trivial as whether to turn on the heating in September or as important as whether to move in with their partner, is very different from the medieval 'whiffler'. The latter was generally armed with a javelin, battleaxe, sword, or staff, and would clear the way for a procession or public spectacle. Rather than taking their name from a puff of wind, however, their prowess was built upon the Old English *wifle*, a 'spear'.

whimsical: playfully quaint; fanciful.

'Not just now. I'm making a whim-wham for waterwheels.' A Northamptonshire substitute for 'I'm busy', this expression was once the ideal if mysterious fob-off for any child wanting attention. There are dozens of similar versions up and down the country, in which 'whim-wham' can mean anything or nothing at all, as well as a sudden fancy. It is the latter that gave us 'whimsy' and 'whim', both shortenings of 'whim-wham'. A 'whim' is a sudden desire or notion, or a change of mind; to be 'whimsical', therefore, is to be a fickle follower of the same desires.

wink: a brief closure of the eyes to convey a secret message.

A 'wink' was originally a full closing of the eyes. This explains why we take 'forty winks' by having a quick snooze, or 'hood-wink' someone by blindfolding them. By the fifteenth century, a 'wink' was more a temporary closing of the eyes – a blink. At this stage the word had already acquired another meaning as a significant glance, whether or not it included a closing of the eyes, used to convey a coded message.

wired: nervous; tense; edgy.

In early twentieth-century US slang, to be 'wired up' was to be 'provoked' or 'really angry'. Decades later, it was to be 'intoxi-cated' or 'high on drugs'. Today you are more likely to be wired by your tenth cup of coffee, but the link between each of these senses is one of being overstimulated, as though plugged into an electric socket.

witty: sharp and inventive.

In Old English your 'wit' was your entire faculty of thinking. It was the seat of consciousness and thought, of memory and attention, and of wisdom – in other words, your mind. 'Inwit' was therefore your inner knowledge or conscience, while your 'outwit' produced your external perceptions of the world. 'Common wit' was simply your common sense. (A 'nitwit', of course, has no wit or understanding at all.)

These earlier meanings explain such prevailing idioms as 'keeping your wits about you', being 'at your wit's end', or 'scared out of your wits'. A quickness of intellect, meanwhile, went on to produce the comedic kind of wit: 'Better a witty fool than a foolish wit,' declares Feste in *Twelfth Night*.

woebegone: sad and miserable.

Tempting as it is to think that 'woebegone' might be a happy word – the result of commanding 'woe' to 'be gone' – its history proves the opposite. 'Begone' here is used in an old sense of being 'surrounded' or beset. To be 'woebegone', therefore, is to be deeply afflicted with grief, and therefore very miserable indeed.

Wohlweh [German: vole-vay]: good pain.

The debatable enjoyments of sado-masochism aside, we are all familiar with the dual response to a deep massage that elicits groans of both pleasure and pain. It is the same feeling that comes from scratching a mosquito bite or intensely rubbing your eyes, or from taking off shoes that are too tight. This is *Wohlweh*, German for 'pleasurable pain'.

woke: alert to injustice.

Few words have undergone such an accelerated shift in meaning in recent times as 'woke'. From its early neutral meaning of being 'awake' to injustice and incrimination, it has become a multi-purpose label with which to insult or, at the very least, pigeonhole someone else's point of view.

The adjective is not new – its first outings in the current sense were in the 1940s. In the 1960s, the *New York Times* was explaining that 'If you're woke, you dig it.' The word was greatly popularized by the Black Lives Matter movement, when 'stay woke' became a rallying cry and a call to be alert to discrimination wherever we encounter it. The singer Erykah Badu also had a hand in spreading the word with her 2008 song 'Master Teacher', which repeats the phrase 'I stay woke' to express a refusal to become desensitized to persistent racism.

Recently, however, the word is being harnessed in different ways, especially as shorthand to describe those on the political left. Together with 'snowflake', it has become a sneering accusation of excessive sensitivity and liberalism, to the extent that those who identify as 'woke' are unlikely now to use it. In other words, it has become what in the US is called a 'skunk word' – one that has begun to 'stink'.

wonder: astonishment; awe.

For children, it comes naturally. Aristotle believed that all philosophy sprang from it, while for the seventeenth-century French philosopher René Descartes, it was the first and most important of the six primary passions of the soul. This is 'wonder', an emotion that has motivated human curiosity, inquiry, and open-mindedness from the beginning.

The ultimate origins of 'wonder' are elusive, which is fitting, perhaps, because in Old English a 'wonder' was also a deed or event brought about by miraculous or supernatural power. Something 'wonderful' was truly astonishing, and as late as the nineteenth century the dictionary definition retained the idea of something that 'excites wonder', whether good or bad. The Wonderful Wizard of Oz was nothing if not awe-inspiring, while Alice's Wonderland is as curious (and mad) as it is wonderful. The Bible has many examples of 'wonderful' things that astonished but certainly didn't please, including plagues and pestilence. By the seventeenth and eighteenth centuries, however, 'wonderful' was becoming the adjective of choice among pamphleteers who frequently touted their wares as 'wonderfull' and 'surprising'. Jonathan Swift topped them all with his whimsically titled 'The Wonderful Wonder of Wonders' in 1720.

Much like 'awesome', however, 'wonderful' eventually became an overplayed adjective for 'extremely good'. It seems that 'wonderful' has lost its sense of wonder, preserved only in 'wondrous', which has all the magic and mysticism of the original.

woofits: an unwell feeling.

Whether or not it is the result of **crapulence**, an attack of the 'woofits' is not to be celebrated. Its definitions range from a feeling of general unwellness to a headache and moody depression. The sound of this twentieth-century word may be as friendly as a cuddly dog, but its effects are definitely not.

wool-gathering: to indulge in daydreams.

If you are a **dardledumdue**, you will know all about 'wool-gathering'. It sits lazily at the extreme end of daydreaming, when your mind is not absent but is instead engaged in idle fantasies and free association. The idea is of unhurriedly gathering fragments of wool from wandering sheep that have snagged on brambles and branches.

worry: anxiety; perturbation.

Both 'worry' and 'anxiety' share an intimidating past. Each comes from the idea of a 'choke' or 'stranglehold'. In the case of 'worry', its meaning shifted from choking on a mouthful of food, to swallowing greedily, and on to seizing by the throat. By the seventeenth century, the verb was all about perturbation and disturbance. For those who feel beset with worry today, the emotion's origins in the Old English *wyrgan*, to 'strangle', will feel entirely appropriate.

wow: an exclamation of wonder, surprise, etc.

Most of us would venture a bet that 'Wow!' began in American English. However, the exclamation, which can express astonishment, pleasure, sarcasm, sorrow, or simple affirmation, has been around in English since the sixteenth century, and its origins are entirely Scottish. 'Wow, that's braw news!' wrote the eighteenth-century poet Allan Ramsay, while Robert Burns offered, 'And wow! he has an unco slight / O' cauk and keel.' By the 1960s, a drawled 'like, wow' was as psychedelically infused as the Beatles' 'Lucy in the Sky with Diamonds'. As a noun, meanwhile, a 'wow' is a sensational success, and having the 'wow factor' is everything.

wynn: delight; pleasure.

The word 'rune', a letter in an ancient alphabet, means 'whisper' or 'secret'. Runic inscriptions may have originally been part of magic and religious rituals as well as serving more practical purposes. Unlike the Roman alphabet, where a letter represents only a sound with no directly associated meaning, runes had names that did mean things. So it was with the runic letter 'wynn', 'ᚹ ᚹ', which resembled a human being and was used to illustrate both the sound of a 'w' and the concept of joy.

For the Anglo–Saxons, 'wynn' had many manifestations. Hana Videen's excellent exploration of Old English, *The Wordhord*, gives us many of them, from the *leod-wynn*, or 'people joy', that comes from a sense of community, to the *lyft-wynn*, or 'air joy', that describes the pleasantness of the air. A *wyn-dream*, 'pleasure-joy', is happiness in abundance.

The rune 'Þ' was eventually replaced by 'UU', which in turn became the modern 'W' and which is pronounced as 'double u'. But the whisper of 'wynn' lingers still in the word 'winsome', meaning 'joyous' and 'delightful'.

xenodochy: a kindness towards strangers.

Had a tired traveller chanced upon a 'xenodochium' in the seventeenth century, they would have rejoiced, for this was a house of hospitality for pilgrims and strangers, such as a monastery or an inn that welcomed anyone seeking relief and refuge.

What was offered there was essentially 'xenodochy', a now-obsolete word from the same period that described a kindness towards strangers. Given the mistrust typically reserved for those from the 'outlands' (producing the word 'outlandish' itself, as well as the strangeness implied in 'stranger'), 'xenodochy' has always been quite special. Its name is based upon the Greek *xenos*, 'stranger', and *dechesthai*, to 'receive' or 'welcome'.

ya'aburnee [Arabic: ya-burn-ee]: an expression of love.

The Arabic *ya'aburnee* literally means 'bury me'. It is said to be one of the ultimate expressions of love for another human, declaring that you would wish to die before them to avoid the sorrow of their loss.

yarooh: a cry of pain.

'Yarooh!' was the customary cry of pain of one of fiction's best-loved characters: '"Oh!" roared Bunter, as Bulstrode's heavy boot biffed on him. "Ow! Yah! Yarooh!"' The Bunter in question is Billy Bunter, the creation of Charles Hamilton, who delights in such exclamations. Hamilton apparently came up with the word by reversing the letters of 'hooray'.

yawmagorp: a persistent yawner.

A 'yawm' is a 'yawn', while a 'gorp', a variation on 'gawp', is delivered with the mouth. Put them together and you have the old dialect word 'yawmagorp', an affectionately mocking term for any yawning, stretching person or sluggard.

yearn: to long for.

A 'yearning' is much more than a craving. Far from being a temporary state of mind, it suggests a deep longing imbued with a sense of wistfulness or melancholy, and an added sense that whatever we are yearning for might always stay elusive. In the sixteenth century, a hunting dog would 'yearn' when it caught sight of its prey; if a human uttered a similar baying cry, they would be said to be 'yearning' too. Soon the word embraced any kind of longing, noisy or otherwise, all extending from the word's Germanic roots and a term meaning 'eager'.

yen: a desire or craving.

The vocabulary of drugs and drug users has loitered around the edges of English for longer than we might think. When we have a 'yen' for something, we long for it – the word is derived from the Chinese *yǎn*, 'craving', which emerged in English in the 1870s. Specifically, it referred to a drug addict's craving for opium – the stuff, after all, of 'pipe dreams', another expression born in the opium dens of the nineteenth century.

zeal: intense emotion compelling action.

As revolutionary France battled the rest of Europe during the closing decades of the eighteenth century, the diplomat Charles-Maurice de Talleyrand-Périgord embarked on a mission to London to persuade Britain to remain neutral. What the country needed, he insisted, was a cool head, not impulsiveness or passion. '*Surtout, pas trop de zèle,*' he said: 'Above all, not too much zeal.'

'Zeal' is a very particular word – it denotes not just intense ardour, but the translation of that into a strong commitment to a cause. It was first used in biblical language, where it described a distinct attribute of God and a powerful love that will tolerate no unfaithfulness or disobedience. When manifested by humans, 'zeal' represents an emotion so extreme it is largely negative, encompassing envy, anger, or obsessive devotion. The root of 'zeal' is the same as that of 'jealousy', the Greek *zēlos*, meaning 'eager rivalry' and 'desire'.

zemblanity: the inexorable discovery of bad things.

Coined by novelist William Boyd in his 1998 novel *Armadillo*, 'zemblanity' is 'the faculty of making unhappy, unlucky, and expected discoveries by design'. Together with **serendipity**, Boyd explains, it forms 'the twin poles of the axis around which we revolve'. While 'serendipity' takes its name from Serendip, an old name for the island of Sri Lanka, Boyd's 'zemblanity' is inspired by a (literal) polar opposite, namely the region of Novaya Zemlya, a vast, isolated archipelago in the high Russian Arctic. Compared to the lush, tropical island of Sri Lanka, it's easy to see how the bleak Russian tundra should inspire a word for the direct opposite of serendipity.

zest: great enthusiasm and energy.

The piquancy of citrus peel lends itself naturally as a metaphor for any kind of flavour or excitement and energy. A 'zest' for life is that invigorating quality that adds considerably to our enjoyment of it. Not only that, but according to Christian Dior, 'zest is the secret of all beauty.'

Zugunruhe [German: tsook-oon-roo-uh]: a keenness to leave.

For many birds, the urge to migrate is irresistible. The build-up of anticipation and tension as a long flight beckons is evident in the birds' behaviour: it is said that even caged robins will turn repeatedly towards the north when their free siblings are making their annual flight. Humans too can feel this uncontainable impulse to move. The German *Zugunruhe* is perhaps best expressed as the anxiety we feel when our current life becomes intolerable and we know something has to change. Even if it's just to go on holiday.

Zugzwang: a no-win situation.

'Zugzwang' is a chess term coming directly from the German *Zug*, meaning 'move', and *Zwang*, a 'compulsion' or 'urge'. It's used for a situation in which any move a player makes will have a detrimental effect on their game.

zwodder: languorous laziness.

The final entry in Joseph Wright's *English Dialect Dictionary* is the perfect expression of slumberous contentment. There, 'zwodder' is defined as 'a drowsy, stupid state of body or mind'. Born for its sound, its roots may lie in the warmth of a pub, thanks to the dialect word **swadder**, 'to grow weary with drinking'. The substitution of a 'z' is surely entirely appropriate for the 'sloomy', slow state of a hot summer's day.

ACKNOWLEDGEMENTS

'People who keep stiff upper lips find that it's damn hard to smile,' wrote Judith Guest in *Ordinary People*. If there was ever a time to let it all hang out, emotionally speaking, it has been the past few years, when so many of us have veered from one emotion to another as haphazardly as dodgems at a funfair. It's a ride we never expected to be on, and I'm hugely grateful to those who helped me navigate it and who stopped me crashing entirely.

First and foremost among them is my editor Georgina – George – Laycock, who once again had an endless supply of encouraging words and clever ideas whenever I need a top-up of either. She, and my agent Rosemary Scoular, are the dream team for any author. I consider myself very lucky to have them.

Tim Waller was the most sure-footed of copy-editors, with a linguistic savviness I can only envy, Howard Davies managed to polish the book as well as wipe it clean, and it is thanks to Ruth Ellis's skilful organization of the text's Thesaurus and Index that the reader can zoom in on the various synonyms for exhaustion or grumpiness, should they need to. Caroline Westmore steered us all with eagle-eyed authority and much-appreciated patience.

Alice Herbert has once again patiently and masterfully managed the publicity of this book, even cajoling me into the odd photo shoot: usually my worst nightmare. And behind the scenes, Diana Talyanina's work has proved vital, not least in ensuring we had books on time.

Thomas Dixon's vast knowledge of emotional histories was indispensable, as was his knack of conveying complex ideas with a common touch, and in compelling detail. Many of the entries on the 'big' emotions such as jealousy and grief were informed by him.

As ever, my daughters have been my go-to repository of smiles, hugs, and biscuits. I have felt many of the joyous emotions in this book because of them. As for the tougher kind, this book is dedicated to the friends who have got me back on my feet more than once.

Finally, I would like to thank my parents, who will never fully realize the extent of the curiosity they released in me on those long car journeys to the seaside. My emotional history was begun by them, which means that ultimately this book was, too.

EMOTIONAL THESAURUS

happiness (*cont.*)
forblissed 121
frolic-hearted 123–4
gaiety 126
genial 127–8
gigglemug 129
glad 130
glee 131
goshbustified 134
gruntled 138–9
halcyon 143
happy 145–6
happy as Larry 146–7
hyppytyynytyydytys 163
jaunty 177–8
joie de vivre 181
jolly 181
jouissance 181
jovial 182
joy 182
jubilate 182–3
kvell 188
letabund 193–4
mudita 221
nikhedonia 231
oblectament 235
perky 252
pleasure 257–8
queem 266
rapture 268
retrouvailles 276
satisfied 285
seventh heaven 297
simchah 301
tickled pink 328–9
tripudiate 334
wynn 359–60

love
amour propre 12
antipelargy 17
basorexia 29
cavoli riscaldati 48
cordial 60–1
coup de foudre 61

crush 66
cupboard love 66
cwtch 69–70
desire 77–8
elumbated 95
engouement 101
finifugal 117
gigil 130
hiraeth 150
limerence 196
love 200–1
love-light 201
mamihlapinatapai 207
mislove 217–18
oeillade 237
passion 247–8
philodoxical 253
redamancy 270
requited 272
romantic 279–80
tabanca 323
teng 326–7
uxorious 341
valentine 343
vernalagnia 345–6
ya'aburnee 363

regret
cacoethes 44
hingum-tringum 150
litost 198
pregret 260
regret 271
remorse 272

sadness
all-overish 10
anticipointment 16
benighted 30
beochaoineadh 30
black dog 33
blahs, the 33
blues, the 34–5
bluthered 35–6

crestfallen 64
dejected 73
depression 76–7
despair 78–9
despondent 79
disappointment 80–1
distress 83
doldrums 84
dumps, down in the 88
Eeyorish 93
grief 136–7
hinayang 149
lacrimae rerum 189–90
liget 195
lonely 199–200
maudlin 208
melancholy 211–13
misery 217
morose 220
mubble fubbles 221
mudita 221
mulligrubs 222
mumpish 222
plobaireacht 258
regret 271
remorse 272
sad 283
saturnine 285–6
saudade 286
sorrow 308–9
subtrist 317
tragic 333
upset 340–1
woebegone 356

surprise
astonish 23
blutterbunged 36
dumbfounded 88
gadzooks 125
gloppened 131–2
nonplussed 232–3
shock 299–300
surprise 318

INDEX

abashed 298
abbiocco ix, 1
abdabs 1–2
abhorrence 2
absquatulate 81
acatalepsy 2–3
accismus 3
acedia 3–4
Adams, Bryan 230
addiction 4–5
admiration 6, 260
adorable 5
aduantas 5
adulation 6
Aeneid (Virgil) 189–90
Aesop 206, 309
Aethelred 270–1
affection 6
affray 114
affronted 6
afterclap 7
after-wit 7
age-otori 8
agelast 7
agony 8–9
alarm 9
Albrecht, Glenn 306
alcoholism 273
Alcyone 143
alert 9
all-overish 10
allergic 9
aloof 10
altruism 10–11
alysm 11
ambition 11
American Declaration
   of Independence
   145
amok 12

amour propre 12
amulets 202
Anatomy of Melancholy
   (Burton) 76, 211–12
Angelou, Maya 168
angina 19
Anglo-Saxons 62, 86,
   89, 148, 270–1, 360
angry 13
angst 13–14
anhedonia 14–15
animated 15
Anne of Green Gables
   (Montgomery)
   277–8
annoy 15
antagonistic 16
anticipointment x, 16
antipelargy 17
Antony and Cleopatra
   (Shakespeare) 239
'ants in your pants' 17
antsy 17
anxiety 17–19
apanthropy 19
apathy 19
apophenia 20
appel du vide, l' 20
appetite 20–1, 29
apricity 21
Arabic words 324–5,
   363
Arcadian 21–2
arguments 38, 45, 47,
   53, 54, 103, 175,
   265–6
Aristotle 57–8, 146,
   357
Armadillo (Boyd) 366
Armstrong, Lance 271

Arnold, Benedict 87
aroused 22
arrogance 259
arse-ropes 141
arsle 22
artificial intuition 174
aspectabund 22–3
asperity 106
astonish 23
astonishment viii
ataraxy 23–4
Athena 15
attractiveness 44, 110,
   229–30
Auden, W. H. 18
Austen, Jane 3, 228,
   229–30, 261, 284,
   293 4
aware 24
awkward 24
awumbuk 24–5

backendish 27
backfriend 27
backwards, going 22
Bacon, Francis 192,
   276
badkruka 28
Badu, Erykah 357
Bailey, Nathan 222
Baining people 24–5
Bakhtin, Mikhail 58
balderdash 260
Ball, Lucille 270
baloney 260
bamboozled 28
Banks, Sir Joseph 234
Banks, Tyra 119
bào fù xìng áo yè 28–9
Barbados, been to 29

INDEX

INDEX